Zeı

and the Art of

Producing

Zen
and the Art of
Producing

Mixerman

HAL•LEONARD®

Hal Leonard Books
An Imprint of Hal Leonard Corporation

Published in 2012 by Hal Leonard Books
An Imprint of Hal Leonard Corporation
7777 West Bluemound Road
Milwaukee, WI 53213

Trade Book Division Editorial Offices
33 Plymouth St., Montclair, NJ 07042

Printed in the United States of America

Cover design by Jeff Mutschler
Book design by UB Communications

Library of Congress Cataloging-in-Publication Data

Mixerman.
    Zen and the art of producing / Mixerman.
        p. cm.
    Summary: "Explores the many roles and responsibilities of a music producer and offers advice on music production"—Provided by publisher.
    ISBN 978-1-4584-0288-2
    1. Sound recording executives and producers—Vocational guidance. 2. Popular music—Production and direction. I. Title.
    ML3795.M57 2012
    781.49—dc23
                                    2012017833

www.halleonardbooks.com

Acknowledgments

Special thanks to:

John Dooher

Bob Olhsson

The Saint

Dave Pensado

William Wittman

Jeff Mutschler

David Wozmak

Jessica Burr

Brandon Gresham

The Womb Forums and all of my friends who run the place with me

This book is dedicated to Max, Colin, *Maya*, Aiden, Tommy, Lila, Bridge, Tairyn and Alex, which will make at least one person on the list *very* happy. I won't say who.

Whom!

Contents

Chapter Three
The Politics

Chapter Four
The Business

Zen
and the Art of
Producing

2 Introduction

When I first sat down to write this book, it was called simply *Zen and the Art of Producing*. Still is. For a while, it was called *Zen and the Art of Producing Bands*, much to my publisher's chagrin. You have to understand that a great deal of prep work is required to release a book like this, and from the perspective of my publisher, changing the name midstream...well, I won't sugarcoat it—it's fucked up. To be clear, that's my assessment, not theirs. They didn't complain a bit when I explained the problem I was having. I must say, as someone who spends his life handholding artists, it's kind of nice to play the role of fussy artist myself for a change.

From the perspective of the writing process, changing the title to...*Producing Bands* made things far simpler for me. For starters, it made the writing flow much better, that's for sure. No longer did I have to stop to add three caveats and two exceptions to every rule in a business that, to some extent, has no rules. I could also concentrate on the politics of band entities, which don't exist to the same degree when dealing with an artist or a singer-songwriter. Bands significantly complicate the politics of making a record.

By the time I'd completed the manuscript, it was evident that despite its slant toward producing bands, the book was still useful for producing in general. Given this, I decided to drop the word "Bands" from the title, which wasn't supposed to be there in the first place. Yes, I will spend much of our time together discussing producing as it relates to bands, but bands are just complicated artist entities, so the large majority of this book should prove helpful for anyone trying to produce any kind of music.

There are all sorts of producing jobs with somewhat different requirements. Producing a pop artist often requires supplying songs, either as a writer, co-writer, or from outside sources. From a creative standpoint, pop is also generally a simpler genre to produce. Programmed music is the norm, and even on those occasions when live musicians are involved, the creative politics are nearly nonexistent until mix time. The producer writes the track, makes the track, has the singer perform on the track, and then the track is mixed. And while, admittedly, major label politics in this arena can be more intense, the actual producing requires little negotiation, and a creative team is mostly a one-man show.

In the past several months of writing this book, the same question has come up over and over again. What can I possibly tell you about programming a track? The answer remains the same: nothing.

This is not to denigrate that kind of production. I have great fun programming tracks. There are no negotiations with anyone other than myself, there's no selling of concepts, there's no coddling necessary, no politics—it's just me alone with the music. *Aaaaaaahhhhh.* So refreshing. But only as a hiatus. When it comes right down to it, the true art of producing lies in dealing with people. The best place to get that kind of action? Producing bands.

Honestly, I love producing bands. I love the politics. I love the camaraderie. I love leading a big team, negotiating, debating. I love the fights, the "Kumbaya" moments, the planning, the creative a-ha's. I love the grind. I love the meals. I love all the people around. Perhaps that has something to do with the fact that the other half of my life is spent either writing or mixing. Maybe all that alone time makes me need some social time for the purpose of balance in my life. I can't say for sure. All I know is that I love producing bands, and there is, without a doubt, an art to it.

There are two kinds of bands. There's the band entity, and there's the artist with a backup band. In some ways the politics are quite different between the two. In the case of the artist, the band is made up of sidemen, who retain minimal stake and no real say in the decision-making process. This considerably simplifies negotiations. In other ways, however, the politics can be quite similar. Band entities often have a brainchild, and this leadership position provides similar power to that of the artist with her sidemen. The biggest difference lies in how everyone gets paid. That difference should not be discounted as insignificant, particularly once everyone realizes the stakes have been raised.

Another big issue I had in writing this book was keeping it useful for more than just the neophyte producer. When I set out to write my previous book, *Zen and the Art of Mixing*, my goal was to provide useful information for the many different stages of a mixer's development. That has proven to be considerably more difficult for this particular subject matter. Producing is a much more involved job than mixing. Budgets vary dramatically, and politics often change based on the money available. Producing a low-budget album for a self-funded band is an entirely different job politically than producing a well-funded project for a major label. Without major label involvement, the producer must act as both good cop and bad. Not in a manipulative way, mind you. It's just that sometimes it becomes necessary to take traditional label positions, mostly because the tension and pressure from a label can be useful for maintaining the balance between creativity and marketability.

It's considerably easier to herd a band when you have a label acting as an implied, if not explicit, backup. Quite simply, the argument is: "The label will never, ever go for that. Forget it." When producing a self-funded band, you're saying no directly to your paying client. Think about that for a moment. I'm suggesting that as the producer on a self-funded project, you must attain and wield some power of veto over the people paying you. That's quite a trick, dontcha think?

My next problem was deciding whether I should approach the book from the perspective of producing for major labels, or of producing for self-funded bands. (I can't do both; I tried and failed on earlier drafts of this book, thank you very much.) I'll spare you the drum roll moment. This was a no-brainer. Clearly, self-funded projects outnumber label projects by nearly a thousand to one. My path was clear. I had to approach the art of producing in a manner that would help the most producers possible. The good news is that most of us pay our dues by producing acts that lack label support.

Further complicating matters, particularly where major labels are concerned, is the current turmoil in the record business. The business side of making and selling music has changed considerably in recent years. Labels are pumping out far less product, and for much smaller budgets, than the "make it rain" madness of the early 2000s. Add to the mix an overpopulation of producers with some modicum of success, and let's not forget the constant flow of new recording school graduates, and you get an idea of the kind of competition you're up against.

At this moment in the history of the music business, the engineering school graduate is competing almost directly with the multi-platinum producer. As if that's not enough, how everyone gets paid has been in complete flux. Producers used to get paid on a percentage of record sales, but these days records are often treated as a loss leader for ticket sales. If no records are sold, then how exactly is a producer supposed to profit-share? And if the entire business is in flux, then how can I possibly provide you with a solid footing for dealing with it?

That's not to say that I won't discuss major labels and touch on how they affect the producing process. I will. But given the dynamics of the business, I must be careful that my advice in this regard isn't rendered archaic before this book is even released. Therefore, most of this book will focus on producing outside the politics of a major label. And frankly, I'm relieved. Not only will it be a far more useful book this way, but it will also be a considerably better read.

Whether or not you work with bands, there is an enormous amount of material in this book that can benefit you in the here and now. The fact is, there will likely come a time when you will be placed in a producing situation that includes organic instruments. And one day you'll find yourself in a recording session with a band for the first time; the information contained here will prepare you for that eventuality. After all, you don't really want to work in just one genre, day in and day out, do you?

Believe it or not, there are certain advantages to working in just one genre. When you have some success with a particular type of music, market forces will work to lock you into that genre. The nature of records that come your way is based on your position, and much of your position is based on your success. Therefore, your position will dictate your career—entirely, if you allow it. Some of you might view this as a positive. I view it as a great way to make sure you have a short career, regardless of how successful the run. Sure, you can always reinvent yourself when that happens, but reinvention can be a traumatic and difficult process. In some ways, it's like starting over.

If the prospect of a traumatic reinvention sounds somewhat distasteful to you, then you might want to consider avoiding it in the first place. It takes both recognition of your position and constant vigilance to have any kind of influence over the kinds of records you win. The problem is that it's difficult to win a record if it doesn't come your way in the first place. While you can certainly generate work for yourself purely by being active and aggressive, there is less time for that kind of self-promotion when you're actually making records on a regular basis.

Your position is also dictated by your knowledge base, both in music and the recording of it. In fact, unless you've hatched your "I'm gonna be a *produsah*" plan as a part of some delusional teenage whim (in which case you might want to go take a music lesson or something), you probably already have a position where record-making is concerned. That position is based on everything you've done up to this point in your career. Whether you've played on records as a musician, recorded tracks as an engineer, or had your songs placed as a writer, your expertise will dictate, to some degree, the kinds of records you fit. The good news is that your knowledge base is easy to change. It's knowledge. Experience alone will cause your position to evolve naturally over time.

The great thing about producing is that you don't have to know everything about everything all the time. That's why you have a team. You can hire someone who is good at recording. You can hire someone to arrange horn and string sections, just as you can hire someone to play the parts. You can even hire someone to take care of the mundane organizational tasks for you. What you can't hire is a leader with the vision necessary to complete the project. That all falls on you.

Vision is probably the most difficult subject to teach. I mean, how the hell do you teach someone vision? How do you teach a person creativity and imagination? I don't think you do. And honestly, if you have limited imagination when it comes to presenting music, then you're not going to be a very effective producer in the short run. If you're not a naturally creative person, and you think that producing is merely a matter of harnessing the creativity of others, think again.

Yes, at times, that's exactly your job—to harness the creativity of others—but one person has to have the master plan in mind; otherwise discipline goes out the window, and the record-making process becomes a hit-or-miss affair. You should know before you set foot in the studio how your album is going to come out, and the answer should be the same every time: great. You can't just close your eyes and hope everything works out in the end—not if you want to actually be good. Furthermore, you can't gain the trust of your brainchild, band, or team if you don't drive the creative vision of the project—a vision that should be stated with absolute clarity, even if no one will truly appreciate it until the record is complete.

Vision and leadership go together. If you have a vision, believe in a vision, and can sell a vision, you can lead. Whatever you do, don't underestimate the importance of leadership and vision in producing. Out of the many roles you have, nothing is more critical to the quality of a record than your leadership. Not even musical knowledge. That's right—I'm telling you that your knowledge of how music works is of considerably less importance than your ability to lead the team toward your vision. That said, even if you know little about music theory, you will need to have some basic understanding of arrangement.

Musically speaking, arrangement is one of your main concerns when producing a track. That's not to say that you must understand how to voice-lead four-part harmonies—that's a skill set that can take years to master. In fact, most musical rules are born out of common sense. A rub is a rub is a rub, and while the educated musician can explain what rule was broken, even the most musically ignorant listener will notice the rub in the first place. In other words, knowing the rules where music is concerned merely simplifies the problem-solving process. Barring the tone deaf, hearing the problem in the first place is somewhat inherent.

I'm not suggesting you should go through your producing career satisfied with knowing little about the inner workings of music. Such knowledge will undoubtedly make your life easier. But the kind of arranging necessary for modern records is not difficult to learn, particularly when you're working within the existing musical structure of a band, where polyphonic instruments reign supreme. This simplifies matters significantly from the days of Beethoven, when nearly every part of a symphony was performed by a monophonic instrument.

There are only five functions in arranging: rhythm, melody, countermelody, call-and-response, and harmony, which we'll discuss in detail later. Once you're able to break down an arrangement in this manner, and once you understand that the human brain can only decipher five distinct parts at any given time, arranging becomes far less complicated to implement well, even if it does take years to fully master.

Still, despite my claim that basic arranging is relatively simple to grasp, people somehow manage to fuck it up on regular occasion. I don't really understand why. If you just evaluate your favorite popular records, you should notice certain obvious similarities that will provide you with some basic "rules." The simplest of all being, *leave room for the vocal.* I mean how hard is that, really? The vocalist sings. The guitar player plays a lick, the vocalist sings again, the fiddle player plays a lick. And while that may be a rather rigid and oversimplified explanation of an "Arranging 101" technique, you are far better off to make records like that than to err in the other direction. If you make it so the instrumentation constantly competes with the vocal for the listener's attention, you will greatly reduce the effectiveness of your production.

I can give you a good leg up where understanding and implementing basic arranging is concerned. After that, it's a matter of learning when and how to break musical rules effectively, and that's merely a matter of listening to the great records that came before you. You can even practice your arranging skills with programs like GarageBand, where you create a production by combining loops. Once you're producing a band, you can always use hit-or-miss techniques in the overdub process to accomplish your goals. Believe it or not, even someone highly skilled in arranging works to some degree in the hit-or-miss modus operandi.

While arranging is the same regardless of what kind of record you're making, it's politics that complicates work with a band entity. You're operating within multiple personalities, all of whom individually affect the artistic product. Everyone has a role, and those roles are not necessarily constant in nature. Some bands, for instance, have multiple songwriters, which can cause a shift in power from song to song. Some bands carry multi-instrumentalists. Some rotate instruments. All of this must be accounted for when producing an album.

Fortunately, even in a highly dysfunctional band (and believe me, they're all dysfunctional to some degree), there is a leadership structure. As complicated as it can be to herd five unique personalities in the same direction, it can be as simple as recognizing who is already tasked with that responsibility. In most cases the existing leader is your conduit to effective politics. This somewhat obvious revelation is not, however, any sort of magic bullet. Your patience and ability both to adapt and to withstand nearly retarded attempts of free will shall be tested within a band entity and on regular occasion, should you allow it. Such is the nature of the beast. If you can figure out how to play politics as an outsider within the band structure, and if you can learn how to use leverage in a wholly honest manner (an oxymoron if there ever was one), then you will be able to adapt to nearly any political situation— both in and out of the studio.

Band politics become easier as your discography expands and improves, but you will never be able to rely solely upon your laurels. Your accomplishments serve only to grant you an initial meeting with an open audience. After that, you are judged on your actions and overall effectiveness as a leader, just like anyone else. Whereas the young producer must work hard to earn the trust of a band, the veteran producer must work equally hard to retain that trust. It is nearly impossible to repair broken trust, especially given the kinds of time frames that exist within the record-making process.

We will discuss politics throughout this book, although if you follow my suggestions when it comes to clear and honest communication, you'll lighten the load considerably. You will also greatly refine your political skill with each and every record you make. For starters, you will recognize potential traps more quickly. Identifying and thwarting hazards before they occur is the best way to avoid them completely.

Effective politics alone will not be your saving grace when it comes to producing. The more understanding you have of the process itself, the easier it is to clearly state your goals before you achieve them. Don't underestimate the power of explanation and communication as far as goals are concerned. Politics are useless if everyone in the room realizes that you're completely full of shit. The more closely your goals match your results, the smoother the process will be throughout. When you prove yourself able to accurately convey in words what you're seeking to achieve with the productions, it becomes difficult for your clients to doubt your method or your madness.

Believe it or not, band politics are simplified significantly when there's a major label involved. A band that's signed to a label has its relationship worked out in the form of a contract. That's not to say that there aren't politics with a signed band. There are. It's just that most of the important systemic hurdles have already been cleared. A signed band entity is for the most part a modified democracy in which everyone has learned to defer and compromise based on her position in the band. I can assure you that the least important person in a signed band will not threaten to quit for fear that he might be taken up on the offer. Such is the burden of unimportance. Conversely, the most important member of the band understands that she will be deferred to well before there's any kind of crisis.

In the case of an artist with a side band, the major label contract exists solely with the brainchild. This makes the politics basic. The only person who really matters is the brainchild herself. Harsh, I know, but also true. This sort of band setup is a sham executed purely for marketing considerations (particularly in rock music). It's really an artist's contract, not a band entity contract. The "band" is therefore work for hire and performs at the pleasure of the artist. That's not to say that the band shouldn't have input. As with any musician, you want to work toward a player's strengths within the context of your vision. But the band politics are as much a sham as the "band" itself.

Some History

Since *Homo erectus* first thought to stretch an animal skin tightly across a hollowed tree trunk and then cleverly bang it with a stick, music has been an important force in human existence. Music became a way for early humans to convey their deepest thoughts, feelings, and intentions, all while celebrating life itself. The medium was certainly useful, whether performed to win over the opposite sex for propagation, to curry favor with the gods for rain, to warn nearby tribes of imminent war, or to express thankfulness for life itself, including the inevitable passing of it. Music was not an arbitrary expression—it had a purpose. It still does.

It seems that the act of sharing music is important to us as a species. It is human interaction and societal culture that propels music, not the needs of any given individual. Music is a communication tool, and as such is meant to include others. Oh, I can hear the arguments now. But what of those who acquire great solace playing their instrument alone? Why, that's nothing more than preparation for an audience. And what of the teenager who listens to sad songs alone in her bedroom? That might be a good point, were someone not actually singing *to* her. A successful performance creates an inherent connection between singer and listener, even in the form of a reproduction.

Of course, long before the drum was invented, man most certainly sang—whistled even. We couldn't live among the birds for very long without attempting to mimic their songs (although it seems to me that song is as instinctual to man as it is to bird). Singing was certainly an important step where the creation of music was concerned, but it was really only half the equation. Man needed something more. Man needed a beat. A *pulse.*

Oh, I'm sure some of you might bristle at the suggestion that a pulse is a requirement for music. Depending on how you define "music," it would certainly be debatable. But if there's a melody involved, there must be a pulse. Without one, note duration is undefined within the melody itself. Perhaps a rubato melody lacking any semblance of time falls within the definition of "music," but unless that melody can be repeated, there is no *song*— an important distinction—and without a performance of that song, there is no *production*.

The moment man first combined improvised singing and drumming, he made a great leap forward where music is concerned, but without some organization and repeatability, that first attempt would travel only as far as the sound itself—perhaps a few miles. Improvised music could not be reproduced, and was therefore local and transitory. But once someone set a definitive melody to a drumbeat, the whole game changed. Not only did we now have a song, but we had a production of it as well. With the production of a song came *repeatability*. Now a song could travel beyond the scope of its initial performance. A song could be reproduced.

Passing a song from one person to another by rote is admittedly a rather crude form of reproduction fraught with problems. If you've ever played the game of "Telephone," you understand it's unlikely that a song survived many generations of hand-me-down reproduction without undergoing some kind of metamorphosis. The first successful songs were likely nothing short of open-source projects subject to constant changes down the line. There's no telling how a particular song might have changed over time. Further complicating matters, as a song morphed, so too did its production. After all, drums were mostly limited to rhythmic function. Eventually, harmonic instruments would come into play.

As man developed tools for hunting and war, his capability to produce musical instruments expanded tremendously. It probably didn't take long for early humans to figure out that they could produce a tone by blowing across a hole in a hollow stick, or by plucking a stretched vine. The creation and construction of scalable instruments, however, required tools. As our tools advanced, so too did the complexity and quality of our instruments. Once ore could be successfully removed from rock, all bets were off. Metal allowed artisans to shape instruments with absolute precision and stunning quality.

Just as the technology of the written word developed, so too did the written language of music. Using reliable, ergonomically precise standardized instruments in conjunction with Western scales and notation, composers were able to write more complex works. A single composer could not only designate who played what when, but also notate it in a manner that allowed for consistent repeatability. This was a major advance in reproduction technology. Now a record of both the song and its production could be preserved and reproduced centuries later, without requiring a direct transfer from one human to another. All that was left to reproduce was a particular performance. That would require electricity.

It's remarkable when you think about it. Thomas Edison wasn't just responsible for harnessing and delivering electricity; he also invented many of the early products that used electricity. This included his 1877 invention of the phonograph (of all things!). With the phonograph in conjunction with the microphone, the world had its first practical recording and playback device. Now, man could reproduce a song, a production, *and* a particular performance. Granted, the recording was a distorted facsimile of the original, limited in bandwidth and smothered in scratchy noise, but that didn't matter. Poor sound quality was irrelevant given the convenience (sound familiar?). Music fans were no longer relegated to localized live performances. Music could now be automatically reproduced by the consumer, and therefore sold. Enter the Music Business.

The phonograph wasn't the only popular reproduction device of the time. The player piano was invented in 1876, and proved to be a remarkably popular form of entertainment. The great thing about the player piano was that it allowed families with limited musical ability to gather around it and sing together…but then, so did the phonograph. And the player piano, with its programmed mechanical reproduction, required human power, while the phonograph offered automatic reproduction. It's no mystery then why the phonograph ultimately won the battle for dominance. Regardless, they were both exceptionally popular forms of entertainment at the turn of the 20th century. In 1902, up to 75,000 player pianos and 1.5 million piano rolls were produced. Meanwhile, phonograph records were selling in the millions.

With the invention of the phonograph, composers no longer required sheet music to convey their vision of a production. They could record an actual performance. Of equal consideration, the end user could automatically reproduce that performance on a later date, at any location, as long as there was electricity available. While this new recording technology opened up the scope of music and the distance that it could travel, there were still physical limitations. A piano and corresponding roll, or a phonograph and disc, were needed in order to reproduce music. Given the times, it seems unlikely that such technology was available to anyone but the very wealthy. Even so, it had to have a stunning effect on how a song was spread.

Before recording technology came into play, a song would have to be passed from person to person—traveler to traveler—over the course of many years in order to reach human consciousness. Even with the public's limited access to phonographs and records, a song at the turn of the 20th century could reach every corner of the Western world in a matter of months. This must have been nothing short of miraculous from the standpoint of art and commerce—that is, until radio came into play.

The first experimental radio transmissions occurred in the late 1800s, but it wasn't until 1920 that the first commercial public radio station—KDKA of Pittsburgh, Pennsylvania—started broadcasting. Few people heard that maiden broadcast, mostly due to a lack of receivers, but this changed dramatically in a short time. Receiver manufacturers had difficulty keeping up with a radio craze so widespread that nearly 60 percent of households had a receiver by 1930. Now a musical performance could be reproduced and broadcast to people separated by thousands of miles. Music could travel the world, not over the course of years or months—but in a matter of days. If the inventions of the phonograph and the player piano led to the creation of the music industry (and they did), the accessibility of radio exploded it wide open. Isn't it ironic that the Internet, for all intents and purposes the 21st-century equivalent of the radio, may have caused an equal and opposite implosion of the complacent, century-old music business?

The New Electronic Instrument

While recording, reproduction, and broadcast technology changed the delivery of music, new instruments changed the music itself. In 1931 George Beauchamp successfully incorporated a magnetic pickup into a lap steel, which was subsequently used heavily in the Hawaiian music craze of the '30s and '40s. Gibson was installing pickups into its archtop series by the early '30s, and for the first time a guitar player could actually compete with the overbearing sound pressure levels (SPLs) of a big band jazz orchestra and drummer.

Modern keyboards were also a product of electricity. In 1929 the Hammond Company was established to build electronic organs. In 1938, the Novachord became the first commercially available synthesizer. The electric guitar and synthesizer would continue to develop for a great many years, and changed music along the way. In the '60s, distortion, which had once been an undesirable side effect of recording, became a new means of artistic expression. In the '70s, synthesizers, which once took up an entire room, became modular, easier to program, and included presets, making them better candidates for touring and recording. Samplers in conjunction with turntables gave inner-city kids lacking access to musical instruments the ability to create technically derivative yet wholly new creative works, such as hip-hop. MIDI allowed electronica to blossom. Drum machines brought us the dance genre (and nearly the entire '80s decade of pop productions). There was, without a doubt, a symbiotic relationship between the technology, musical instruments, and the development of music itself.

Sorry to whip through 100 years of musical instrument history in just two paragraphs, but the basic point is that instrument technology has had a great effect upon music. So too has recording and reproduction technology.

Recording Technology

Over the past 100 years we have made numerous advances in audio technology. From the advent of magnetic tape to more sensitive microphones to improvements in amplification to stereo and multitrack recording to digital recording—advances in technology have brought us new instruments, new music, and new techniques for recording music. Unfortunately, there were negative side effects to these new recording technologies—in particular, the elevation of the producer and technician over the artist and band in the creative process.

Magnetic tape allowed a producer to edit a recorded performance, which had the effect of elevating the producer's role in the artistic process. Multitrack recording gave the producer more control over the process of recording. Now the producer could put recordings on top of recordings, dissect an arrangement into its individual parts, and then put it all back together again in the mix. This placed some of the actual artistry in the hands of the producer and his recording team. Automation allowed even more control over the mix. This greatly amplified the importance of the mix, and thus the mixer was born—a specialist. Drum machines, modular synthesizers, and samplers made it possible for one person to create an entire production without a band or sidemen of any kind. A producer could create a work without musicians. DAWs allowed a band with limited playing skills to be presented perfectly in tune and in time, making the producer more important than the band itself in the creation of a performance competitive in all the wrong places.

Further muddying the waters, advances in technology often came with negative side effects. DAWs with unlimited tracks, along with cheap hard drives, led to bad recording habits, such as the practice of delaying decisions until later in the process (you might as well shoot darts in the dark if you're going to make a record like that). Early digital technology, while more convenient, was inferior in quality to analog reproduction. The debate over which is better—analog or digital—continues to this very day, although even the die-hards have begrudgingly accepted the widespread transition to digital recording. Yet more than three decades later, with vastly improved technology, we're still delivering product in a rather flawed and limited format. Forget about that improving any time soon—consumers currently accept low-quality compressed MP3s as a reasonable alternative to full-size WAV files.

MP3s may be convenient for the consumer, but to keep their file size small, they omit "unnecessary" audio information. This information was somehow deemed superfluous by technicians who were unqualified to judge what was important when it came to *music*. As a result, the emotional impact and overall inviting nature of music are severely compromised in these compressed formats—in digital media in general—yet we continue to act as if none of that matters, just because a bunch of code monkeys figured your average punter couldn't hear a difference. Meanwhile, those of us who attempt to invoke emotional impact on a daily basis are doing our best to point out that you shouldn't evaluate how something *sounds*, when the point of music is to affect how you *feel*. But I digress, as is my way.

Additive Technology

Despite the advances in instruments over the centuries, it is relatively easy to find a drum made from hollowed-out wood and animal skin. More stunningly, a playable million-year-old drum would not seem out of place in even the most modern production. For the most part, our rich history of musical instrument technology has been additive in nature. Very few instruments, if any, go the way of the dodo bird. New instruments don't replace the old ones. Sure, for short periods of time, fashion might dictate the overuse of a particular instrument—and the near abandonment of others—in popular music, but the old instruments are never replaced or forgotten. Even a Theremin will occasionally make its way onto a record, and no instrument was ever made with the same uselessness to difficulty ratio as the Theremin.

Like musical instruments, microphones are also additive in nature. A microphone is essentially the musical instrument of the recordist, and age has little bearing on its usefulness. A quality, decades-old RCA 77 is still a wonderful piece of kit, one that I would very much prefer to have in my arsenal on any given session as a recordist. Granted, given their age, there are good ones and not-so-good ones. Maintenance and history determine the overall quality of a 70-year-old microphone. But then, an improperly stored Stradivarius will be rendered valueless.

Whereas even the oldest microphone can be an important part of your mic collection, the same can't be said for recording media. The phonograph and wire recorder, while interesting today as novelty items, have long since been replaced. Even magnetic tape is perilously close to its full demise, given the utter lack of demand for it. It's doubtful that technologies such as the CLASP system, which allow a producer to seamlessly lock up an endless loop of analog tape with Pro Tools, will be enough to save magnetic tape. At some point, it won't be economically feasible to make tape, even as a boutique manufacturer. Believe me, I take no pleasure in predicting tape's demise, and I hope to be proven laughably wrong on this by the "great tape resurgence of the twenty-tensies." I won't hold my breath. You shouldn't either.

Clearly, technology has had a profound effect on the creation of music. With the price of admission into the world of recording at an all-time low, and with direct access to information and skilled professionals on the Internet, the production of music has exploded as a hobby. Unfortunately, reading as much (mystifyingly flawed) information as possible about gear on the Internet is an inadequate and inaccurate way to learn about the artistry involved in record-making. Producing music requires a modicum of people skills. Learning how to operate a DAW doesn't. Producing is far more complicated, and frankly considerably more difficult, than any other skill in the recording business.

The Requirements of Producing

Producing requires equal parts obsessive attention to detail and reckless abandon. It requires the ability to communicate vision without getting in the way of the message. It requires strong leadership and an innate ability to follow. It requires an enormous ego in conjunction with absolute humility. It requires strength of conviction coupled with a willingness to compromise. It requires both forethought and the ability to improvise; calculation and kismet; aggressiveness and passivity; strength and sensitivity; refinement and brashness; creativity and organization; masculinity and femininity; power and frailty; passion and . . . well, more passion.

That may sound rather dramatic, but look at what you're getting yourself into. Music manipulates emotions. That's the very definition of drama. And while you should do all you can to limit the drama to the product itself, some personal spillover to the process is expected.

The goal is to keep all the emotion in the music, but as anyone who has produced more than one record knows, that's an unattainable goal. While we can't eradicate the toll of misplaced emotions, we can certainly *diminish* it—that starts with you. I mean, if you're passionate about music, you're going to allow your emotions to take over, particularly early on in your career. But given the nature of the job, it is incumbent upon you to reduce both the frequency and severity of blow-ups, and this can't be achieved if you're part of the problem. Your artists will get emotional. You will get emotional. If you can direct those emotions into the music and avoid exacerbating them with your own baggage, you'll have a far greater chance of success. You'll have a better time too.

Music is music is music. It doesn't matter whether you're producing a country album or a hard-rock album: the goal is to communicate with the audience in a manner they understand. From a producer's perspective, the difference between these two genres is merely presentation. Therein lies the crux of our job description.

The producer is responsible for the ultimate presentation of the music. Can you imagine suggesting to a hard rocker that you want to replace the distorted guitars with a clean pedal steel? Or attempting to sell the concept of "screaming the lyrics" to a country crooner? This is not to suggest that the cross-pollination of genres is a bad thing. It's not. In isolated instances, somewhat counterintuitive suggestions (like the screaming crooner) might be pure genius. Genre tapestries, as I like to call them, can be exceptionally effective in creating fresh music. Still, your artist has chosen an overall genre, which not only appeals to her, but also fits in well with her message and audience. Working against your artist's general strengths is a great way to make music that appeals to no one. Not that you'd get the chance to actually complete the work. You'd be fired during preproduction, and rightly so.

Strict adherence to genre can be just as foolish as abandoning convention entirely. I assure you, any record that stands out begins with a standout artist. That said, even a standout artist can come off as downright generic, given the wrong producer. If you merely make a safe, generic, derivative record, indistinguishable from other records of the genre and prevailing fashion, you will only serve to reduce the impact of the record. This is an absolute recipe for failure. At the very least, it's a recipe for mediocrity—and in my book, mediocrity is failure. If your artist is special, this must be made obvious to anyone and everyone. Special artists come along infrequently. You certainly don't want to be the person who presented that special artist in the most mediocre way possible.

Conversely, if you make a record that has no basis in precedent whatsoever, you might as well build a wall between the artist and the consumer. I say "consumer," because your artist won't have very many "fans" (that is to say, people who are fanatical). A record that is so far outside the mainstream as to be almost unworldly is difficult to connect with.

Given the two extremes, a successful producer will balance originality with convention. The exact ratios between the two are, at best, ambiguous, and wholly reliant on the times. But unless your artist plans on using a new musical scale with more than 12 notes, I'm thinking the ratio will lean heavily toward convention. Our creativity exists within a slightly malleable set of variables, musical rules being one of them.

The Musical Rules

I'll warn you now, if you know nothing about music, you're not likely to understand a whole lot in this next section. Read it anyway, and don't get discouraged.

As much as some of you will scoff at the suggestion, music has rules. I'll even give you one. A flat 9 is not an available tension in a major 7 chord. If you don't know music theory, that rule means nothing to you. Depending on what genres you work in throughout your career, it's possible that situation may never even come up, partly because the combination sounds so bad (which is the reason for the rule), and partly because that rule mostly has to do with jazz. The *real* kind—not today's adult contemporary version that often features a player who wouldn't be allowed to carry Charlie Parker's saxophone case. It's also possible that someone will play a flat 9 on a major 7 chord, and you'll pick out and eradicate the rub without ever learning the rule. Like I said, it's a rule for a reason.

Here's another rule: don't cross the harmony voicing with the melody voicing. I'm going to discuss basic voice leading later in the book, but essentially, if the harmony starts above the melody, it should stay above the melody line at all times. I can assure you that this is a very good rule. You will confuse the listener if you allow the melodic and harmonic musical lines to cross. You never want to make the listener think about the music. Crossing lines will most assuredly make them think, if nothing else, that they should hit the Skip button.

Now, do you need to know that rule in order to produce? No. In all likelihood, if you have a good ear for music (and let's hope that you do, given your aspirations), you would notice the problem without knowing the rule. This means you would define the rule for yourself, and the next time it happened, you would recognize it instantly. In fact, it's such an obvious rule that I've only ever seen one person try to break it. That's because musical rules are typically based on common sense. They weren't born out of academia.

The maddening part about music—or the beautiful part, depending on how you look at life in general—is that all rules should be broken. Notice I didn't say all rules *can* be broken. That's a given, and irrelevant, due to free will. No, musical rules *should* be broken, because there will be situations in which any given rule is invalid and wrong. For example, it's a musical rule to avoid parallel fifths in voice leading. This is a good rule in Western music, since moving in parallel fifths sounds Chinese to our ear. But what if you want the part to sound Chinese? Perhaps that's the point of the musical section—to sound Chinese. In that case the rule becomes invalid and *should* be broken.

As much as the Western 12-note scale currently dominates music, it doesn't define how different cultures hear music. An "A" note at 440 Hz is the same note as an 880 Hz "A." They're both "A," just an octave apart. As much as an "octave" is a human definition, it's also a physical law, much like gravity. An octave is an octave. No matter what culture you're from, it's all the notes between the root and octave that define the scale from a cultural perspective. The quarter-tone scale from 18th-century Arabic music, for instance, divides the octave into 24 notes, which is twice as many notes as what most cultures currently use.

Some scales completely avoid certain notes. The pentatonic scale, a staple of traditional Chinese music, and oddly enough, Western rock music, has only five notes within the octave. Then there's the blues scale, where the third of the scale is bent down so it falls directly in between the minor third and the major third. We call this the "blue note." Since the third defines the major and the minor, which in turn determines whether we hear "happy" or "sad," respectively, the blue note provides some ambiguity as to the nature of the key.

This might all seem like Chinese to you. If that's the case, worry not. It doesn't preclude you from producing. It does, however, at least for the time being, limit *what* you can produce. Don't let that discourage you. I promise that's not the only place you're deficient (feel better now?). Every producer has deficiencies, and your position as a producer will largely be defined by your perceived weaknesses. The good news is that your position is constantly changing, particularly if you're motivated.

Since you've reached the end of this introduction, I'm thinking you're motivated. Let's get to it.

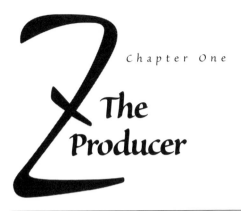

Chapter One

The Producer

Positioning

"Positioning" is a well-established marketing term. It refers to your position in the market (go figure). For instance, a Volvo is positioned as a "safe car." A Lexus is positioned as a "luxury car." All successful products have a position in the market, and that position offers appeal in niche markets.

Despite their specific positions, the Volvo and Lexus are both cars, and perform the same overall function. Yet, the makers of these cars focus on one specific selling point in order to attract a particular customer. Generally, the position of a product is purposeful. Lexus loads its cars with features that make them luxurious, and advertises them as such. Volvo makes sure its cars get high safety ratings, and markets that safety record to stay-at-home soccer moms seeking to protect their children. As service providers, we also have a position. We just have limited control over it.

If you want to be a producer, the first thing you need to address is your positioning, both real and perceived. You know what your capabilities are. Unfortunately, the primary way others judge you is through your record of past work. Further complicating matters is the relatively short shelf life of that work. Yes, the "What have you done lately?" attitude is alive and well in this business—it always will be.

Your position determines the kinds of records you will most likely win and lose. If you're known first and foremost as an engineer (based on your discography), you're not likely to produce a singer-songwriter seeking a co-writer/producer. You could be a fantastic songwriter, but if you're not known as a songwriter, your position is as an engineer, whether you like it or not. Conversely, if you've spent your career writing highly successful vacuous pop songs (I'm not criticizing), then you're going to be virtually hog-tied to that kind of record—that is, until you can convince someone otherwise. If you've spent your career producing records that are über-edited and tuned with Beat Detective and Melodyne, you're going to have a difficult time winning a wholly organic roots record. If you're bristling at the suggestion that you'll be pigeonholed like this, good. That's the first step toward fixing the problem.

Changing your perceived position is not an easy task. It takes time, and you don't have a tremendous amount of control in the process, although you do have some influence. The first step is to figure out your current market perception. If you feel you have no position at the moment, worry not—you probably do.

Most people don't wake up one day and decide that they want to produce records when they know nothing about the process and have spent no time in a studio whatsoever. Typically, producers transition from some other profession in music. Given enough record-making experience, songwriters, musicians, engineers, and studio owners are all in a reasonable position from which to transition into producing.

There are many different kinds of producers, and we should define them in order to better understand positioning. I'll warn you now: very few people fit neatly into any of these categories. They are wholly unfair stereotypes, and I promise you that my intent isn't to further propagate pigeonholing in this industry. Unfortunately, we must deal with realities here, and you will be spoken of, and about, in these terms as you are considered for projects. Worse yet, most of the time you will not be present to defend yourself or correct the record. Therefore, as unjust as these representations might be, they're also very real, and are often bandied about outside of your purview. If you want some control over your position, the first step is to understand how the market perceives you, regardless of whether it's fair.

The Musician Producer

The Musician Producer comes from a music background. Some musicians migrate to producing because they were unable to achieve any success whatsoever as a performer. Some migrate because their run of success as a musician has either ended or peaked. Some transition to producing because it interests them. Regardless of the reason, those known as Musician Producers are highly proficient at an instrument (maybe several) and are often hired because of this proficiency. There is much respect in the music industry for well-regarded musicians and artists who become producers, making this one of the better positions from which to start.

While the ability to play an instrument is not a prerequisite to becoming a producer, it sure does come in handy when you need to converse with your players without looking like an idiot (not that looking like an idiot should ever stop you). If your goal is to become a producer in any genre of music, you should learn an instrument—preferably piano or guitar, given their flexibility as harmonic, melodic, and rhythmic instruments. You can get started producing without any musical knowledge, but if you wish to open yourself up to a broader swath of records, learning music should be part of your regimen.

For the most part, this position has no stigma, unless you end up performing on every record you make, and then you will be limiting yourself to a certain sound, and to those artists who want you to perform on their album. You should be careful about how often you play on records, and be certain you're not overshadowing the artist as a musician. Otherwise, you will cut yourself off from a great many records.

The Engineer Producer

In general, it's rare for me to use the term "engineer," as I prefer recordist and mixer, but Engineer Producer is an already established category within the industry lexicon—a term I have no control over. Frankly, the pure Engineer Producer is my least favorite kind of producer. This breed of producer doesn't tend to come from a musical position. He rarely has any kind of proficiency on a musical instrument. She tends to focus on sound more than performance, and is generally weak at arranging. Given these perception issues, the pure Engineer Producer is typically limited to producing bands. Of course, there's nothing wrong with that! Bands come with songs and even arrangements, and therefore aren't typically in need of a musical expert as much as someone who can act as both arbiter and arbitrator.

If you're an engineer wishing to transition into a producing career, and you worry that this perception will limit you (and it will), then the only way to broaden your appeal is to learn music. Just for the sake of client perception alone, it's helpful if you're able to converse musically. Otherwise you'll have no way of overcoming the stigma attached to engineers. I would know. If you look at my discography, it appears that I come from an engineering background. Despite the fact that I'm proficient in multiple instruments; have studied music, harmony, and arranging at the college level; and have a 20-year career making records, I still deal with this particular stigma to some degree.

It's always amusing to me when I'm on a session, and the musicians assume I know little about music. They take me far more seriously when I shatter that misconception with a well-timed comment. The best is when I can call out a particular note or interval by ear, and then explain why it should or shouldn't be in a particular chord. The change in attitude and respect is immediate. From that moment on, I'm one of them, and I have their full faith and trust. Perception matters.

The Music Fan Producer

While you would think that this is an impossible position from which to become a producer, I happen to personally know some exceptionally talented Music Fan Producers. In fact, I've probably worked with the best there is when it comes to this particular breed of producer. J. P. Plunier, for one. He produced the first four Ben Harper albums and Jack Johnson's highly successful first album, and his only musical expertise before making these records was as a dance club owner in France.

The strength of this position comes from a deep-rooted understanding of music and production history. The Music Fan Producer gains all of her musical knowledge by evaluating records. She is so keenly aware of the production techniques that have been used over the years that she has an invaluable and innate sense of what works, even if she has no idea why. Furthermore, the Music Fan Producer is typically exceptional at combining genres and styles, and brings to record-making what an interior decorator brings to a living space: vibe.

Don't underestimate the power of this position. The Music Fan Producer can bring a fresh vision to a record through his historical knowledge of music. While it's true that this producer is extremely limited in the kinds of records he can accept, a good team of musicians and engineers can compensate for his shortcomings. Personally, I would much rather be involved with a Music Fan Producer than an Engineer Producer, mostly because the results with the former are far less predictable.

Despite the fact that J. P. originally came from the position of music fan (as well as professional photographer and artist manager), he has always worked hard to fill in his holes. Since I first worked with him, he has learned and practiced multiple instruments, and educated himself musically.

The Songwriter Producer

Songwriter Producers, particularly ones who have had a successful songwriting career, are exceptionally strong when it comes to working with solo artists lacking material. A solo artist doesn't *require* a Songwriter Producer, since songs can be acquired through a publishing company. Overall, however, the Songwriter Producer is a good fit for the solo artist, particularly when development is involved.

Unfortunately, producers who come from a pure songwriter position are often weak creatively, and bring little to no vibe where production is concerned. While I can think of several Songwriter Producers off the top of my head who don't remotely fit this description, below the upper echelons of the breed an inherent lack of creativity tends to be the norm.

Professional songwriters must constantly make demos. There is a psychology to making a good demo, and it usually entails dumbing-down the product in an effort to attract both an artist and a producer. The worst thing a writer can do is turn in a demo so fantastic that no one dares to touch the track for fear of failing to improve upon it. As a producer looking for songs to produce, are you going to select a track to recut that you think is so phenomenally executed that you can't imagine producing it better? You shouldn't. Demo-making requires an entirely different muscle from record-making. As a result, the transition to record-making can be difficult at best.

Also problematic is that songwriters on publishing company rosters tend to write exceptionally formulaic songs. This is an occupational hazard, which often translates into recording similarly formulaic, one-dimensional productions. Coupling a formulaic song with a formulaic production is a great way to make mundane music that offers instant appeal but little to no staying power.

This description may seem particularly harsh, but it's a perception that must be dealt with, particularly if it is somewhat accurate as it pertains to you. A songwriter migrating to a producing career must address this perception problem, especially if it exists. The best way to accomplish your goals is to produce an album that has undeniable vision. Once you've established yourself as a creative force in record-making, you'll be free of this stigma. If you're a good songwriter, you're likely a creative person. It's just that your creativity has been focused over time to meet the craft needs of songwriting.

The Default Producer

If you're working for a studio, and you end up as the house engineer on a project without a producer, you become the producer by default—without credit, of course. If you prove yourself valuable, you can sometimes negotiate a co-producer's credit from this position once the album is done. If the idea is met with resistance, worry not! You gained valuable experience. Nearly every young studio engineer has acted as Default Producer on numerous occasions, and that includes me. It's part of paying your dues.

Just keep in mind that as you work on records, you're defining your position. If you're credited regularly as an engineer on these records, guess what? You're going to be positioned as an Engineer Producer in the future. If you can take steps to broaden your appeal, this is the best time to do it. If you already know music, make sure that you use that knowledge regularly to boost your perceived position.

The Studio Owner Producer

The Studio Owner Producer's only qualification for producing is a capital investment in audio gear. While it's possible to become a successful producer from this position, the amount of learning necessary is monumental, to say the least. Overcoming the lack-of-knowledge stigma is even more problematic. Starting out weak in both musical knowledge and engineering is a difficult position from which to learn. The Studio Owner Producer's monthly nut alone often forces him to concentrate on filling studio time first and foremost. Typically, this means that the Studio Owner Producer is renting the artist time in his studio in exchange for experience and the title of producer. That said, it's a completely legitimate way for you to become a producer. Just understand, your improvement and success rate will likely be slow as you learn every aspect of record-making concurrently, on the job.

I don't care how experienced you are in the studio—producing is a long development process coming from just about any position. But at least with the other positions, one already has a proven skill set useful for record-making. If your only qualification is a collection of gear in a treated recording space, then that makes you more of a studio owner than a bona fide Engineer Producer.

Further complicating matters, given the need to meet studio overhead demands, the Studio Owner Producer will often have a long succession of critical failures. These can be difficult to overcome, and greatly minimizes her chances of success. You are far better off learning the engineering side before you define yourself as a producer. As the engineer, you'll often be put in the position of Default Producer. This is good. You can fuck up a great many records this way and not take any of the blame for it. Of course, if the record turns out great, you'll be able to parlay that engineering credit into other records. In other words, you can take all of the credit and none of the blame early in your career. In the meantime, you're getting much-needed experience under your belt. Good for you. Just make sure that you take some music lessons too. Understanding music will greatly accelerate your transition to legitimate producer.

The Gridiron Producer

The Gridiron Producer purposely seeks out acts that are in need of excessive computer enhancement. This breed of producer is interested in one thing and one thing only—a look. As far as the Gridiron Producer is concerned, musical talent and skill falls within his purview, not the artist's.

The DAW is the main weapon of choice for the Gridiron Producer. Drums are sliced and diced, and nearly all parts are aligned to grid. Bands that can hardly play are fair game, if not desirable, to the Gridiron Producer. No performance is sacrosanct. The Gridiron Producer is beholden to good timing and good tuning over any other production technique. As such, she seeks out and attracts bands that play poorly and rely on technology. Becoming known as a Gridiron Producer is a self-fulfilling prophecy, one that all but guarantees that good musicians will avoid you like the plague.

If you want to spend your life being the only talent in the room (and I'm being kind, since it requires little talent to edit to grid), then the Gridiron Producer is a great position to take. If your goal is to work with great musicians, you're making a big mistake. You will be completely discounted and get no respect from real musicians who have no need of your computer.

The bitch about being a Gridiron Producer is that it only takes one record to get branded as such. Once this happens, getting out is nothing short of a monumental task. So be extremely careful about this particular perception, unless it's one that you relish, because you're going to be stuck with it for a good long while.

The Luddite Producer

Luddites, by definition, shun technology. The Luddite Producer will avoid editing within the computer at all costs, and believes that there's a certain beauty to bands that are slightly out of time and tune. The hardcore Luddite Producer won't alter a performance at all, and seeks vibe over all else. Analog tape is usually the preferred recording medium for this breed of producer, as it bypasses the seductive and slippery slope that is computer editing.

Frankly, this producer is all but extinct in her purest form. You might find producers with Luddite tendencies, but it's almost impossible to maintain a career today as a pure Luddite. You might find yourself acting as a Luddite Producer on a particular project that warrants it, but that's about the extent of it at this point.

For the most part? Extinct.

The Hip-Hop Producer

The Hip-Hop Producer is, by default, the person responsible for creating the beat. It is not unusual for this producer to have stock-piles of beats that she can shop to rap artists. A hip-hop artist's rhymes are often written to existing tracks, and as such, the producer isn't attempting to make an arrangement that works with the lyric and melody, but rather a beat that inspires the artist to flow.

This is not to denigrate the role of the Hip-Hop Producer in any way. It's a highly creative medium where the process is the very definition of teamwork. In fact, the producer who makes the beats is also listed as a songwriter, since his role is so crucial to the existence of the work in the first place.

Most rappers spend their time developing their ability to flow in rhyme. The best rappers can rattle off a rhyme on any subject at any moment, and in a compelling manner. Developing this skill is a full-time job in its own right, and given the urban roots of the art form, it allows young artists to be creative with minimal monetary investment. Even the buy-in requirements of a Hip-Hop Producer are considerably lower than in any other genre. It's an art form that was created on the streets, one in which sonic clarity is secondary to a powerful beat and rhyme. Often, the more fucked up it sounds, the better.

If you're not intimately familiar with what it's like to grow up in an urban setting, this can be a difficult genre to excel in. That's not to say that growing up in the hood is a requirement, but not growing up in the hood certainly puts you at a disadvantage. If black urban music is what interests you, and you don't have any kind of street cred, you're far better off working on hybrid music, which melds R&B, soul, rock, and/or funk with rap.

I worked on many rap projects in the early '90s, and was immersed in the lingo and the culture. Even with that cred, I was still considered an outsider by people who had a genuine (and mutual) respect for me. I never took offense. I mean, I was a young 20-something who came from a middle-class suburban background. I didn't know a single person who actually spent time in jail, and that alone set me apart from my clients and their posse. As much as I could empathize with the plight of these inner-city rappers, as much as I could recognize the injustice of what they live with in the United States, it would be impossible for me to fully relate to their experience. They knew it and I knew it. That made transitioning into producing pure urban hip-hop a nonstarter for me. Interestingly enough, transitioning to Country Music Producer as a cultural outsider is also problematic (unless you're Mutt Lange and you're banging Shania Twain—then you can count on yet another 25 million albums, even as an outsider).

Just so we're clear, I'm not saying that if you're a white kid from a suburban neighborhood you can't become a Hip-Hop Producer. Not at all. But you will have considerable cultural challenges to face. Of course, overall you'll most assuredly have far fewer challenges in life than the inner-city African-American and Latino kids with whom you'll ultimately compete. But then, therein lies the rub.

The Absentee Producer

This is the rarest breed of producer in the business, and for good reason. You pretty much can't get away with being an Absentee Producer unless you're so successful that you're literally a mogul in the industry. Yes, the Absentee Producer doesn't even bother to show up to sessions, except occasionally. Rather, he works from his house and hires a highly qualified engineer to act as the Default Producer (for no credit). Seeing as the fun part of producing is what actually goes on in the studio, I'm not sure that this is something to which one should aspire. While I'm hopeful that you'll become so successful at producing (don't forget to thank me at the Grammys) that you can make the transition to Absentee Producer,

I'm equally hopeful that you resist the temptation to operate in this manner.

The Hands-on Producer

The Hands-on Producer is the exact opposite of the Absentee Producer. The Hands-on Producer never wants to leave the room. Ever. For anything. He never wants to miss a great moment, and is at all times involved in nearly every aspect of the recording. Oh sure, she'll delegate certain tasks, but not without taking the time to carefully inspect the work upon its completion. Even on those occasions when the Hands-on Producer temporarily passes his producer's scepter to the recordist or artist, you can usually find him lying on the couch in the back of the room, attentively listening, as he appears to sleep. I'm quite familiar with this type of producer. It describes me.

On the surface, there's nothing wrong with being a Hands-on Producer, so long as you don't get a reputation for being so detail-oriented that you lose sight of the big picture. We will be discussing how you do that throughout the course of this book.

The Self-Producer

There are perhaps a handful of people in the world that would get my blessing to produce themselves. For everyone else, I advise against this.

Now, don't get me wrong. There is nothing wrong with producing your own material if the purpose is to gain experience. But if your goal is to be a successful artist, you should leave the producing to others. Producing is a full-time job, with requirements that cannot be performed by the artist. It is nearly impossible for a producer to talk an artist down from a metaphorical cliff when she's talking to herself. There is no instant external feedback available to the artist without a designated producer. There's no one to take care of all the mundane but necessary organizational requirements. There's no one to keep the pulse of the session and make smart, rational decisions on how to change course for the sake of morale. There's no one to offer encouragement. There's no one to propel the vision forward.

This leads to an album or track that takes far longer than it should to make, and the process is fraught with bad decisions made due to the artist's particular set of weaknesses. Only a super-artist, with strengths in musicality, songwriting, and engineering, has the requisite skill set to adequately produce himself, and even then it's not advisable. And let's not kid ourselves. When an artist brings the studio engineer into the fold, she's basically just hired a Default Producer who has no power in the process.

If you're reading this book because you intend to produce yourself for the purposes of becoming a successful artist, I encourage you to read on, because by the time you're done, you'll likely change your mind. A team offers an artist the group's collective strengths to overcome any given individual weaknesses, and unless you've been making records for decades, you likely have a great many holes in your skill set. Any of you who shun this commonsense notion are merely letting your egos get in the way. As far as I'm concerned, that's just further evidence that you shouldn't produce yourself.

The Armchair Producer

The Armchair Producer is that guy, usually a friend of the artist or the band, who thinks that his input into the process as an outsider is just as valuable and appreciated as the input coming from within the team. While it's unlikely that you would buy this book specifically to make the transition to Armchair Producer, it's important to understand how to deal with this particular breed of producer.

The most problematic part of dealing with an Armchair Producer is that they often have the trust of the band, or at least one member of the band. If that member happens to be the brainchild, then it's critical to deal with this producer as soon as possible—otherwise your decisions are going to be second-guessed the whole time.

Given the relationships between everyone involved, castrating the power of a legitimate and trusted Armchair Producer requires a politic approach. Often, the best course of action is to give that person some of your busy work. There's nothing better than translating the enthusiasm and energy of others into a reduced workload for your team. Editing tracks for timing and tuning can often be left in the hands of the Armchair Producer, as he usually has the chops, and will likely work hard to please you. Once you have the Armchair Producer reporting to you, he will relinquish his influence with the band or artist, because he's basically bought into your leadership. This is good.

The Band Member Producer

The Band Member Producer is similar to the Armchair Producer, only he typically has fewer skills, less understanding of the process, and a big fucking ego. As such, offering a Band Member Producer busy work is often a risky call, unless you want to have to redo it, and then suffer through the ramifications of his bruised ego. Most problematic of all is when you upset the Band Member Producer. If you piss off your Armchair Producer, he'll just leave. Problem solved. If you upset the Band Member Producer, you're stuck with him. *Uy yuy yuy.*

The Band Member Producer is also far more overbearing than the Armchair Producer, and for some inexplicable reason, she believes part of her role is to run the session. As much as diplomacy is the preferred method of dealing with problems, there is nothing more maddening than having one part of the team fucking up the general flow of your session. As such, it is not unreasonable for you to yell at this person. Yes, I'm giving you permission to yell, and in the very first chapter of a book on Zen producing. This *must* be some sort of record.

Whether you choose to yell or not is up to you, but there will be times when you must take the drastic step of asserting yourself in such a manner, that there is absolutely no confusion whatsoever as to who's in charge. As much as record-making is a team effort, there can only be one person running a session at any given time. I even go out of my way to dub members of the band "temporary producers," just so it's crystal clear who's in charge at any given moment. I also reserve the right to revoke that privilege, as there must be only one person "at the con," as it were. As long as everyone on your session understands this, you will maintain a much-needed efficiency within the confines of a rather inefficient creative process.

Sitting down with your band or artist to explain how your session will be run is a good start for dealing with any potential, or realized, Band Member Producers. Unfortunately, this heart-to-heart is typically not enough to prevent uncomfortable situations—hence my permission to yell.

I will acknowledge that in general, it's inadvisable to yell at your band or artist, but it is even more inadvisable to relinquish your control, particularly to the one person who is guaranteed to fuck everything up. The way I see it, anyone brash enough to try to take over your session will generally respond well to a stern reprimand. Therefore, it's best to take a rather unyielding position, stated in uncompromising terms. And while it's totally unnecessary to raise your voice the first time you say, "I'm running the session," it's nearly unavoidable the 10th time you have to say it.

I suppose you could consider throwing the Band Member Producer a bone and letting him take over the producing reins occasionally, but he typically has his head so far up his own ass that the result is often disastrous. Furthermore, you'll piss off the rest of the band, subjecting them to his tyranny. This will serve to create chasms within the band (if not widen existing ones), and will often result in a band intervention. This is a risky move when making an album, and I highly advise against forced interventions during the recording process. They have a nasty way of backfiring. Welcome to the world of producing.

The Hybrid Producer

While it would be nice to categorize people in such clean terms, the knowledge base of any given producer is often considerably more complex than the classifications I've laid out above. The problem is that we are at all times dealing with others' perceptions, and while we have some control over those perceptions, that control is akin to pushing a rather heavy vehicle: you can move a stalled car on flat ground in neutral—some distance, even—but it requires a great deal of effort for little relative movement. Still, we must try.

I can assure you, there is nothing more maddening than being pigeonholed. As your name begins to be bandied about, you will often be relegated to one of the rather unflattering categories above. If you work in only one genre, the problem is even worse. You really only have two ways of dealing with how you are perceived. Go with it, and allow the simplistic perception to define your position and brand. Or, take active steps to overcome such unfair positioning. In the short run, the easiest solution is to go with the perception. Unfortunately, that will likely prove problematic in the long run.

If you really just want to make a particular kind of record, or work within a single genre, then capitalizing on a stereotypical position based on your background can yield good results in short order. While such a position can make you highly sought after by certain clients (like major labels), you will find yourself producing rather uninventive and safe projects. These kinds of projects will often yield good, but formulaic, results. The problem—aside from "good" being a rather lame goal—is you put yourself entirely at the mercy of an ever-changing industry. Once your style of production goes out of fashion, you're fucked.

Like basketball, producing at a high level is often a game of runs. Unlike basketball, you might only get one run. Two, if you're lucky. Three, if you become adept at reinventing yourself. Unfortunately, even if you can manage three runs, you will have to survive the painful periods between them. After a while, you might actually regret the decision to make the same record over and over again, ad nauseum. This is particularly true when your run ends, and you discover that not only are you viewed as a one-trick pony, but your trick is no longer desirable. Once this happens, you have limited recourse: you can either retire and do something else, or reinvent yourself—a process that can take considerable time and vigilance.

It can take years to overcome the perception issues associated with a discography laden with one particular style and genre. Not only will it seem as though you're only capable of producing one record, but in a style that is somewhat undesirable. And while one well-timed record can change that stigma, it must be a rather successful one. The more likely scenario is that you'll have to make several records outside of your genre in order to overcome your established position. Not only will those records be more difficult for you to win, but you'll likely end up having to reduce your rate to secure them. That is why it's so critical for you to continually evaluate the perception of your brand within the community. If you're not vigilant with regard to your position, you can literally kill your career, and for good.

Overall talent and a keen ability to sell yourself are important traits that can come in handy. Sadly, if you don't get the call in the first place, selling yourself is fairly useless. You can't close a deal that you don't know is on the table. I've caught wind of more than a few situations in which I was up for a gig that I never had the opportunity to pitch. Absent the ability to sell yourself, you are at the mercy of any and all perception issues associated with your name and work. So, discount how you are perceived within the community at your professional peril.

Getting past perception issues is best achieved by defining yourself through the records you make. The more diverse your discography is, the more difficult it will be to classify you beyond your all-around abilities. And while you will never be considered an "expert" in any particular genre, I would rather have that stigma than be considered an expert in only one genre. But that's me. You need to figure out what works best for you. Clearly, you have very little ability to dictate what opportunities will arise as you progress through your career and life. Your only control lies in preparing yourself for the moment when those opportunities arise.

If you're finding yourself dismissed because of your actual weaknesses as a producer, then you have to work to eradicate those weaknesses. If you don't write music, if you're a weak arranger, or if you don't even play an instrument, you can clearly improve in these areas. If you're completely unfamiliar with a particular genre, spend some time evaluating it. A good knowledge base in all genres allows you to use cross-genre techniques in your productions. You never know when that knowledge will prove useful—my own career trajectory serves as a good example.

In the early '90s, after four years of recording and mixing in Boston, I moved to Los Angeles. At the time, rock was king in LA, and breaking into recording, mixing, and producing without a respectable discography in the genre was a difficult prospect at best. There was substantial competition for these positions. Not so in hip-hop, which was still a relatively young genre, with little to no competition for people interested in mixing and recording. So when the opportunity presented itself to record *Bizarre Ride II the Pharcyde*, a successful album often touted as being one of the top 25 quintessential hip-hop albums of all time, I was not only ready, I was completely willing. Clearly, at the time, I was unaware of the impact this album would ultimately have. I liked the music and wanted to work. Go figure.

After three years of mixing and recording hip-hop almost exclusively, I was given the opportunity to mix Ben Harper's *Fight for Your Mind* album. This was Ben's sophomore effort, and the goal was to make a rock/roots album heavily influenced by hip-hop production techniques. With three years of professional hip-hop mixing under my belt, and a knowledge base in rock music, I was in the perfect position to mix it. Given its overall success, the album redefined me as a rock mixer. In fact, I haven't done a hip-hop album since then, and that wasn't necessarily by choice. That's how powerful perception and position can be.

Speculation

You can't just wake up one day, announce to the world that you're going to get hired on a hip-hop album, and expect it to happen that very day. Life doesn't work like that (usually, anyway). You can, however, set a goal to work on some hip-hop music (or any other genre), and actively work toward that goal. One way to accomplish that is to find an artist that interests you and develop her. This is called working speculatively, or more commonly, "on spec."

There are several reasons to produce an album on spec: Because you believe in the project, and you think you can make money on it at a later date. Because you want to expand your discography for positioning purposes. Or, if you're a very new producer, because you want to gain experience in that genre. These are all legitimate reasons for seeking to produce an album in a particular genre on spec.

There will be times in your career when you come across an act so undeniable, you're compelled to take a chance on them. There are basically two ways to handle this as a producer. You can do a straightforward Producer's Agreement, where you lay out how you'll get paid on future sales, and then beg, borrow, and steal to get the project done. Or, you can sign the act to a Production Company Agreement, in which case you fund the entire record and try to make money by convincing a label to sign the act. Both of these scenarios require a contract, which we will touch on later in the book. The point is you have to be willing to take a chance now and then to further your career goals.

If you want to break out of a perceived position, a speculative project is a great way to do it. And why not? If your discography is in desperate need of diversity, you may need to take some proactive steps. Unfortunately, if you've never worked in a particular genre, it can be difficult to sell yourself for that kind of project. Even if you did the project on spec, you'd need to sell yourself. It just happens to be a rather easy sale since it's not going to cost the client any money up front.

Very few record producers are on a payroll. For the most part, producers are independent and work for themselves. That would make you a business owner, not an employee. If you want to have a successful business, you have to be willing to take chances. Sometimes that means investing your time on a record in the hope that you can get it noticed. Any time the industry is aware of a record you've done that falls outside of your position, you've made inroads toward changing your perceived position. If the record ultimately blows up, you've managed to *redefine* your position. Of course, at that point you're going to be approached with records that fall within the scope of your *new* position. You see why maintaining your discography takes vigilance?

It will take a long time before you can rest on the laurels of your discography, and even then you'll often be judged by what you're doing now far more heavily than by what you did years ago. Of course, the more successful and mature your discography, the less likely it is for a bad record to change your position, so long as you don't follow up one stinker with another.

As much as you can take an active role in shaping your perception within the industry, if you're ill equipped to make a record in a particular genre, you're not necessarily doing yourself any favors. How are you supposed to produce a hip-hop album if you never really listen to hip-hop, and if you don't make beats? Granted, making beats isn't all that difficult, but making great beats that aren't dated requires knowing the general progression of the genre.

Your skill set comes into play as well. How are you supposed to co-write an album if you've never even written a song? The answer is you can't and you shouldn't. You can certainly go to a publishing company and look for songs that your artist likes. But you're not going to be a very effective co-writer without some experience writing.

At the very least, working outside of your general knowledge base is going to increase your costs. If you decide you want to get some rock bands on your discography, and you have no skills as an engineer, you'll have to hire a recordist, and then ultimately a mixer. It's one thing to do a project on spec. It's another to fund a project, including all the personnel needed to fill in the areas where you're deficient. But hey, if you have the backing, then by all means do it. Otherwise, you need to come up with reasonable goals that fit within the reality of your circumstances and knowledge base.

Much of what you learn about producing you'll learn as you produce. "Earn while you learn" is alive and well in this industry. That doesn't mean you shouldn't take steps to learn more, particularly if you wish to expand the kinds of records you can make. I've already suggested that you should learn an instrument, or even basic music theory. You can also start writing songs purely for the experience. You can hold jam sessions to experience performing in a group setting. Your only real way to combat perceptions that prevent you from winning particular gigs is to improve in all areas important to producing. You don't have to be a world-class musician. You don't even need to be a decent one, really. But you most certainly need an appreciation for what goes into *being* a musician.

There is so much to know when it comes to producing, that even if you plan on hiring other people to fill in where you're deficient (which you should and you will), you ultimately need a working knowledge of everything that goes into making a record. This takes time, but it also takes perseverance on your part. The good news is, no matter how deficient you are in certain seemingly important areas, you can still produce. I'll bet you're happy to read that!

The Many Roles of a Producer

There are a great many jobs that must happen concurrently when producing. You are in charge of every aspect of the recording. This means you must straddle the line between having the technological savvy necessary to record, and the inspirational persona needed to get the best out of your performers. The two go hand in hand. It's difficult at best to inspire a singer to perform if she doesn't like what's coming from the monitors. While a stellar performer and a crappy recording rig is a far better combination than a crappy performer and a stellar rig, you will neuter your fabulous performer if the technology is constantly in the way.

Producing is not purely a creative job. It's half organizational in nature, for good organization promotes exceptional creativity. There is nothing creative about making your singer wait during her moment of inspiration all because you weren't prepared. It is through organization that you make the technology invisible, and this allows your artists to concentrate on simply delivering a great performance.

Let's face it: all but a handful of records are made within the constraints of a budget. As the producer, you not only need to operate within a budget, but you also need to create the entire game plan for accomplishing the record within the proposed budget. This requires a modicum of efficiency, and a willingness to stick to the basic structure of the plan. I've worked with producers who were completely lacking in organizational skills, and their records suffered as a result. It's not enough to be a creative and visionary genius. Producing requires the ability to work politically to keep everyone on task without making the process so rigid that it stifles creativity. Believe me, that's a balancing act of epic proportions.

Certainly, vision and leadership require creativity, but you cannot lead if your actions are so unpredictable and nonsensical that no one can keep up. Making a record requires some order, as does music in general. One of your main jobs is to keep everyone comfortable and working together. If you leave all logical convention behind, you'll stress out your band.

Suppose you plan to cut three songs a day in tracking, and then you inexplicably abandon that notion to begin overdubs on the first song. Not only is your band likely to revolt, they're going to wonder what the fuck is wrong with you. You're paying for a tracking room. You have a limited number of days in that tracking room. Why are you doing overdubs? Because you're "feeling it"? All you're going to be feeling is the metaphoric equivalent of a boot upon your ass, and rightfully so.

That said, there are times when momentarily abandoning a plan makes sense. If the horn section you intend to hire is going out of town, recording them a day early is a reasonable change in plan. If your artist just started playing the most amazing song you've ever heard, then there's a good argument for taking some time to investigate it, no matter where you are in the process. There's absolutely nothing wrong with taking a two-hour detour if you're convinced it could result in the best track on the album. As the producer, you must constantly weigh creative payoff against organizational discipline.

Overall, you have two main jobs as the producer: organization and leadership. These two jobs, however, break down into a number of specific roles. Not only are you in charge of the budget, but also the time, personnel, politics, and overall musical vision of the project. How you approach each of these jobs will have an effect on the quality of your output, and it all starts with the budget.

Budget Manager in Chief

You cannot produce an album if you don't have complete control of the budget. All decisions are made based on the funds available. But let's not kid ourselves here—time is money, and many of your calculations where budget are concerned have more to do with time than any other factor. If you figure you need 30 days to record an album with a particular group, and you can only afford 15 days of studio time, clearly you're either going to have to expand the budget, or come up with creative ways of reducing the overall cost of your recording time.

If you don't have control over the budget, then you have no way of budgeting your time, which means you have no way to gauge where you're at in the process. If you're unaware of where the limit is, you have no ability to plan ahead. You are at the mercy of the person controlling the purse strings, and at all times in danger of not completing the project. A great way to reduce your career to nothing more than ashen embers is to produce two projects in a row that are never completed.

The only feasible way to produce a record is to control the budget, and to include your fee in the budget—either on a per song or per project basis. When budgeting for an album, you need to guarantee that you'll deliver a certain number of tracks. Given this, you should plan to record more tracks than your artist intends to put on the album. If you agree to deliver 10 tracks, and you only record 10, you have absolutely no room for error. One problem song alone can blow a large hole in your time budget, particularly if you're forced to complete the track. I know. I've done it.

When I produced Australian superstar Pete Murray's multi-platinum *See the Sun* album, I had to deal with just that. The label had gotten a hold of a demo for Pete's song "Better Days," and decided the song was going to be his next big hit. While it was certainly a catchy song, it was a problematic one as far as I was concerned, mostly because it was a bit too adult contemporary for him as an artist, and particularly for his youthful fan base. As such, I felt the track could alienate his audience.

The original demo was a skippy, sweet pop production, and while Pete is certainly commercial, he's not pop. As if that wasn't bad enough, the first two lines of the chorus melody weren't as interesting as the verse, which meant the melodic payoff really didn't enter until halfway through the chorus! Between the skippy beat, the delayed chorus payoff, and a label hot for the track, I had a challenge on my hands.

I won't go into all the sordid details, but out of a 28-day session to record the album, I spent 7 of those days on that stupid fucking song (and I only denigrate it in this manner because of what I went through to make it right). I cut it four times. At one point, his manager asked me incredulously, "You're cutting it again?" Yeah. And I would have cut it a fifth and sixth time if I thought it was necessary. Of course, wouldn't you know it—the track was Pete Murray's biggest hit to date. I'm glad we spent some time on it.

I fixed the delayed vocal entry and payoff by writing a counter-melody on the piano. Given the somber nature of the part, Pete suggested we have it played by a cello. Sold! We traded the skippy beat for a powerful eighth-note pedal, and kept the arrangement bare-bones simple. That was less of a well-thought-out choice than a necessity, given that every time we tried to lay down anything other than bass drums, guitar, cello, and vocal, the track immediately went into the pop/country realm.

Fortunately, none of the other tracks caused us such fits. In fact, we finished the album without going a single day over our allotted time. If politics didn't force me into producing that song, I would have abandoned it before cutting it that many times. I certainly wouldn't have spent seven days on the track. Engaging in such madness (and believe me, I acknowledge it was madness, possibly even my own) is a great way to blow your budget. In this case, we were so efficient on all the other tracks that we had the time to invest on the one. I can assure you, I knew at all times where we were at on time. It was no accident that we finished on time and on budget.

Record More than You Need

As I've demonstrated to you in the Pete Murray example, if you only cut the minimum number of songs per your agreement and one doesn't go your way, you're fucked. On a 10-song album, it's best to cut 12–14 songs so as to guarantee that you end up with 10 phenomenal tracks. This way, if any particular track gives you fits, you can easily dump it and concentrate on the others. Don't feel compelled to work on or finish all 14 tracks in the overdub sessions—that is, unless you're coming in under time and under budget.

I've worked on albums in which we've cut 18 songs, but those days are over. Shrunken budgets from an industry in the middle of its own reinvention have made an 18-song album all but impossible to do well (not that I'm crying about this—that's too many songs!). Besides, from a publishing standpoint, the artist and band only get paid mechanical royalties on 10 songs. Artists and bands are far better off putting out two 10-song albums in a three-year period than one 20-song album in the same period. This makes sense for a number of reasons. For starters, recording 18 songs in one session is a mammoth and expensive undertaking. Secondly, out of 18 songs, there are usually 6 or more that are below the standard of the others, and those tracks should be chucked, not preserved on an album. Thirdly, from the perspective of a music fan, a 10-song album with a run time of 45 minutes is a better experience than a 72-minute, 18-song album. Lastly, your band is only getting paid mechanical royalties on 10 songs! (Did I mention that?)

The budget will dictate how many songs you can record more than any other factor. That said, you should be mindful that you don't put yourself in a position where your song count diminishes the quality of your overall product. It's better to do a stellar job on 10 songs than to accelerate the creative process to accommodate 15 less-than-special productions.

Making a Budget

Before you ever walk into the studio, you need to make a budget that accounts for every possible expense. This includes tape costs, hard drives, equipment rentals, engineers, tracking studio time, overdub studio time, mix studio time, estimated overages for those days you need to work more than 12 hours, sidemen, licensing costs for samples (although estimating this is difficult, and will likely be paid for by the label outside of your part of the budget), food, alcohol and/or weed, hotels, airfare, per diems (if any), your producer's fees, and rehearsal space costs for preproduction. Mastering and reproduction costs don't go into the recording budget.

When estimating how much studio time you'll need to book, you should take a look at a number of factors. How tight is the band? Are they strong players who can nail takes with very little editing? Do the players have good tone? Are you planning on editing your production to grid? Are you working with a singer who generally only needs a few takes to compile a killer performance, or are you going to have to handhold him on a line-by-line basis? Are the arrangements mostly worked out, or are you going to be experimenting with the arrangements throughout the overdub sessions? How many songs will you be recording? How long are the songs on average? A song with a run time of five minutes takes considerably more time than one with a run time of 3:30. Seven-minute-plus songs are time sucks of epic proportions. I'm not arguing against songs this long, but you need to take the extra time required into account. Will there be an excessive amount of tedious Science Experiments? Will the arrangements generally be sparse, or dense and multi-textural?

You can't determine all of the answers by merely listening to the demos. You need to get into a rehearsal and see how well the band takes direction. If you're hiring outside musicians, the calculus is generally simpler. Professional studio musicians tend to work fast, have good tone, and don't require as much love as your typical band musician. Bands, on the other hand, are one great big X factor, and a single weak player can expand your time requirements significantly. Furthermore, if your band will be subjected to heavy-handed Gridiron editing and tuning, this must be accounted for within your estimations. Editing takes time, and while Beat Detective can reduce the time sap, it also tends to completely eradicate all musical feel from a performance. In general, the more editing and/or computer manipulation required, the longer the overall recording process will take.

I can promise you, anyone who makes their living as a Gridiron Producer will take issue with the idea that their productions take longer. I've made albums in every way imaginable with all skill levels, and I can assure you that any album that requires Gridiron techniques will take considerably longer than an album with quality musicians. If you choose to live the life of a Gridiron Producer, that's fine by me, but don't think for a minute that it's a faster process. It's not. That said, there are ways to reduce the extra time required, but that just shifts your costs from time to personnel.

If you're a Gridironer, one great way to cut down on your track-ing session time is to hire an editor who can work in the next room as you cut tracks. This way, you're not paying top dollar to edit in a room that you primarily rented for acoustical purposes. It's far cheaper to hire an editor to work as you continue to record than to stop recording in order to edit in an expensive tracking room.

Editing strictly to grid requires little to no talent whatsoever, so there's really no reason for you to be there for that part of the process. All you need to do is oversee the results. If the goal is to leave the "good" time discrepancies intact, you need to find someone who is not only skilled in editing by hand, but also able to make those kinds of judgment calls on your behalf. You may want to make sure that you've established a protocol with your editor before releasing her to make subjective decisions for you. Once she understands your preferences, she should be able to work on her own without constant monitoring.

If you were thinking it might be a good idea to record your basic tracks and leave the editing for later, I would seriously advise against this. It's critical that you know exactly where you are at all stages of the recording process. Breaking down a session without solid beds runs counter to that principle. You could very well find yourself at home with a compromised track. This can be exceptionally problematic, particularly if it's an important song on the album—a colossal mistake on your part. The mere act of setting up a second tracking session to repair your error will be so costly and disappointing that you could greatly reduce your artist's trust and morale. Don't risk it. Make sure you have everything you need before packing up your tracking session.

As the Budget Manager in Chief, it's important to realize that you don't budget money without budgeting time. They go together. Time is money. How much you have to spend daily on a tracking studio has everything to do with how much time you need to track. This is where estimations get a bit tricky. I hesitate to offer you any rule of thumb, because there really is none. So much of it depends on the abilities of your players, the density of the arrangements, the run time of the songs, and your ability to make quick decisions. A band like Radiohead, which tends to record on two-inch tape with minimal editing (if any), reportedly only needs a day per track. That's an exceptionally fast pace in the grand scheme of things. It also happens to be a good pace for them, because a time restriction like that forces an appropriate product. Conversely, a band like Linkin Park, who are heavily manipulated and polished in a computer, could require as many as five days per track, if not more.

Sometimes it's easier to budget your time into separate tracking and overdub sessions. You can get a reasonable idea of how many days you need to track in the rehearsals. If the band has no problem performing the songs and you're looking for a reasonably polished product, you should be able to record three beds a day during the initial tracking session. Of course, you may only end up with usable drums on those days. It really depends on the kind of record you're trying to make, as well as the abilities of the band.

Sidemen

Sidemen are musicians for hire. They are not a part of the core group, and do not have a direct stake in the project. It's not uncommon to bring in sidemen for horns, strings, percussion, and specialized instruments. Sidemen can be rehearsed, or come to the session unfamiliar with the music. This depends on how comfortable you are with working on the fly. I personally prefer to work with sidemen on the fly, particularly during the overdub phase. If the sidemen are also the tracking band, then I prefer to rehearse them like any other band, although the budget can make a rehearsal prohibitive.

Scheduling sidemen for an overdub session can be somewhat problematic, given the necessary coordination and preparation.

You're limited in what you can do shortly before a scheduled sideman session, and poor planning can result in the interruption of a productive session or cause an unproductive one. Then, of course, there are the listening sessions that usually ensue after each and every sideman records (which can be a great morale boost for your artist, so I'm not knocking it). Just from the standpoint of logistics, the more sidemen you'll need as part of the overdub process, the more time you'll need to budget.

Sustenance

I almost always include food in the budget. It's worth it to set aside enough money to feed everyone two proper meals a day together. This ensures a higher-quality diet and consistent blood sugar levels, and prevents disparate and out-of-sync eating. It's better to schedule two thirty-minute sit-down meals as a team than have someone eating at all times during the session. Besides, there is nothing like the camaraderie of breaking bread together to help maintain good morale within the group. Eating together gives you time to socialize and connect with your entire team. On those occasions when things aren't going as smoothly as you'd like, think of dinner as one giant reset button.

Rentals

Depending on where you're located, you can usually rent equipment and instruments that will help speed up the process. In this sense, rentals are a reasonable and often worthwhile expense. If you're working with a band, and they have shitty instruments, or a limited supply of decent amplifiers, then you should consider renting some more appropriate equipment. If spending $500 on instruments is going to save you half a day of dicking around while simultaneously improving your results, then that's clearly a worthwhile expense—

especially if it benefits the product. While there's no doubt that the player will be the biggest factor where quality of tone is concerned, a fine instrument is often easier to play. That alone makes it worthwhile. Of course, if the record is in need of a ratty guitar tone, then you would be foolish to spend money renting a high-quality and well-intonated vintage guitar.

Beg, Borrow, and Steal

If rentals aren't readily available because of your location, or if they just happen to bust your budget, then you need to do what I do in that situation: beg, borrow, and steal.

This is where networking comes in handy. If you build relationships with the musical people in your area, there isn't much gear you won't find. Granted, you might not be able to find a specific and valuable piece, like a 1959 Les Paul, but even if you can, I'm not sure it's a good idea to borrow a $250,000 guitar and put it in the hands of an 18-year-old punk rocker. I believe there are comparable and less costly instruments you could borrow for that situation. There are musicians everywhere in the world, which means there are fine instruments within your vicinity; you just have to find them. The best way to do that is to network with anyone and everyone who likes to make music.

Local music stores are a good place to start. Not only will they have equipment that you may be able to borrow or rent, but the staff and owner will also likely know all the local musicians, engineers, and producers. They'll probably even know who owns a particular instrument in the area. Most local stores will also have a bulletin board for people to post flyers and business cards. Contact them all. Invite them to your production room if you have one, or meet for coffee. But get to know everyone in your local scene. You'll need them one day, and they will likely need you in return.

Local clubs are a good place to frequent, too. Especially if they book acts from out of the area. Live shows are a great way to make connections, and can widen your networking scope significantly. This also happens to be a fabulous way to find talent, especially if you use the Internet to do your research on a show. Of course, if you're so isolated that none of these suggestions are useful, I have to wonder how the hell you're supposed to start a producing career in such a remote location. I suppose there's always the Internet.

It's staggering how many professional relationships I've made on the Internet. All that's required is a willingness to participate in audio boards, engage in discussions, and build relationships with people who also make music. We run events on thewombforums .com that allow people to mix it up with other musicians, recordists, producers, and songwriters from all over the world. If I find myself in need of some professional help while I'm in a remote location (and it happens), I can put up a bulletin on the forum and have 10 names within an hour. There are millions of people involved in music all over the world, but involvement in the Internet community should reduce connections to one or two degrees of separation from just about anyone in this business. I needed a tuba player in Asheville, North Carolina, and a single post on the Internet garnered me three names in under an hour. Bam!—I had a professional and wholly competent tuba player on my session before the end of the day. Granted, I'm pretty well known in audio Internet circles, but then that's the point. Make yourself a part of the community, and you'll make all sorts of new and symbiotically useful connections.

If I need something really big, I'll make a direct trade. Say, a mix for some musician services. For smaller requests, the trade is implied. I mean, if you're going to borrow a fine instrument from a veritable stranger—or even a buddy, for that matter—then you'd better be prepared to do the same in return. Sometimes you don't get the opportunity to pay the favor back directly, so I view the loaning and borrowing of gear as part of a greater good. I borrow from some. Some borrow from me. All is good in the universe.

If you've never been on a session in which you had to beg, borrow, and steal, I'll tell you now, it's a major pain in the ass. It's also oddly fun, challenging, and remarkably rewarding. If you believe in the music, it's a worthwhile endeavor. With a little ingenuity and creativity, you can pretty much get anything you need to accomplish your goals, no matter how impossible they may seem. Suffice it to say, the line item on the budget for beg, borrow, and steal is zero.

Time Manager in Chief

Budget constraints largely translate into time constraints. Given this, time management is one of the more critical organizational roles of a producer.

Whether a project is large or small in nature, studio time is a significant expense in the budget. It's also the trickiest expense to gauge accurately, particularly since studio time estimates can be blown to smithereens due to circumstances beyond our control. This can be particularly problematic with a small budget, as there's little to no room for error. I mean, if the singer gets sick the week you intend to record vocals on a nonrefundable lockout session, guess what? Unless you have a particularly good relationship with the studio owner, you've just completely fucked yourself out of several days of studio time. Given a substantial budget, the loss of a few days isn't the end of the world. But if you're working with a minuscule budget, you may have made a serious error by leaving the vocals to the very end. As a freelance producer, you're in a position where you have but a few viable options: go over budget (if that's even a choice); pay for the overages yourself (and you wanted to be a producer); or beg, borrow, and steal in order to finish the project.

The size of your budget will greatly affect how you choose to work. The recording schedule can't be based purely on what's ideal, but rather must also take into account the overall budget. A generous budget allows you to camp out in a large tracking room and record one song at a time, if you like. A modest budget will force you to track in a large room, and then move the operation to a considerably cheaper overdub room. This is a common method of working, regardless of budget size. It's just that a limited budget forces the issue.

In order to plan out studio time, you need to gather as much information as you possibly can about the project. How many songs do you intend to track? How many do you intend to finish? How well does the band play? If you plan on three days of tracking time for drums and bass, that determination needs to be made based partly on the abilities of the band, and partly on how well they know the material before they walk into the studio. Given that the tracking room can be three to five times more expensive per day than the overdub room, you can really bust your budget if your band is incapable of achieving quality beds in the time allotted.

No matter how good you are at reading the tea leaves, you can still misjudge things. You'll make your time estimations based on incomplete and imperfect information. The more information you can gather before you set foot in the studio, the more accurate your estimates will be. Regardless, you must leave yourself some wiggle room, and this is achieved by padding the budgeted time.

If you believe it will take the band three days to make 10 takes, you should budget for four or five days. This may force you into a slightly less expensive tracking room. As long as you're meeting your acoustical needs where the recording is concerned, this compromise can save you from a difficult budgeting situation.

Whatever you do, don't completely sacrifice your acoustical needs due to time and budget constraints. You're not doing yourself any favors by recording in an inadequately sized room, particularly if your vision is for large, bombastic drum tones. Budgetary decisions must be weighed against the overall needs of the recording, and time is only one consideration.

Whenever you're looking at possible tracking rooms for a low-budget project, you must also meet your musical gear requirements. If the project features a pianist, there's really no point in investigating studios lacking a piano unless there's room in the budget to rent one. Once you have a list of rooms that meet your needs, you must weigh the costs against all other factors. You certainly don't want to be penny wise and pound foolish. Saving $100 a day in studio time is useless if you find yourself renting a piano for $300 a day, or if you have to put the band up in a hotel just to work there.

The studio equipment list must also be carefully considered. Depending on the quality of the band's gear, it could be worthwhile to select a room stocked with high-quality musical instruments over one packed to the gills with recording equipment. Badly intonated guitars, or drums that rattle, will cost you valuable time, and let's face it—young musicians often have fucked-up equipment. You can have the greatest microphones in the world, but all they're going to do is an exquisite job of capturing crap instruments.

These days, many of you reading this book probably have a space of your own. While this can certainly help with budget constraints, it doesn't necessarily prevent you from renting outside studio time. If your recording space is inadequate for accomplishing your recording goals, you should probably rent an outside room. When your budgetary compromises prevent you from making the record you envision, you're not doing your job. Not well, anyway. To cut corners on a low-budget project is a necessity, but you must execute those cuts in the places that will least affect your product. And when you find yourself unable to make the record you envision due to an inadequate budget, then it is incumbent upon you to present this information to your client.

Look, no matter how much you want to make a record, if you can't make the record you envision, then you're failing. What are you going to do? Put a disclaimer next to your name in the liner notes? "This album would have been exactly the way we intended it, had I just 3,000 more dollars with which to make it." I'm thinking not. So, if the budget isn't sufficient, you need to propose one that is, and if that's not a possibility, you should pass on the record.

Let me repeat that. If you can't make the record you envision, you're wasting your time by taking on the record. So, if you *really* want the project, then you either need to help your client secure more funds, or you need to reduce your fees, even if that means working on spec. If you can't or don't want to work on spec, then I contend the band isn't that undeniable in the first place. Move on. If you're thinking you can take the gig and then just go over budget, I suppose that's an option, but it's a rather risky one. It's also downright slimy.

There's no doubt that even the best planning can prove inaccurate, and there will be times when you will go over budget. Shit happens. So why not move forward with the project, wow your client, and convince them to pay more for the album once everyone is fully committed? Setting aside the moral issue for the moment, if you've made an agreement to deliver X number of songs within a certain budget, then your client is well within his rights to take the overages out of your back end. You would have been better off working on spec. It's actually unusual for a client to penalize your back end like this, mostly because when it's clear that you're going over budget, you have time to renegotiate terms. But I would highly advise against ever purposely taking on a project that's obviously inadequately funded.

One of your most effective tools for keeping a project on schedule and under budget is day-to-day time management in relation to the full schedule. On occasion you'll find yourself spending an inordinate amount of time on one track or even one part. Exploring and working out parts is to be expected. You can't reasonably shut down what could be a brilliant game-changing idea just to keep to a rigid schedule. You must leave yourself time to be creative, otherwise what the hell are you making? A widget?

Falling behind on a project is a given, and can be a useful session tool, as it tends to ratchet up pressure. It can also bring down morale, particularly if you get too far behind. Getting ahead relieves pressure, and allows everyone to relax. Between the push of falling behind and the pull of getting ahead, you can manipulate the forward push of your session. If you base your day-to-day time-management decisions on this principle, you will at all times know where you're at on a session in regard to time. So will your team. If you allow yourself to fall way behind, you will be so focused on catching up that your decision-making will suffer. Parts that should be investigated could end up being sloughed off for time considerations. This is exactly what you want to avoid.

While you don't have total control over how things go on a session, you do have considerable influence. You should certainly have some idea of which tracks will be a breeze and which a struggle. Of course, you'll be totally wrong at times, but that goes both ways, and will ultimately result in a wash. Simply put, if you're ahead, work on something that you believe will require time. If you're behind, knock out something easy.

There's a certain ebb and flow to the creative process and recording sessions in general. Working 12-hour days on a creative project will all but guarantee hours in which seemingly nothing is accomplished. This is a given, and such waste can't be eradicated from a recording session. In a 12-hour session, the most efficient work is often done after dinner. A slow start to the day is common, although many producers are their own worst enemies where this is concerned.

One of the more atrocious habits you can get into is to work more than 12-hour days, regardless of your client's wishes. Any hour of real time you might gain at the end of the night will almost always be lost the next day. Worse yet, the more long days you work on a given project, the more inefficient and exhausted everyone on the session becomes. Even at those times when you're on hour 14 and kicking ass, you will surely pay for it the next day. That said, there are occasions when it might be well worth it.

Deciding when to cut off the session for the day is a judgment call, one that you will fuck up many times in your career. At least, you'll think you fucked it up when you find yourself in hour 6 with nothing accomplished, all because you didn't have the discipline to shut your session down at a reasonable time the night before. Often, the solution is to start later, but that only works so many times before you've completely flipped everyone's schedule around. You don't think you're going to cut the session off at hour 10 when you lacked the discipline to leave hour 12 the day before, do you? Of course, that's probably what you *should* do, but that inefficient first 6 hours looms large at hour 10.

Every now and then I come across producers and engineers who prefer to work 10-hour days, or worse yet, 8-hour days. Working too few hours can be equally inefficient as working too many. If your most efficient time is in the last 6 hours of a 12-hour day, then logically speaking, an 8-hour day provides just 2 efficient hours. The argument for the short day is that of a well-rested team. This assumes 1) that your band isn't going out and partying every night (now that they have the extra time); and 2) that you want everyone well rested. As much as you don't want your entire team exhausted, you don't necessarily want them perfectly rested either. Too much rest can be equally debilitating to a session.

Creative projects require a certain amount of obsessive qualities, and I'm sorry, but you can't compartmentalize your obsessions into eight-hour blocks. It's important to the process that you immerse yourself in a project; otherwise, you risk losing motivation and inspiration. Besides, lack of sleep tends to enhance the creative state of mind. Not to overstate the obvious or anything, but that's a good state to be in when producing a record.

Whereas a reasonable amount of sleep deprivation can prove useful, the same cannot be said about food. Low blood sugar will make the entire team sluggish and cranky. Even the simplest track can become nothing short of a clusterfuck given food deprivation. This means you have to include the food schedule in your calculations. It also means that you have to think ahead. When you're completely focused on a track, the last thing you're thinking about is food. Given this, you should consider delegating someone to keep on top of food timing.

If you can manage regular eating times, that's best, but I offer my advice as someone who is relatively terrible at accomplishing that particular feat. Of course, that just means I'm decidedly experienced in what happens to a session when low blood sugar hits. If you wait until you're famished to order food, you will find yourselves working in a volatile state of mind at least twice a day.

If you delegate your assistant to take food orders at designated times, you'll reduce squabbles if not prevent a total blowout. Let's face it, some people get downright ornery when their blood sugar is low, and life's too short to *not* have fun making records. Eat.

Breaks are also useful for keeping a session on track. Given the nature of the creative process, calling breaks at regular intervals is a nearly impossible task. It's hard enough to work around dinner. You're going to work around a set break schedule too? Besides, the last thing you want to do when your session is going well is to call a break. Your group might have had another hour of efficiency in them! We can't time our need for a break with anywhere near the same kind of accuracy as we can predict hunger. Given the challenges involved, full-team breaks are usually best for "reset" purposes.

If your team is going strong, and you find yourself in need of a break yourself, delegate the producer's role for a few minutes and take one. It's important that you get out of the room on occasion. For the most part, your band and artist will have all sorts of down time. You need some yourself, but you don't necessarily want to bring the entire session to a screeching halt just so you can take a quick breather.

Be Flexible (Just Not Too Flexible)

As much as you must adhere to a budget, it's useless to be militant in your approach to time management. No one makes a list of songs and records them in that order. No one schedules two meals and three breaks and works rigidly around them. At least no one should! In fact, your management choices should generally be based on the band's overall state of mind. If your whole team is beat up from hours of working on aggressive tracks, finish the day on something mellow. If the band is up and inspired, pull out an energetic track—one they can nail in short order, especially if you're up against the end of the day. This can have the effect of sending your team home on a high, which has the benefit of translating into an efficient start the next day. If everybody's totally fucking stoned, pull out the stoner piece. If the singer is absolutely inspired to sing on a track, let her, even if you're on your tracking session. Give her two takes, and call it a day.

If you haven't figured it out by now, let me just say it plainly: time management in record-making is about keeping the team in the right headspace. The goal is to make constant adjustments in order to keep the team and the project on track. "Win One for the Gipper" speeches as Motivator in Chief can help, but ultimately, the project itself must be the most motivating factor. Countless hours of inefficiency has the debilitating effect of lowering spirits. If you don't make the necessary calibrations, you risk feelings of despair from your artists. To date, you're recording the most important work of the band's career. This is how they see it, and frankly, so should you. As a result, slow progress can freak your team right the fuck out. I can assure you, a freaked-out artist is a fabulous way to bring your session to a grinding halt.

It's pretty simple: people tend to get along when everything is going great, and are at each other's throats when it's not. So, if you want to keep your session running smoothly, you must adjust course when necessary, if only to eradicate the relatively poor mood of your team.

Personnel Manager in Chief

As the producer, you're in charge of the entire team. This includes the musicians, engineers, and studio personnel involved on your session. That's right: you're the boss. But don't get a big head. The kind of boss you are will have great ramifications on how well your team will work for and with you.

Assistants and/or Interns

If you treat your assistants like second-class citizens, you could inspire them to work against you in the most insipid ways. You should be exceptionally nice to your assistant. That doesn't mean you shouldn't ride them hard when you need to, but that must be counterbalanced with kindness.

I rely heavily on a good assistant, but then I'm usually recording my own sessions, which means I'm doing two jobs. You can't reasonably judge the performance of a take if you're checking levels, or worse yet, fucking with tones. My assistant is therefore critical in watching my back on the engineering side.

When you find yourself in a situation where you're both the producer and the engineer because of budget constraints, and particularly if you're not actually a qualified recordist, delegate many of the engineering duties to your assistant. If you're booking a room for a tracking session, request an assistant who is a somewhat bona fide engineer, interested in an engineering credit (like that'll be hard to find!). The studio manager will typically be more than happy to accommodate you, and the staff assistants will be ecstatic to act as recordist, particularly if they know up front that they'll be credited for their work. Credits are worth more than money early on in an assistant's career, since this is what allows an assistant to make the much-desired transition to engineer.

The most important attribute I look for in an assistant is vibe. There is nothing worse than attempting to record a project with an irritant in the room. Personally, I'd rather have a green assistant with a great attitude who at all times appears to be into the project than a super assistant who annoys the shit out of me and my clients. Both have their problems, but the latter is cancerous to a session, and will have an obvious negative impact on the work.

The longer someone has been an assistant, the more likely it is that he will bring a bad vibe to your session. Obviously, that's not always the case, and in smaller markets this is less true, given the lack of opportunities. But typically, if you find yourself with a surly longtime assistant, it's probably due to career frustration. You really only have two options. Bring him under your wing and involve him as an engineer. Or request someone else. Be forewarned: if you don't get some basic respect from your studio assistant or engineer, you must replace them.

If you're working in your own room and you don't have an assistant, then you should take steps to get someone to help out. The local recording colleges are a good place to start. There are far too many recording graduates for the jobs available, and the competition is so steep that you can get help for short money. The trade-off is that your assistant learns as she earns, but then don't we all?

Engineers

I stopped using the term "engineer" long ago. Mostly because I find it insulting to both the person who's spent four years in college and the guy in charge of recording "the coolest project ever." To find work as an "engineer," one needs a degree, and for good reason! Actual engineers are in charge of shit that, done improperly, will result in death. You know, like designing bridges and building jet engines. All an audio engineer can kill is a record—that is, barring some bizarre studio accident or an A&R rep intent on murdering you (that's a story for another book). Besides, specialization has rendered the term nearly archaic. These days, you have recordists, seconds, mixers, and masterers.

My friend Joe McGrath often scolds his recordists for being "engineyes." "You're an engin*ear*, not an engin*eye*," he likes to say.

Despite my feelings regarding the word *engineer*, I find that a particularly salient point. Given the advent of DAWs, recordists are all too often preoccupied with what waveforms *look* like rather than what they sound like. On those occasions when I find my team surrounding the computer screen during playback, I shut the damn monitor off.

Those waveforms will influence what your team hears. That's because we tend to rely on our sight first and foremost. This may seem rather obvious when spelled out like this, but it's critical to make audio evaluations by ear. To some extent you can learn to ignore the visual cues, but that takes years of practice, and even then you're still influenced by what you see. It's perfectly acceptable for an engineer to use visual information, but only to confirm or verify what's coming from the monitors. In reality, this is far more difficult than it sounds (pardon the pun). Anyway, I digress.

The job of recordist is largely a left-brain one. In simplistic terms, the left hemisphere of the brain is the analytical side, responsible for minutiae and detail. Whereas the recordist is recording and capturing *sound*, the producer is recording and capturing *performances*. Now, sound and performance are inextricably attached, but capturing sound requires attention to the technology, and evaluating performance requires attention to musicality. Conversely, the right hemisphere of your brain is responsible for evaluating the big picture. It's also where most of your creative thinking occurs. As a result, producing is largely a right-brain-dominant activity. It's actually impossible to concentrate on the details and the big picture at the same time. If you're focused on the details, you're metaphorically zoomed in. If you're focused on the big picture, you're metaphorically zoomed out.

I've been recording and producing simultaneously for 20 years now, and I can tell you, at all times one of those jobs suffers.

Ultimately it all gets done, but I must consciously slip between my producer's brain and my engineer's brain to achieve this. I can get away with it partly because both the producing and engineering are almost second nature to me, and partly because I make sure my assistant can adequately cover some of the engineering duties for me. That said, if you have room in the budget for a recordist, that is always best. Ten years ago it was unheard of for a major label record to be produced without a recordist. This has changed considerably in recent years.

A quality recordist can make your life considerably easier, particularly if you don't have a tremendous amount of experience in that arena. Your recordist can be your most valuable commodity on a session, since she can cover much of the left-brained thinking as you stay camped out comfortably in your right hemisphere. Unfortunately, not all recordists really grasp the producer–engineer relationship. Therefore, you need to choose carefully, and spell out your expectations clearly before you set foot in the studio with your recordist. You may have your own ideas where this is concerned, but here are my expectations for a potential recordist:

1. **I want you to have an opinion, and you can state your opinion in front of the team, but if I'm clearly in a debate of a critical nature, I need you to either back me up or stay out of it.**

Some producers like constant opinions. Others prefer that the recordist do as he's told and shut the fuck up. Personally, I like free-flowing opinions and ideas, but I certainly don't want to debate ideas with my recordist, especially if I'm clear in what I'm trying to achieve. How you run your session in this regard is up to you, but it's a problem when you have a recordist who seems to be on a different page. You also don't want your recordist to somehow become the de facto tie-breaking vote against your favor. Making a record isn't a democratic process, but when your recordist is weighing in against you, it can become one. If this happens, you need to have a conversation with your recordist (away from the band) in order to reset the protocol.

2. **Please watch my back. If I'm doing something that you know is not my intention, or if you feel I'm forgetting part of the stated plan, let me know. In other words, don't let me fuck up! I'll do the same.**

At any given time on a session you can have 20 things on your mind. Fuck-ups happen, especially early in your career, but they need to be minimized. It's up to you and your team to work together to accomplish that. If you somehow forget to record an overdub on an internal chorus, your recordist or assistant should catch that before you move on. Under normal circumstances, this shouldn't happen, but if you're working against the clock for some reason, or if it's late at night, it *can* happen. Not only will such a mistake make you look incompetent and less than professional, it will cost you valuable time.

I'm reticent to name the whole host of stupid errors I may have made in my career, for what should be obvious reasons. We all make errors. Everyone. The process of producing a band, however, is a team process, and the team must work together to prevent mistakes. Yes, you want your recordist to watch your back, but you also need to watch his. Given that record-making is a creative process, it can be slightly lax at times, and that's when mistakes happen. The trick is to keep up the illusion of a relaxed atmosphere while constantly paying attention to everything that's going on around you. But you can't be the only one. Everyone needs to participate in this, particularly your recordist. Explain it in exactly this manner.

3. Document, document, document.

There will be times when you'll want to revisit a part, or match a particular sound. I've recorded rock sessions in which there were 100 guitars and 20 amps. Even as few as 5 guitars and 5 amps allow 25 possible combinations. Add to the equation mics, mic pre's, compressors, pickup choices, tone settings, etc., and it becomes nearly impossible to return to a particular sound. You need your recordist to document the entire chain, starting with the source. This way you can get back to it later.

There is no avoiding the occasional change of mind that occurs in a production. If you ever need to change a part later in the recording, you'll need to get back to a particular tone. Sometimes you merely want to streamline the process. You may like the guitar tone on one song, and desire a similar one for another song. If the combo and chain are documented, you can be up and running in a matter of minutes. The same goes for synth patches, snare drum choices, vocal mics, bass settings—you name it. If it's something you might want to return to, it needs to be documented. You only need to experience the "matching tones" game once before you decide that this is something to avoid. Sure, you can just re-record a part, assuming it was a breeze to lay down in the first place, but the new tone (and certainly the new performance) could very well be second-guessed for the remainder of your session and beyond. There's nothing worse than that nagging feeling that your track isn't as good as it would have been. No matter how preposterous or irrational that might be in reality, this is a mindfuck of epic proportions. And even if you find yourself comfortable with it, your band might not be.

As you listen to a take, you want your recordist to document your thoughts. If you state aloud that you like the second take, then that should be documented immediately. If you seem excited about a vocal take, there should be some notation made. The more your recordist can document, the better. If she wants to assign this job to the assistant, that's fine, but that doesn't absolve her from the responsibility. Furthermore, if the assistant is doing something else, the documentation job must continue. If this all seems a bit silly, I can assure you that these notations will save you untold hours over the course of a session.

4. **Never send an artist into the room to actually perform before you're 100 percent ready to start recording. If you need time to get tones, let everyone (particularly me) know, so that no one gets frustrated.**

This is my biggest pet peeve with recordists. I'd rather have a killer take with less-than-optimum recording quality than have a shit take that presumably sounds fantastic (it doesn't). This rule goes for you, too. If you or your recordist sends the artist to stand in front of the mic only to wait as you all get your shit together in the control room, you risk frustrating them. I promise you, of all the emotions that can be used for an effective performance, frustration is rarely one of them. On those occasions frustration is called for, you now know exactly how to get it.

This particular error in judgment makes you far less likely to get that magical take from your artist. So have your recordist get into the habit of making all the necessary preparations before the artist enters the room: make sure the headphones are working; superfluous headphones are unplugged; mics are ready and scratched out; water (or tea) is available in the recording room; pencils are on music stands, etc.

When your recordist needs to get tones with the talent, she needs to be told this in advance. The recordist needs to get tones as quickly as possible, but take as much time as is reasonably necessary.

5. Trust me.

You're the one with the vision, and you may not always know the exact path to get that vision, but when you hear it, you'll know it. The more experienced you get, the quicker you'll figure out how to fix a problem. Your artist has hired you to produce the album. By the time you're hiring a recordist, your artist will have trust in you, and you need the same from the rest of the team. If you know you'll be employing a recordist for your project, there's nothing wrong with bringing her to rehearsals or preproduction, although as we will discuss later, there are no guarantees that the session will happen until preproduction is completed. If you feel like you're about to hire an engineer who is dubious of your skills, move on to the next interview.

6. Do not undermine my authority. You work for me.

A quality recordist won't undermine your authority. Sadly, not all recordists can be described as "quality."

You should be wary of ambitious recordists. If your potential recordist tells you that he too is a "producer," you might want to look elsewhere (and I say this as a person who was for hire as both a recordist and a producer for a time). The sad part of this recommendation is that if you can find an engineer who understands producing and is willing to stay out of your way, then you could be passing on a huge asset.

Frankly, if you're lacking experience, you should try to hire a veteran recordist if you can. Guys who have made a career of recording tend to know how to operate with a producer. You don't have to shy away from hiring someone who knows more about record-making than you do. This can be beneficial to your session, and a veteran can keep your session on track in an invisible manner. Of course, an experienced recordist should have plenty of references.

If you can find a recordist who gets good tones and is willing to accept those terms, then that's the person you should hire. That said, you must be willing to let your recordist do her job. While all aspects of the recording are within your purview, the recordist is there to cover much of the left-brain minutiae. As such, the recording process choices are within her purview. So, let your recordist use the tools she prefers. If you're unhappy with a particular tone, it's fair to make a suggestion, but it's more important that you present the problem and allow your recordist to come up with a solution.

Musicians

Whether you're working with a band entity or a band made up of sidemen, you're in charge of the musicians. So long as you have some basic understanding of music, you shouldn't have any problems leading your musicians. Where things start to get a bit fuzzy is when one or the other of you is unfamiliar with basic music lingo. I've worked with producers who have little to no musical knowledge other than what they like and dislike. This always makes for an interesting, if not amusing, session. Equally amusing are those sessions with a musically illiterate band member. And if everyone on your session proves equally illiterate? A thesaurus might be the best solution. That's because bizarre adjectives become the only viable way to convey a musical concept. Get used to it.

A musically illiterate musician is not necessarily a poor one. It just means you're going to have to communicate through demonstration and the use of colorful "feeling" adjectives. Believe it or not, there are plenty of great players out there with absolutely no grounding in any kind of music theory whatsoever. They play by ear and feeling alone, and are free from musical rules beyond their own innate recognition of them. At times, that can be a disaster. Other times it can prove both refreshing and beneficial to the session as a whole.

Even when dealing with knowledgeable musicians, adjectives are often the best way to get across a concept. If a guitar player is too constrained on what is meant to be a raw rock track, I might suggest that he take off his "red velvet tuxedo" and start to play with "reckless abandon." If the bass player is a bit herky-jerky on the groove, I might recommend a more "soothing" part. If the singer isn't delivering a compelling vocal, I might ask her to sing it like she means it.

Concrete examples are an exceptionally good way to communicate. I produced an album recently where I spent an hour recording a guitar solo, to no avail. That may seem like a long time to invest without intervening, but I didn't have a solution myself. Sometimes producing isn't about knowing exactly what you want at a given moment. Sometimes it's about waiting to hear what you want. (Obviously, you can only wait so long.)

When you're dealing with a struggling musician, you must weigh the consequences of pulling the plug. Whether you pull it early or late, either one can frustrate a player. In the case of my struggling soloist, I probably could have stepped in earlier. My hope was that the guitar player would hit on something by accident, some theme that we could build upon. I would much rather wait for an accident and build upon it than spoon-feed a part to a competent if not downright inventive guitarist. Unfortunately, after an hour of solo wank, we didn't even have a musical phrase worth building upon.

In this particular case, we were recording a track that had been completely reworked in preproduction. The track was originally a rather mundane country/folk song. For purposes of a richer production, and in order to accentuate the band's rather eclectic ways, we added some disco and ska elements to the production. Regardless of what you might think of that decision in the abstract, the guitar player had no clue what to put on this rather new interpretation of the song. To be perfectly honest, I was equally clueless at the time. Perhaps that was the most compelling reason to let him struggle for an hour. If he couldn't take it, I would have stepped in earlier.

With a guitarist moments away from suggesting we cut the solo (okay, okay, maybe I did let him go too long!), I had several options. I could move on and revisit the solo later. I could write a solo myself, which could take even longer. Or I could give him a concrete example that might inspire him.

"You know the solo on Michael Jackson's 'Beat It'? The one that was played by Eddie Van Halen, and that is so outside the scope of the song itself it's almost comical, yet somehow it works? Give me something like that."

He laughed at the suggestion, not because he thought it was ridiculous, but rather because he somehow understood it. How do I know that? He played the perfect solo in one take, and frankly it was nothing like the Eddie Van Halen solo. My example pulled him outside of the box that was constraining him (and me). He was still stuck on his approach to the original demo. A single simple suggestion like that, based on something concrete and well known, can immediately break down communication barriers.

Now, I purposely didn't play the Michael Jackson track for him. I didn't want him to play a solo similar to Van Halen's. What I wanted was for him to draw from the feeling he *remembered* from that solo. Feelings are powerful, and even the most illiterate musician will understand this. In this particular case I wasn't dealing with an illiterate musician. Far from it. But too often we try to communicate in specific theoretical terms, and sometimes all of that crap needs to be tossed aside.

Had the guitarist continued to struggle, I might have considered other examples, or I might have actually played him the Michael Jackson track. There are no guarantees that a particular solution will magically work. This just happens to be a nice little success story that I can share with you. I guess the point is that you can't just beat the shit out of a player for hours on end. You're going to destroy the morale of your musicians and artist. They look to you for guidance when they struggle, just as you should look to them for guidance when you have similar issues. At some point, however, as the producer, you need to be willing to come up with a concept, anything that might inspire the right performance.

Recording Sidemen

Recording a band of sidemen in the tracking session is not much different from recording a band entity. Actually, it's considerably easier, since they're working for you, rather than the other way around. Rehearsals and preproduction are still a good idea, even with a band of sidemen, although it's often cost-prohibitive to bring sidemen into rehearsals, especially if they're union players.

When working with a band entity, it's not atypical to bring in sidemen as part of the overdub phase. The exception to this is when the sideman is a somewhat regular guest of the band. In general, you should have a fairly good idea of what you're looking to achieve with a part. Sometimes you may have specific parts in mind. I recommend keeping those to yourself until you hear your musician's take on it. This has more relevance in the overdub phase, given that you're often hearing a sideman for the first time, without the benefit of rehearsals.

Every musician has a unique personality, and brings some of herself into the session. Good musicians tend to listen and react to what the other musicians are playing. In an overdub situation, your player has a concrete bed from which to work. As a result, the musical interactions only go one way. As you layer new parts on your record, the new players will interact with what's already there. I'm always interested to hear the musician's take before I offer my own, and there are good reasons for this. I don't want the production to be one-dimensional; I never want to limit a production to my own preconceptions; and I don't necessarily want to influence a musician with those preconceptions.

In all but the rarest of cases, I recommend that you allow your sideman at least one pass before you offer direction, and at least several passes before you decide to dictate parts. To assume that you would come up with a better part than someone who has actually mastered a particular instrument is not only myopic and egotistical, it's downright foolish. You're not there to dictate parts. Yes, sometimes that's part of the gig. But overall you're there to recognize greatness and build upon it. Allowing a sideman to play the track down a few times not only familiarizes her with the track, it also provides you with an opportunity to get her flavor on a track. This methodology allows you to compare what's in your head to your sideman's initial musical response to the track.

Oftentimes a quality sideman will come up with something brilliant, and guess what? You just managed to improve the record by staying out of the way. Of course, sometimes you get nothing even remotely useful, at which point it's time to offer some guidance.

Pull that great part from your back pocket and give it to her. If she's a good musician, she'll shape the part in a manner that works best with her instrument. In fact, you should encourage that. If she's unable to make the part her own, then you'll either have to try something else, or spoon-feed her the part. Sometimes a simple part is what the track needs. Of course, you very well could have the wrong instrument, or even the wrong player. At that point, you can consider your other alternatives, including a new and improved sideman.

I always cringe when I bring a sideman into a session and a band member offers direction before we've even heard a note. Musicians tend to play to their strengths, and you are well advised to find out exactly what those strengths are and how they might fit with your production before you start fucking with them. You could very well decide your sideman is far better suited for another track, even if that goes against the original plan. As you use different sidemen, you will start to acquire favorites. Even so, you will often find yourself in a session with a player you've never worked with before. Find out what he brings to the party, then use him for his strengths.

A session player who is either underqualified, or who brings the wrong sensibilities to the track, is not worth the time sap. Some people have far more patience with this than others, and while several hours of hard work might yield you something useful, perhaps even something brilliant, the more likely result is lost time. Unless you have a limitless budget, it is not a sum win to end up with a single magical (and seemingly incidental) note that happens once in the song—especially if you spent hours to get there. *You* could have played that!

The longer you produce, the less patience you'll have with musicians who don't fit the project. Veterans will cut their losses early and come up with a new solution. This scenario tends to happen most often when the band brings in a buddy, or you somehow must hire an unknown entity, particularly on an unusual instrument. Don't get me wrong: these situations have their benefits. At the very least, they're often downright comical, and can reset the headspace and morale of your entire team. But comical tends to quickly transgress to painful, followed by annoying. What's worse is when your brainchild is the one who brings the sideman into your session. She will tend to feel a responsibility to get something useful in order to spare the feelings of her hire (artists are sensitive folk). If firing the sideman is politically problematic, this is often a good time to pass the producer's baton to your brainchild and take a break.

Even if you're initially dubious of your sideman's abilities, make sure you provide him enough time to acclimate. Oftentimes, he's hearing the track for the first time, and some people find their place later than others. This is particularly true for musicians with minimal studio experience. If the musician is seemingly competent, give him the time he needs to work out a part. If he's clearly incompetent, take two takes, and move on. Like anything in producing, you have to make a judgment call based on both the politics and the budget.

Now, some of you might be reading this and wondering why I wouldn't send a rough to a potential sideman in advance. This can sometimes be the best option, particularly if the part is complex and exists in demo form. In the real world, however, sending tracks ahead isn't always an option. In my world, it's rarely a preferred option.

Personally, I like to be there for a player's first musical response to what she's hearing. Good musicians have keen instincts, and if I send a track ahead, I miss out on their gut responses. The sooner I can get the sideman on the mic and recording something—anything—the better. After a few passes (maybe less), I'll invite her in to listen to what she's done. This gives me the opportunity to point out what I like, and the musician can hear for herself what she's bringing to the track. Whatever you do, please never, ever, ever let a musician play to a track in the recording space without recording her.

Union Musicians

There will be times when it's necessary to pay your sidemen through the American Federation of Musicians union. There are different scales for musicians, depending on the type and purpose of the session, but they are far too numerous to list here.

Union sessions are defined in three-hour intervals. If you go over three hours on a session, by even a minute, the musicians must be paid for another three-hour session. Some musicians command multiples of scale, depending on their demand. Typically, the best musicians get triple scale for sessions, and that can amount to nearly $1,000 per three-hour session.

You also have to pay one of your session musicians "Leader" scale. If you hire a group of string players, for instance, you will designate one of those players as "Leader," and he will be paid double scale. Oftentimes, the leader will put together the group of players for you, so this is a worthwhile extra expense. The leader can also help you with scoring, and if you're going to bring in a plethora of string players, regardless of scale, you'd better have a score. String players in general aren't that great at winging it. Your results will likely suffer without a score. You've been warned.

You can mock up your score using MIDI, or you can hire someone to write the arrangement for you (often the leader is the arranger). Either way, there are too many musical rules involved in four-part harmonies to leave this to chance. Horn players, particularly ones who typically perform rock, pop, or funk, are often able to play by ear, and if that's the case you can get away with bagging the score. You'll have to listen carefully for rubs, but a good horn section will naturally stick to the voice-leading rules.

Paying for musicians through the union is usually more expensive than negotiating outside of that structure. Even union musicians will work for less than scale on certain projects, but if you're making a record for a movie or a major label, you will be required to adhere strictly to the union rules. Frankly, that's good for our business, because if quality musicians can't make a decent wage, then our pool of great musicians suffers. You want to get paid. Why shouldn't your musicians?

Editors

Editing can make or break the feel of an album. It can also be an exceptionally time-consuming job. An aggressive edit job on drums, performed by hand (as opposed to through Beat Detective) can take hours for a single track. Frankly, it doesn't make much sense to bring your tracking session to a grinding halt in order to edit drums. For starters, a tracking room serves as a grossly over-priced editing suite, and you risk stale, if not deflated, musicians if you use it as such. The best solution is to have the tracks edited elsewhere as you continue to make takes.

Every kid who goes to recording school knows how to edit. Not only is it the easiest job to learn, it's also the safest job to perform, given the nondestructive nature of it. Given this, finding a good editor should be neither difficult nor expensive. The tricky part is finding someone who is both musical and able to follow direction.

If you're looking for a slight nip and tuck on only the most egregious drum timing errors, you're not going to be satisfied with a Gridiron edit job. Conversely, if your desire is to have a soulless feel, and you want that wonderfully robotic Beat Detective sound, then you should hire an editor capable of such atrocities. Not everyone can perform within both sensibilities (or lack thereof). A highly experienced professional editor should be able to quickly adjust to your preferences and needs on a per track basis. There should be no need for hours of handholding. Frankly, just five minutes of your time should be adequate. Besides, whether your editor errs on the side of aggressive or conservative, it's easy for him to make the necessary adjustments upon getting your feedback. If your project requires considerable editing, or if you have a budget that can afford it, you are well advised to hire a designated editor. If not, your assistant should be able to help.

I'm not trying to slough off the importance of finding a good editor here. Certainly, it doesn't do you much good if your half-priced editor takes eight hours to do a four-hour job. Nor does it make much sense to hire an editor who can't get the job done right the first time. If your project will likely require heavy editing, it's best to find someone who can do the job both quickly and properly. This is true whether the budget is $500 or $500,000.

Mixers

As someone who has been a professional mixer—exclusively for certain periods throughout my career—I can assure you that there is nothing more difficult than mixing your own productions. Yes, even for me. If your experience in mixing is limited, you should seek out a third-party mixer—preferably a great one. Unfortunately, great mixers are few and far between.

A great mixer can read a well-arranged and well-organized production like a book. A great mixer can also save you from a confused mess of a production. The job requires musical sensibilities. As the producer, the vision of the album may be yours, but you must rely on the mixer to frame that vision for you. That said, there are strategies you can follow in order to make life easier for both you and your mixer.

Rough mixes that closely represent your vision can be helpful to a mixer, although some mixers will prefer not to listen to your rough, myself included. This is especially so on the day of the mix, mostly because I don't want your rough to influence my decisions. Some mixers aren't as precious about this, and admittedly, if a producer insists, I'll listen. Whatever you do, don't give your mixer a rough that you've determined is completely off base. It will only serve to confuse him. No mixer wants to listen to a track only to be instructed, "Mix it nothing like this." That's really not helpful.

In general, you should avoid giving the mixer a list of conceptual instructions before a mix. Words can often serve to confuse and improperly influence people, particularly when presented in the abstract. If you've done your job properly, the needs of the track should be readily apparent. The only time you should give prior instructions are on those occasions when your tracks don't match your vision without significant alteration. For instance, if you've decided just prior to the mix that you want the bridge of the song to sound filtered, this would be good information to offer the mixer in advance.

Do not, under any circumstances, provide the mixer with rejected parts. Any part you provide a mixer should be fair game for the mix. There is nothing more aggravating (and rude) then giving a mixer a shitload of parts that you dislike intensely. You're all but guaranteed to hear a mix that you dislike as much as the parts themselves. Of course, if you're *unsure* about a part, then it's fine to give the mixer. Let her decide if the part is worth using or not.

Conversely, don't give a mixer a session missing parts that your band is used to and expects to make the record. You might as well run him over with a bus. This happened to me once, and I was some pissed. I spent a full day on this particular mix, and it was rejected outright by both the band and the label. Not because I did a bad job, but rather because the producer didn't provide me with about 20 parts that existed on the roughs (which also weren't provided to me). To make matters worse, the producer neglected to inform the band of this fact. Nice.

As the producer, it's a given that you have power over the mix. But the mixer must enter into your realm as producer in order to do his job. You want a mixer involved with the arrangement decisions; otherwise you're completely neutering him. Furthermore, it's critical that you give the mixer space and time before you start second-guessing his decisions. A good mixer can explain all of his decisions. That doesn't mean he's right. Nor does it mean you're stuck with his mix. You're the producer. But the mixer must have the time and latitude necessary to present a mix from his unbiased position first. Then, if he's missed the boat completely, you can address the issues with him.

On those occasions when there's some question regarding the importance of a particular part, your mixer will generally ask you about it. Believe it or not, it's quite easy to spot a controversial part. It's also quite apparent when a part will evoke a mass mutiny were it to be underdubbed during the mix process. Controversial or contentious parts are confusing to a good mixer. Critical parts are typically precise, obviously well thought out, and best featured. Wait until your mixer is ready for notes before you start messing with his process. As your mixer completes mixes, he'll start to adjust to your preferences. That said, if your mixer's first mix is so far off base that you don't even recognize the track, you've hired the wrong mixer.

In general, you want to allow your mixer the latitude to process parts. For instance, you may have had a filter strapped onto the output of your vocal as you created the track. You should provide your mixer with both the processed and unprocessed vocal. In general, given the choice between using a producer's filtered vocal and recreating it, the sane mixer will choose the former. The unprocessed track merely gives the mixer some extra flexibility in case he needs it.

Don't ask your mixer to remake a part that you spent hours getting just the way you like it. I call these Science Experiments, and there's no reason to think the mixer can do a better job of them during the mix phase. You will exhaust him unnecessarily. No mixer wants to spend three hours recreating an incidental part that already exists on some earlier session. If he thinks he can do it better, he'll tell you. Then (and only then) should you give him the unaffected Science Experiment.

The better the recording, the better-sounding the mix. The more precise the arranging, the more likely your mixer will deliver a mix that's true to your vision. That said, I've done plenty of solid mixes on tracks containing no arranging discipline whatsoever. Unfortunately, that means there was no vision, and if there was no vision, then the production was left up to chance. It's just that I, as the mixer, was able to salvage the production. A mixer can save your ass, but if you continually leave the vision in his hands, you are making your mixer more valuable to the project than you are as the producer. I advise against this. Worry not: we will talk at great length about vision.

I'll be hammering on this particular point on more than one occasion in this book, but you should know exactly where you are in your production at all times. Even after recording bass and drums, it should be pretty clear whether you have the bed necessary to build an effective production. You're not working totally in the dark here. Preproduction and rehearsals should provide you with enough insight to imagine the other parts as you evaluate your bed. Any time you find yourself unable to put up a static mix that is more exciting than the last, you should be overcome with a feeling of discomfort. You don't have to deal with that discomfort right then and there. You can put away your track and come back to it fresh. But you should never send a track you're uncomfortable with to a mixer for fixing—that is, unless you're in a position to drop that track from the album once the mix doesn't come off as you hoped.

Your mixer may have his own thoughts as to the kind of track he'd like to begin with, but it's usually best to start him off with a well-arranged one. Mixing requires a flow, and you want your mixer to get into a groove sooner rather than later. As it is, the first track of a project often takes longer than the others, especially if the mixer is in an unfamiliar environment. The mixer needs time to get acclimated to the project, the people, and the room. Even a relatively simple track can potentially take the full first day, even for a mixer who tends to mix fast. Therefore, you don't want to start him on a track requiring excessive busy work and production decisions.

Choosing a mixer is difficult at best. If you don't have someone you can rely on, or if for some reason you think you need fresh blood for a particular project, how do you pick? You could look at the liner notes of your favorite records. You could ask around. You could search on the Internet. But ultimately, once you have a list of mixers, you must select one of them. That's where shootouts come in handy.

A shootout is like a mini competition for which you are the judge. Many mixers will participate in shootouts against other mixers, and this can be a good way to make a tough call easier to make. Whatever you do, don't do a shootout between more than two mixers. Evaluating more than two mixes is a headfuck of epic proportions, and you will find yourself liking different things about the different mixes, making the decision even more difficult. Furthermore, never do a shootout purely for budgetary concerns. I can tell you without equivocation, if I do a shootout for you, I won't be negotiating my price down to that of the losing mixer. We will establish the price in advance, and once you decide you want me to mix the record, that's what I'm charging. I mean, think about this for a moment. You like my mix better, but I'm too expensive? Then you shouldn't have had me shootout in the first place. Besides, it costs more to have it mixed twice than to have it mixed right the first time. As a potential mixer I'm sure to point that out.

Under certain circumstances, a mixer will be willing to perform a test mix for you, free of charge, or at least for a temporarily reduced fee. There's a very good reason for this. If you don't like the first mix, you're going to fire the mixer anyway. So, why not test the waters for little to no money before making a two-week time commitment that could result in a one-day failure. However, it's unreasonable to ask a mixer whom you have a relationship with to perform a test mix, unless it's to ease the concerns of your artist, and if that's the case, it should be presented in that manner. Whatever you do, *never* engage a mixer in a shootout under the premise that it's a "test mix." Whereas I might be inclined to do a test mix knowing that I'll win the gig if you like the mix, I may not be similarly inclined to do a shootout. To ask a mixer for a test mix under false pretenses is both scummy and reprehensible, and will not win you any friends. Be honest and forthright about your intentions, especially regarding the budget, and the number of mixers vying for the gig.

Mastering Engineers

Frankly, you should allow your mixer to choose the mastering engineer, particularly if he has a preference. The mixer is the one responsible for framing your production, and if he did a great job, you certainly don't want someone else with far less control coming in and dramatically altering your product. If you don't have a mixer, or if the one you do have is somehow clueless about mastering (this happens), then you need to find a mastering engineer you can trust for the job. The easiest way to do this is to look at the liner notes of your favorite-sounding records, relatively modern ones.

We'll talk about the mastering process in considerably more detail, discussing loudness in particular, what that means, and how it affects your record, as this is critical to understand before you select a mastering engineer.

Product Manager in Chief

As the producer, it's up to you to guide your band toward their most effective songs. I've never heard of a band that performs songs written for them. Even if such an animal exists, it's too rare to quantify. Typically, it's the solo pop artist who doesn't write songs, at which point your job is to help her find a suitable collection of them. Publishing companies keep a stable of songwriters who can either work directly with your artist or supply demos. While you won't get an unpublished Diane Warren song for an unsigned and unproven artist, there are plenty of quality writers willing to take that kind of chance.

With bands, your job is to sort through existing material. You want to listen to every song the band has, including previous releases and every demo in existence. If they have a number of songs lacking demos, have them performed for you in a rehearsal or gig.

Gigs are particularly useful for evaluating a band, mostly because you can watch the reaction of the audience. Of course, if your band is of the hard rock persuasion, watching them play at a country bar is unlikely to tell you much as far as audience reaction is concerned. Furthermore, a poor reaction from even an appropriate audience doesn't necessarily mean it's a song problem. That's why they're hiring you, right? A poor reaction shouldn't automatically disqualify a song, particularly if you have a vision for changing that. Of course, a positive reaction should rarely be discounted.

When evaluating a band for the first time, it's not unusual to pore through as many as 30 songs. That's way too many songs to do anything with, so you need to whittle the list down to the most viable songs in order of priority. Just be careful not to single out a particular song as the "most important," and if you do, *don't tell the band!* This puts too much pressure on that song, and works to the detriment of the project as a whole. Besides, at this stage of the game, you're not in a position to determine which is the best track. There are too many variables to make such a blatant predetermination.

Your song prioritization allows you to compare how you see the band with how they see themselves. If your priority list doesn't remotely intersect with that of the band, then you either need to sell them on your vision, or pass on the gig. Whatever you do, don't realign your vision to match that of the band. Your gut instincts are almost always right, and if you ignore those instincts, you risk regretting it later.

Choosing songs with a band is often a bit of a negotiation process. Unfortunately, if your favorite songs continually fall off the list at the insistence of the band, you're probably not the right producer. Think about it. If your vision is significantly different from theirs, you'll find yourself at odds with the band throughout the entire recording process. You can't implement your vision if you find yourself recording the band's least compelling songs. Avoid this scenario like the plague.

There will be times when you'll need to get involved in changing the song itself. This can be uncomfortable territory for both artists and bands alike. A great song requires a strong melody and strong lyrics. If one or the other is weak, it's incumbent upon you to address that problem. You don't have to get involved with the actual songwriting process, but if you're going to record a track, you need to convince your artist to fix systemic songwriting problems, particularly on songs that have considerable potential.

When you do get involved in the songwriting, you're entitled to a credit and publishing, but this must be worked out in advance and should be in your contract. Bands will likely balk at this suggestion, particularly if you don't have a definitive track record as a writer or producer. Furthermore, the lines aren't always clear. I wrote the cello part that was integral to the payoff of "Better Days" for Pete Murray. Should I have gotten writer's credit and royalties? Possibly. But I didn't negotiate this at the time, and there's a strong argument that the cello part functions purely as a countermelody.

Tempo and key are also important considerations. Singers will often overshoot their range. The true range of a singer is what she can sing on a daily basis, not what she can sing on her best day. If the singer is struggling on a track, you'll want to change the key before recording the track. Just keep in mind that the key can affect the emotional impact of the song.

A few years back, an Australian band called Speedstar hired me. While this was a mixing gig, they were unhappy with the production of their single, and asked me to help them pinpoint the problem. In comparing the demo to the rough mix, the problem was obvious. They were in different keys! The most staggering part of this revelation? That the song was more compelling in the original key.

We pitched every track on the master recording using time compression. The audio took a hit from this, but I was able to handle that at the mixing stage. That was far easier problem to deal with than changing the key itself, particularly since re-recording wasn't a viable option. That said, don't go testing every key for every song. You only want to change a key if there's a problem, and the singer's range would be the number-one reason for that. As much as I may buy into the notion that one key can be better than another for a song, I'm not so sold on it that I'm going to waste my time trying out every single key for a particular song.

It's far better to implement any key changes during preproduction than during recording. If there is even a minute amount of harmonic bleed contained on the drums, changing the key is an impossibility without re-cutting them. The rub will be untenable. We'll discuss preproduction at length later, but use this time to evaluate your singer's ability to hit her notes. If she's struggling, consider bringing the key down. Just make sure you're not bringing every key down to accommodate a sick or fatigued singer. Fatigue can be fixed through rest, and a virus will pass. It's highly unlikely that your singer will try to sing every song out of her range. It's equally unlikely that you'll need to change the key for more than one song on an album, and you will do many albums in your career that require no key changes. So don't go crazy now.

Arranger in Chief

Aside from politics, the single most important aspect of producing is arranging. The song and its arrangement should focus the listener's attention and propel him forward through the song. Because songs unfold over time, they must keep the listener's interest, and this is achieved through both writing and arranging techniques.

Great songwriters use musical tools to propel the listener forward. For example, a writer can achieve a more effective payoff melodically if she avoids the tonic (the root note) until the chorus. The tonic represents "home" or resolution in music. Even a passing tone, where the melody briefly touches upon the tonic, can retard forward motion. The tonic is so powerful that it can stop all forward motion entirely when it completes a melodic phrase. Of course, sometimes this is the desired effect (like at the end of a song!).

The rhythmic structure of a melody can provide forward motion as well. The most common example is an acceleration of the rhyme structure in conjunction with the melodic rhythm, particularly in the pre-chorus (or B section). Suppose the rhyme structure of the verse is ABAB, with melodic phrases neatly spanning four bars. It's not uncommon for the rhyme structure to accelerate in the B section to AABB, with shorter, more punchy melodic lines that span two bars. This has the effect of hurling the listener into the chorus.

There are many ways to write a song. Not all songs have B sections, and some songs don't have a chorus but rather a refrain (which is basically a one-line chorus). Some songs have a bridge, which by definition is a unique section that occurs only once in the song. Sometimes the true payoff is reserved for the end of the song. There are entire books on the subject of songwriting alone, and if you are having trouble following me on some of this, you'd be wise to investigate a few of them.

The point is, a good songwriter uses various techniques to push the listener forward. You can tell when it's happening innately; if you couldn't, you would need a musical degree just to listen to music. These techniques are merely tools to manipulate the listener, and if you're astute, you can at least recognize when you're being manipulated. Your arrangement should mirror, if not enhance, the forward motion of the song. What if there is little to no forward movement? Then you'd better manufacture some.

Believe it or not, you don't really need to go to music school to learn arranging in regard to producing modern records. Sure, you'll need to hire arrangers on those occasions when some scoring must be done, but there's nothing wrong with that. I mean, I can score, but I'm far more likely to hire someone for this purpose than do it myself. That said, you need to have a basic understanding of arrangement, particularly as it relates to stereo record-making.

If you really want to learn all you can about mixing, even if you don't plan to mix yourself, you should probably read my book *Zen and the Art of Mixing*. I realize this is a somewhat self-serving suggestion, but if you're serious about producing, you definitely want to understand the art of mixing. Besides, the two books will look quite nice together on your mantel, and you'll be exceptionally well educated in the major aspects of record-making to boot.

Function

There are five basic functions in any given arrangement: melody, harmony, rhythm, response, and countermelody.

The melody, which is usually carried by the vocal, is not only the most important function in the song, but also defines the song, along with the lyric. Given its overall importance, it's our goal to make the listener focus on the melody. This can be achieved by highlighting the melody prominently in the production, and consciously designing the arrangement so it doesn't distract from it.

Harmony is basically the chord changes. Polyphonic instruments like guitar and keyboard, while often referred to as rhythm instruments, can also provide the entire harmonic structure of a song. Monophonic instruments like horns and strings must be grouped in order to offer full harmonic support.

Rhythm is the structure in which the melody operates. A rubato (or free-form) melody is neither satisfying nor readily repeatable. Modern music in particular is based on a strong rhythmic component. This is what makes us move. While drums and percussion are the most obvious rhythmic element in a production, rhythm can be provided by nearly any instrument or part, even if it has another function. The bass, for instance, often supplies both harmonic support and the rhythmic foundation of a track.

Any music with a defined pulse has accents. Given four beats per measure, pop and rock tracks tend to accent the two and the four while hip-hop tracks often accent the one and the three. In the case of a waltz, which has three beats per measure, the accent is on the one. Working around the accents are the internal rhythms. These are the rhythms that help define how the listener should move. Within a drum pattern, the internal rhythm is typically provided by the hi-hat, ride, and sometimes even snare ghosting. Percussion, guitar, and keyboards are also good candidates for providing internal rhythm.

Response, as in call-and-response, is an important part of Western music. It is prominent in gospel music. The preacher sounds the call, and the "chorus" behind him offers the response.

The Who's "My Generation" is a great example. Roger Daltrey sounds the call: "People try to put me down," and the band sings the response: "Talkin' 'bout my generation."

Response isn't limited to a chorus of singers. In Led Zeppelin's "Black Dog," Robert Plant sounds the call, which is followed by the band playing an infectious riff. This kind of musical response is designed to momentarily grab the listener's focus and pass it right back to the vocal.

The countermelody is a separate melody that plays in conjunction with the vocal (or primary melody). A great countermelody can work as a melody on its own, but is by design subservient to the melody, and I mean that literally. Basically, when the melody moves, the counter typically holds, and when the melody holds, the counter usually moves. The countermelody tends to weave around the vocal to avoid stealing the listener's focus. The more effective a countermelody, the louder you can place it in the production without distracting from the melody.

A part can serve more than one function in an arrangement. A guitar part can serve as both rhythm and harmony. A tom beat can serve as both rhythm and countermelody.

Planes of Space

In a stereo image we use planes of space to create a four-dimensional image (the fourth dimension being time). All in all, five basic planes of space can be replicated by two speakers:

1. panning—left to right
2. frequency—up to down
3. contrast—sparse to dense and bright to dark
4. reflectivity or reflection—far to near
5. balance—front to back, large to small

PANNING—LEFT TO RIGHT

There's only so much space available to us in our mixing palette. Using the full spectrum of left and right is just as important as using the full spectrum of the frequency range. As far as I'm concerned, anyone who would consider using less than the full width of panning available to them might as well also consider using filters to cut off the very top and bottom frequencies of the mix.

Panning is the most underutilized plane of space in a mix, particularly by neophytes. It's a mistake to not use the entire width of the stereo field, because you're abandoning valuable space. For many professional producers and mixers, myself included, the pan knobs are rarely anywhere but left, center, or right, and there's even a name for mixing like this—it's called LCR mixing (which stands for left/center/right). This isn't to say that there aren't times to soft-pan parts, but any part that is soft-panned will tend to react within the room as if it were placed center. The soft-panning can only be pinpointed from within the stereo field.

Young producers and recordists are often compelled to record parts in stereo. Unless you're recording a rather large instrument, like a drum kit or piano, or an instrument that uses left-right movement, like a B3 or a Rhodes with tremolo, you should avoid loading your productions down with stereo recordings. This is especially true with instruments like acoustic guitar. Without getting into the technical details, two mics in close proximity on a single mono source will react in such a way that the source will appear to come from no particular place within the stereo field. I call this faux stereo.

True stereo requires some distance between microphones, and that distance equates to a time differential. There is not enough of a time differential between two mics in close proximity to adequately represent stereo. This translates into a part that lacks directionality, and what's worse, the part will shift positions within the stereo field in an unpredictable and distracting manner. You never want the listener to notice the recording, and a lack of location can make the listener uncomfortable.

The strength of the stereo field comes from the panning of mono sources. Not the combination of stereo ones. Even keyboards are often best placed as a mono source within the mix, especially if they're not the most important part of the song. A piano that fills the entire stereo field makes sense if it's featured, but if it's a guitar-centric track, there's no reason to give the piano such importance. You're better off placing it as a mono part within the stereo field, and possibly even hard-panning it, as long as it's not fighting a guitar on the same side.

FREQUENCY—UP TO DOWN

Just like we have width in a mix, we also have height, and this is an illusion that's created by frequency.

We can hear frequencies from 20 kHz (kilohertz) to 20 Hz (Hertz), although that's exceptionally charitable, even for a young child. For recording purposes, anything lower than 20 Hz is nothing more than rumble, and anything above 20 kHz is nothing more than spitty noise. And while there's a reasonable debate over how frequencies outside our range of hearing affect the ones within our range, it is not of significant consequence where the art of producing is concerned.

What's important about frequency in the context of space is directionality. High-frequency waveforms require far less space (distance) to fully develop than long, drawn-out low-frequency ones. Consequently, high frequencies are quite directional in nature. They're similar to a garden hose set to jet. The water has a focused directionality on this setting, and when the water hits a hard object it reflects. When it hits a soft object, like a towel, it's absorbed. Conversely, if we set the hose to spray, the water has no directionality, tends not to reflect (even off hard surfaces), and gets anything and everything in the general area wet. This is precisely how low frequencies work, which is why you can place a subwoofer just about anywhere in a room. The low end goes everywhere, traveling easily along (and through) walls and floors. You have to actually be in line with the tweeters, or horns, to get the full brilliance of your high-frequency information.

Given the directionality of sound, frequencies within the stereo field will create the illusion of a vertical plane of space. If you sit between your monitors and close your eyes, the highest frequencies will appear at the top of the sound field (level with your tweeters), and the lowest frequencies will extend all the way down to the floor.

Frequency also relates directly to music. All notes occupy a fundamental frequency. The open E string on a bass has a fundamental frequency of 41 Hz, which is quite low. That means the E string is vibrating 41 times every second. Above the fundamental frequency are overtones, which extend upward in static values. The first overtone is always an octave higher than the fundamental, and an octave is nothing more than a doubling of frequency. In the case of the low E, the octave above it has a frequency of 82 Hz. The next harmonic is a fifth higher than the first octave, and the next a fourth higher than that (which together equals an octave, and thus the third overtone on that low E is 164 Hz). The overtones continue infinitely, and are mapped out in what we call the harmonic series. You can do more research on this, but it's the overtones that define a sound. Without them, a piano would sound no different from a guitar.

Since different instruments occupy particular ranges of notes, by default they also occupy a particular range of frequencies. For instance, a bass covers the low to lower midrange frequencies. Yes, we can boost 5 kHz on a bass and bring out some upper harmonics and string noise, allowing the note to cut more, but when playing in its normal register, the bass doesn't fundamentally occupy the upper midrange space. Kik drums also cover the low to lower midrange frequencies, and although we've all heard plenty of clicky kik drums, those particular upper frequencies are transitory and therefore don't take up an exceptional amount of frequency space unless they happen in quick succession.

We deal with about eight octaves within the range of human hearing. Some instruments have a limited range, like a violin. Others work within the full range, like pianos and B3 organs, and therefore can take up an inordinate amount of frequency space in a production. It is part of your job as producer to consider frequency in the context of your instrumentation. An arrangement that contains crashing cymbals, screeching violins, a wailing B3 in its upper register, and a ripping guitar solo will be compacted in the mid and upper frequencies, which will be difficult to separate sonically. It could also have the effect of tiring your listener (and you!). An arrangement that contains a djun-djun, bass, cello, and toms will likely result in an undefined, muddy mess. There must be some separation of the frequency ranges within your instrumentation or you will have little clarity among the parts.

How you combine frequencies from an arranging standpoint will greatly affect the listener. A high, screeching violin in conjunction with a low pedal tone leaves such a large hole in the middle frequencies that it will actually make the listener uncomfortable. If you've ever watched a slasher movie, you've experienced this.

While equalizers may lie within the purview of your recordist and mixer, frequency should play an important part in your decision-making process as the producer. If you're in need of a rhythmic part but already have an excess of high-end information, you should consider finding an instrument that sits lower in the frequency range. This will make that part far more effective, since it doesn't have as much competition for space. Not only will such a strategy make the part easier to fit within the mix, it will also provide you with a bit more frequency balance.

CONTRAST—SPARSE TO DENSE AND BRIGHT TO DARK

Contrast is the relative comparison of balances over the course of time. We can listen to a mix and immediately hear frequency, panning, and balance decisions, but contrast reveals itself over the course of the production.

Contrast is used to produce excitement and dynamics in a production. A sparse verse, comprising nothing more than bass drums and a single guitar, contrasts considerably with a dense chorus of crunch guitars, a B3, a choir, and a string section. This can provide the illusion of a dynamic, even if there isn't a considerable level difference between the verse and the chorus. Of course, if there is a level difference, then the contrast is even greater. Asymmetrical panning contrasts with symmetrical panning. A single guitar panned to the left with no other part to counterbalance it will sound asymmetrical. Add another guitar of similar level to the right, and you have contrasting symmetry. Frequency can be contrasted as well. A warm verse containing very little high-end information will contrast exceptionally well with a bright and gritty chorus.

Contrast, while most certainly a definitive plane of space, is nothing more than a tool. Some records don't require contrast, but if you're looking to get more dynamics out of your track, contrast is a great way to accomplish it. Frankly, the more powerfully the song itself pushes the listener forward, the less you'll need to concern yourself with contrast in the arrangement.

REFLECTIVITY OR REFLECTION—FAR TO NEAR

Reflectivity is the illusion of space. Whereas we accomplish the three-dimensional illusion of width, height, and depth through panning, frequency, and balance, respectively, we accomplish the illusion of reflectivity within all three dimensions plus the fourth—time.

Sound doesn't exist in a vacuum. We can hear the direct sound waves of a source directionally, but the reflections surround us based on the space we're in. A kik drum in a large concrete room will resonate and reverberate in a completely different manner from a kik drum in a small, carpeted living room. It's difficult to go through life without figuring this out. How a room reverberates depends on a great many factors. The frequency response of the source, the size and shape of the room, the materials contained within the room, and even the placement of the source within the room will all have some bearing on how we hear the natural room ambience. These factors will not only affect the decay time of the reverberation (the time it takes for it to dissipate completely), but will also affect the most prominent resonant frequencies.

Just as the contrast plane relates to time, so too does the reflectivity plane. In fact, the way that we perceive reflectivity is defined mostly by decay time. The smack of a snare drum will bounce around a room and dissipate over a quantifiable amount of time, often in under a second, or 1,000 milliseconds.

Reflections will appear to us as reverb in enclosed spaces and as delay (with the possibility of some reverberation) in open spaces, particularly where there are obstacles nearby. While reverberation is the quick, successive bouncing of a sound wave throughout a space, delay is a singular reverberation caused by a sound traveling for a significant distance, hitting an object, and returning back to us.

Whereas in real life reverberations surround us, coming from all directions, in a stereo production their spread is limited to left and right. We can create the illusion of distance using reverberation, but both the source and the reverberation must be balanced lower relative to the other parts. Otherwise, the illusion is blown. Furthermore, as sound travels, the top end dissipates along the way, so attenuating the top end of the source is an important part of representing distance.

Our control over reflectivity is a one-way street. We can add reflections, but we cannot take them away. Yes, we can use mutes or gates to reduce the length of time of a recorded reflection, but we can't remove the audible room reflectivity while a part is actually sounding. Most recordists will close-mic and even baffle a source in order to reduce the problems of excessive reverberation. Room ambience can always be recorded separately with distant mics, giving you more flexibility down the road, although there's nothing wrong with committing to an ambient source if you're certain it's what you want.

If you're looking for a big, reverberant sound, then you should record in a room that offers you this option. Room mics are far more natural than a digital reverb placed on the source after the fact. Even the best convolution reverbs pale in comparison to natural ambience. There is a certain marriage that exists between source and room that cannot be replicated. Not to date, anyway. So, if you're looking for a big, natural rock drum sound, record the drums in a big room.

While it would seem to make sense to record the entire band in the drum room, you generally want to avoid ambience on every track. Crunch guitars are often bone dry in comparison to the drums, and for good reason—they become a smeary mess otherwise. Reverberant crunch guitars would tend to smear the overall sound to such a degree that the listener would have great difficulty making out the nuances of the performance.

You should also consider the feelings that a space will evoke. Dry—that is, non-reverberant—tones create a sense of intimacy. Reverberant and reflective tracks create a sense of larger-than life drama. Furthermore, reverberation tends to soften tone. A violin devoid of reflectivity is considerably more aggressive than one placed in a large hall. The '80s hair bands are often doused in reverb, not just because that was in fashion at the time, but also because it softened the tone, allowing them to appeal to a broader audience.

Balance—Front to Back, Large to Small

Balance is a game of relativity and is the holy grail of the five spatial planes. I've left balance for last since it affects everything in the mix of your production.

Fundamentally, the balance of an instrument has to do with how loud it is in comparison with all the other parts at any given moment. The loudest part in a mix is going to get the most attention. This is true whether it's a final mix, a rough mix, or even a monitor mix for the purposes of overdubs. In the case of the monitor mix, the part you're working on is typically the loudest, which allows you to focus on the part at hand. In a final mix, the loudest part is what the listener will tend to focus on. This is why the vocal is usually the loudest part in a mix. It contains the melody and the lyric, and that defines the song itself.

All balances are an exercise in relative comparison. An exceptionally loud acoustic guitar can easily dwarf a drum kit, particularly given the inherent disconnect between their relative sizes as instruments in comparison to the space they take up in the mix. Furthermore, how your band is monitoring their balances can have a significant effect on their ability to perform. An off-time and out-of-tune singer is often the result of too much vocal in her cue balance.

When you think about it, every adjustment we make is a balance adjustment. If you pan a guitar to the left, you're bringing up the balance on the left, and bringing it down on the right. Boosting or cutting a particular frequency is literally altering the balance of that frequency within the context of the part you're processing.

Your balance decisions must make sense not just to your mixer, but to you as well. If, upon completing your last overdub, you have no earthly idea how you want your tracks balanced, then you have been completely ignoring how the track is supposed to make you move and feel. As the producer, you don't have to be a great mixer, but you must be able to balance your parts in a manner that allows you to make sense of your own production. Therefore, you should be toying with your balances each and every time you touch the track.

Now, if you have a recordist, she is likely going to set the balances for you as you work. But once you're finished working on a particular track, you should take some time to mess with the balances before moving on to something else. This will allow you to determine exactly where you're at in your production. Part of your job is to make sure that the track offers forward motion, just as the song should. The arrangement alone doesn't accomplish this. It's the arrangement in conjunction with balances that pushes the listener forward. So, before you ever pass a track off to a mixer, you want to be absolutely sure you have all the elements necessary, with a firm understanding of how they work relative to each other. This means you must be able to balance.

Worry not: balancing isn't actually all that hard, particularly in the recording phase of a production. In fact, bad balancing decisions are in some ways more revealing than good ones, and there's no such thing as permanent balances until the CD is made. So, don't be afraid to get your hands dirty and move some faders every now and then. You're in charge, so you have to understand how balance works in relation to the mix.

To review: We have five planes of space that fit neatly within the four dimensions of width, height, depth, and time. Panning uses balance across the speakers to provide us the illusion of width; frequency uses balance across the spectrum to supply us with the illusion of height. Contrast is balance relative to the next event in time, which provides us with both real dynamics and the illusion of dynamics. Reflectivity creates the perception of space based on how it's balanced within all four dimensions of the mix. And balance in conjunction with the other four planes offers us the perception of depth, making balance the driving force behind all five planes.

Leader

If you haven't figured it out by now, as the producer, you're the leader. As such, you must lead. Now, I admit, that sounds pretty stupid. But somehow, there are all sorts of people who think that one can lead by following. One can't.

As the leader, it's your job to keep your finger constantly on the pulse of your session. Even when you're just having a good time with your band, you should be monitoring the session itself. It doesn't take long before this becomes second nature.

Any time you allow your session to come to a momentary halt, whether to watch a funny YouTube video in the back of the room or just to order food, either something else should be happening (like your engineer should be setting up a mic), or there should be a need for that general break. That doesn't mean you should become a militant prick. On the contrary, allowing moments of camaraderie on a session is important to the session itself. It's part of keeping morale high, and morale patrol is one of your more central leadership jobs.

All sessions have an ebb and flow to them. There are highs and lows. If there weren't, your session would be dull and severely lacking in passion. When morale is high, productivity tends to be high. When morale is low, productivity can be nonexistent. Conversely, when productivity is high, morale stays high. When productivity stops, morale can tank.

As you're producing, you need to watch for indications that morale is headed in the wrong direction, preferably before it bottoms out completely. Still, there will be times when your session will slow to a crawl, no matter how skilled you are at judging morale. Don't bother beating yourself up over this. It happens to everyone, and when it happens to you, your job is to get your session back on track by any means necessary. Just make sure you're not addressing morale as a means to avoid tough work.

All things being relative, there will be tracks that give you little to no resistance, and tracks that make you wonder why you got into this business in the first place. You can often predict which tracks are going to prove difficult, but not always. Either way, on those occasions when you find yourself mired in a difficult problem track, you can't simply set it aside for another day. I mean, you can, but I promise you that this will diminish spirits far more than working through the problem. Besides, if you spend your session avoiding the difficult work, all you'll manage to do is pile it all up to the end.

Hopefully, you're not working with a crew of dainty little flowers, unable to deal with the natural headwinds of your typical recording session. I mean, the goal here is to create music. Not only is that hard work, everyone on your session is likely aware of this. The more seasoned your band, the more of a workhorse mentality they'll typically have. A veteran understands and expects the grind. Fortunately, these days, even the greenest bands have some experience in the studio.

Personalities will also dictate how hard you can push. If you're working with a musician who takes every criticism personally, or who gets frustrated at the first hint of any problems, then you'll have to adjust to that particular reality. If you're working with a supremely optimistic workhorse, you can push hard.

I suppose the point is that you should allow your session to alternate between the tough work that retards flow and the seemingly effortless work that flows free. This way, the aggregate of your session is kept on a somewhat even keel. Just as important, don't ignore how a session is affecting *your* judgment. If you're in a shit mood, or down in the dumps, you're not helping your session morale. This I can promise you.

Conflict Resolution

Conflict happens. Sometimes you're in the middle of the conflict. Sometimes you're the arbitrator of the conflict. And if you believe you have a personality that can avoid all conflict, think again.

I'm not saying you should constantly engage in fights. That's just stupid. But if you give in to your client's every whim, then how exactly are you serving their needs? What are you going to do when the singer decides he's going to take over the session because he has a bug up his ass to do something else? This happened on one of my sessions, and I'm not sure whether it was a test or not, but I can assure you I didn't let it happen.

What are you going to do when the artist wants to put a violin response part right on top of the fucking vocal? Are you going to allow it? It's a response part—it should go between the vocal lines. That's Arranging 101. So, when you run into controversy, are you going to shy away from it? Of course not! You're going to stand up for what you know is right. Situations will arise on sessions when you must make a political calculation, and sometimes in politics things can get a bit ugly. Even if you whisper your objections, you're still in the midst of a conflict. The definition of "conflict" does not include yelling. It's a disagreement that must be negotiated and resolved.

If you find yourself in the position of Default Producer (the studio owner/engineer), you pretty much work at the pleasure of the band. If you're actually the hired producer, you're responsible for delivering a final product on time and on budget. So, you don't always have the luxury of letting your artists experiment with breaking tried-and-true arrangement rules. And while yes, you still work for them, they've hired you for your expertise. If you don't stand up for your expertise, then you're not really helping the band. Worse yet, you risk going over budget.

At the same time, you have to recognize when to give your band a bit of rope. I mean, if your brainchild wants to hear a trombone on a particular track, and you're going to be hiring a horn section for other tracks anyway, then there's really no reason not to indulge her. It could be genius. You rarely want to get into a conflict over something abstract, at least not if you can possibly avoid it. Any time you're debating a part that doesn't currently exist, you're merely speculating. It's better to spend an hour recording the trombone part than to shoot it down based on nothing more than a guess. If it works, great! If it doesn't, at least you can express an argument based on demonstrative realities.

Bands as an entity are often conflict machines. Of course, if they've been together a while, they're typically good at settling their conflicts on their own. But if you have a strong opinion one way or the other, don't let your band argue for an hour before weighing in. That's just a waste of everyone's time. Put up your opinion (or solution), and move on. That's part of leadership.

With bands, there is almost always one person who wields more power than the others. Occasionally there is a duo of power players. Typically the power player is the brainchild, songwriter, singer, or any combination of the three. It's pretty easy to pick out the power player, because she's the one to whom the band acquiesces. She's also the one you've probably been talking to from the start.

Frankly, you should be able to assess the personal dynamics within the band in the first two minutes of rehearsal. Once you've pegged the bandleader, that's the person you want to develop a relationship with. For starters, the brainchild's opinion will naturally have more weight with the band. Secondly, there's already an established hierarchy, and she already knows precisely how to lead the band. Therefore, nearly anything that you work out with her, she can then work out with the band. And when you find yourself at odds, you can always use the band for leverage.

It's not that you have to do everything through the power player in the band. You work with the entire band, and you develop your relationships with them all. But when there's a dispute between you and another band member, she will have the weight necessary to help resolve the issue. Hopefully, so do you, but you're not a dictator in the process. For the purposes of making the record, you're the leader, but there is already an established leader of the band, and that person can make the session considerably easier or more difficult. So lead, but don't discount the need for politics.

Honesty

In my experience, the best way to deal with bands (or any artist, for that matter) is to be completely honest and blunt at all times. It may be shocking at first, but your band will soon realize that they can trust what you say, and this is crucial to making a great record. Here's why: If you tell a band outright your negative feelings about their work, they'll believe you. If you only offer them positive words of encouragement, they will wonder, deep down, whether you're just saying that to gain their favor. Therefore, you must at all times be brutally honest, so that your encouragement can be trusted and believed.

You must never lie to your band. If you don't like something, tell them. If you think something is terrible, don't sugarcoat it beyond, "I've heard better." If you think something is mediocre, say it straight up. When a band member does well, tell him what he did, and why it's good. I promise you, no matter how sincerely you can present a falsehood, your artists will know when you're lying to them.

Trust is the cornerstone of your relationship with an artist or band. If you don't have their trust, you can't operate effectively as their producer. You will be second-guessed at every turn. Trust is so critical to the working relationship between performers and producer, so necessary to the process, that you shouldn't even consider engaging in contract discussions until that trust has been firmly established.

If you take nothing else away from this book, take this: Do not squander or risk established trust under any circumstances. Don't blow smoke up you band's collective asses. They'll know it. They'll resent it. And they'll never trust your encouragement again. Even if you are somehow incredibly talented in your bullshitting abilities, at some point you'll be caught, and everything nice you've said to that point will be tainted and questioned as to its sincerity.

Don't patronize your musicians by praising an idea you have every intention of muting later. When you're honest, it gives your artist a chance to reconsider her approach, which could ultimately lead to something brilliant. If you cheat your band out of a compromise, you risk a confrontation later. You might even box yourself into needing a part that you hate come mix time. After all, every subsequent overdub will be recorded with that part in the equation. You don't do yourself any favors by shying away from your true feelings.

The most compelling argument for total honesty is that it tends to open the channels of communication in both directions. You lead by example here. If your singer is uninspired by the track, and doesn't feel she can be fully forthright about it, then all your hard work could be for naught. You can't reasonably demand honesty from your artist if you're not setting the tone.

Now, just because you're honest, even brutally so, doesn't mean you shouldn't select your words carefully. Of course, how carefully depends on the personality of your artist. If proclaiming "That sucked" is going to send your singer reeling and unable to perform for the rest of the day, I would suggest softening your delivery a tad. You're not engaging in effective communication if your criticisms bring the session to a screeching halt. That said, I have to wonder how this dainty singer is going to survive a career in music if she can't take direction from an ally, no matter how seemingly harsh.

Just to be clear, we all have different personalities, so if you can't fathom proclaiming "That sucked" to even your worst enemy, not to worry. You can say it as you like. How you couch your criticism is up to you. Just don't shy away from the truth of the matter. There isn't enough time in your budget to fuck around. Spit it out, and move on.

In general, you should tailor your style of communication, and even your working methods, to the musicians. A singer in need of constant encouragement and direction is not a good candidate for setting the recorder to loop. Conversely, a singer who takes direction well, but often needs a moment to work out the implementation, would probably love it if you looped a section. That's not to say you should never push your musicians outside of their comfort zone. It means you need to pay attention to what that comfort zone is in the first place.

In general you want to gauge what works best for your band and its members, and work within those confines, even if it takes you out of your own comfort zone. When criticism becomes a problem, you should likely seek out positive examples of what you're trying to express. Rather than focusing on how badly the artist performed the second verse, you could present the first verse as a positive example of what you seek. "Sorry, but you did such a killer job on the first verse, that this is now the bar," is considerably more palatable for the Dainty Artist than "You call that performing?!"

Fortunately, the Dainty Artist isn't all that common. Besides, if you're straightforward right from the beginning and your artist accepts this about you, even the Dainty Artist can handle a direct style. Just make sure you're consistent in how you communicate. You don't want to be pure sweetness during preproduction and abrasively blunt during the session. Let them see who they'll be working with, and if you lose the gig, that's probably a good thing.

The Struggle

There will be times on just about every session when your artist will struggle. As much as I'm a big fan of playing the Dad role on the session, occasionally you need to tap into your inner Mom. Father's "smack." Mother's "coddle." Regardless of your gender or parenting style, let's stick with those definitions for the purposes of a recording session. When your artist is struggling, it might be time to coddle him.

All artistic people need occasional coddling. Even you. This is all part of the leadership job. Sometimes a good 10-minute love fest is exactly what a stalled session needs. And why not? You chose the project because you loved it, so it's good to express adulation every now and then. Let your artist know you still adore the project and why. Remind him of everything that's going right with the album. Take a moment and review your successes. Play the tracks that are kicking ass, regardless of what stage they're at in the recording process. Explain what's good about them, how they make you feel, what kind of physical reactions they cause. This sort of positive feedback is a great way to reset, and can often serve to inspire your talent enough to get you through the tough times.

Track review is also a good idea when you're the one struggling with a particular track. At the very least, it gives you a basis of comparison and a break from the grind. More important, this can help you recognize an undiagnosed problem more readily. You might even decide your problem track is a lost cause. I mean, if you listen to three tracks that are kicking ass, and then go back to an inherently broken track, at least you can cut your losses then and there. Once you've determined there's a systemic problem with a track, what's the point of wasting more time on it? This is the whole point of cutting more tracks than you need for the album. Sometimes you record a dud.

Now, if your dud track happens to be one of the more important songs, then dumping it isn't a great option. Neither is freaking out over it. As the parent, you need to act like the parent. Review your options, and choose a course. It's not the end of the world to recut a song, particularly if it's not living up to everyone's expectations. Your job is to make sure that everything is great before you put out the CD. What are you going to do? Pretend like there's not a problem? The moment you realize a track isn't up to snuff, you need to deal with that problem, and sweeping it under the rug to save face is shortsighted. Would you rather the band know you're not perfect, or everyone who listens to the final product?

If you realize you fucked up a track, or you made a bad decision, fix it. If that requires starting from scratch on the track, do it. This is why I'm so insistent that you know exactly where you are in a production at all times. This way, you rarely end up at the end of the process with something unusable. You and your band discover a problem along the way, which gives you the opportunity to do something about it. Everyone fucks up. It's how you deal with those fuck-ups that sets you apart.

The Big Superfluous Change

Since we're talking about fuck-ups, I'm going to take a moment to save you from one of the bigger mistakes you can make as a producer. One of the best ways to end up with an uninspiring record is to completely overhaul your talent to the point that they're performing well beyond the limits of their strengths. If your whole purpose for taking a gig is so you can turn an act into something completely new, don't. This probably has more relevance when producing an artist than a band, but it's an important concept just the same.

It makes no sense to take a strong, riffing singer and constrict her to singing a rigid melody in a light and airy tone. A style outside of what she naturally does well will lead to poor results at best. Yes, you want to follow the song, but you also need to do so in the way that best fits your talent. Besides, a drastic change in style would require an immense amount of preparation and practice by your singer, and if that learning process occurs in the studio, you're not going to get a compelling performance.

You can't reasonably turn a hardcore band with weak melodies into a polished pseudo-punk pop act. That's not what they do. That's not what they hear. And that's not going to be what they perform best. And if they don't resent you during the process for trying to make them something they're not, they will certainly hate you for ruining their record forever after that, and rightly so. You will likely have ruined their record.

Young producers often feel compelled to make an indelible mark. There is no reason for you to feel superfluous to the process even if your only role is to merely confirm goodness. That's important feedback. The longer you produce, the more content you are with staying out of the way. An experienced producer will get his hands dirty when needed, but would prefer to do the least amount of work necessary. Believe it or not, that's not laziness.

Staying out of the way requires more discipline than just about any other skill in producing. Even if you find yourself on a project in which an aggressive touch is necessary, there should be times when you don't have to do anything beyond offering a few well-placed suggestions. The old adage "If it ain't broke, don't fix it" is one to live by when producing, although I would add: "If it's systemically broke, don't take the gig in the first place."

All bands and artists need guidance, no matter how great they are. I promise, I promise, I promise, you will never cut an album in which your only role is to sit and admire the work of your talent. There will, however, be *moments* like this, and when those come, enjoy them. And I mean *really* enjoy them. Lie down and take a nap, if that's the only way you can shut the fuck up. But don't muck things up by sticking your nose into a process that's working beautifully without your guidance.

The one time it's acceptable to bring an artist to an entirely new place is when it's time for a reinvention. Alanis Morissette was a Canadian teenage pop singer before she co-wrote her album *Jagged Little Pill* with producer Glenn Ballard. That was a total reinvention of her. As it turns out, a far more appropriate and successful model for her, since she'd outgrown the whole bubblegum-pop angle. Even with the changeover, Glenn did not ask her to work outside of her strengths. If anything, he helped her make both music and productions that fit her abilities in the best way possible. That would seem to explain the album's massive success.

As long as you work within your talent's strengths, you'll be okay.

Visionary

Vision, quite simply, is your ability to picture the final product before recording a single note. Vision alone is your most powerful asset as a producer, and more specifically, as the leader of a project. Without vision, you are like the blind leading the blind. If you don't know how to present an act, if you don't have a clear concept of the project at hand, then you have no business producing it. Period.

Whereas you can produce a record with large gaps in your knowledge base, you cannot produce a record without vision. Certainly not well. As we've already established, an Engineer Producer could have minimal knowledge of music and still produce a record. A Musician Producer can have little knowledge of the craft of recording and still produce an effective record. Those gaps can be compensated for by employing others. Who are you going to hire to fill in for your lack of vision? A producer? That's you!

I can promise you this: if you don't like the act, the song, or even the genre, then you will have no vision in regard to the project. You can't possibly. How are you supposed to make a great production out of a song you think is awful? Does that make a whole lot of sense? You can't lead if you don't know where you're going, and you can't possibly know where you're going with a production if you don't adore the material. And I mean *adore.*

Clearly, your vision for a project is not so clear that you can predict with absolute accuracy the final result. There are far too many variables for that. The free will of your talent alone would make that impossible. So, vision isn't some form of clairvoyance. Vision has to do with the basic conceptualization of the album, in both sound and approach.

Your vision should take into account the likely, or even preferred, audience demographic. Again, you're not trying to completely change the band, you're trying to present the band in a way that strengthens their musical appeal, and to a particular market. A hard-rock band requires a different approach than a pop band. The genre will dictate which conventions you adhere to, but music is far too complex to stay rigidly within the stereotype of a genre. Besides, how boring is that? Your goal is to create something stunning and new, but also recognizable. You must operate within and outside of convention simultaneously.

The recording process itself can and will carry great influence over the final product. Thirty days of recording time will yield a considerably different record from 10 days of recording the same band. The shorter time span with limited overdubbing gives you less time for polish. This will produce a far rawer product than that of a highly textured and painstakingly overdubbed product. Unfortunately, if you have an act that requires 30 days of polish in order to meet your vision, and a budget that barely covers 10 days, you could very well be unable to accomplish your vision. In other words, vision dictates budget, and budget dictates vision, and if you can't reconcile the two, you can't make the album. Not properly, anyway.

Now, you don't typically conjure your vision out of whole cloth. All the information is there for you in the form of the band's past records, demos, and live performances. You just have to figure out what it's all telling you. This is true even if the band's vision is on point. Merely recognizing this is a contribution on your part.

When you listen to every available track from a potential band, you should begin to get a clear picture of how you wish to approach the album creatively. It's not enough to listen to one track and decide you have a vision for the entire project. That may be a fine vision for one song, but that song could also prove an anomaly in the grand scheme of things. If you don't immerse yourself in the complete recorded history of the band, you won't have the benefit of understanding how it developed and transformed over time. This is true even if your band has only recorded demos.

Listening to demos and previous recordings is an absolute treasure trove of valuable information. Band strengths and weaknesses will become apparent. The style that fits them best will be revealed. Subgenres will be discovered. All of these realizations go into the making of a vision.

For instance, you may discover that the singer sounds best in a particular range. This could make certain songs pop more than others. You will find songs that you think fit the band better than others. Helping a band to home in on a set of songs that seems to fit them best is a major part of carving out a vision. The band may have a tendency to cut their tracks too slow across the board. This could drastically change the audience a band attracts. If a band's style and genre don't jibe with their approach, they could very well make themselves unattractive to all.

Your band's arrangement choices can also be quite revealing. As you investigate an act, you should find little threads that make them more interesting than the generic standard of their genre. It is a band's uniqueness that sets them apart from every other band in their genre, and if you can find all those glorious distinguishing characteristics, you can take advantage of them in your presentation. It's not enough to accept what makes a band different from everyone else. You want to *exploit* their differences.

Some of those tiny threads are considerably more obvious than others. If you dig a little deeper, you will likely find influences that fall outside of an act's overall genre. A country act could have blues influences. A hard-rock act R&B influences. These could be obvious or subtle, but they're important to both recognize and include as part of your vision. Cross-genre influences are like threads in a tapestry—they add color.

There will be times when a cross-genre influence is a sum negative for a given production. You could conceivably wish to quash a particular influence if you think it's getting in the way of the intended audience, or even the feeling you wish to evoke. Certain parts can change the overall genre landscape of a song. A piano on a roots song can pull it into the country realm, and could alienate the appropriate audience. It could also be fresh, and work brilliantly despite being wholly inappropriate for the desired audience. Only you can make these determinations.

Genre influence can be contained within the fabric of the music too. Certain melodic modes, chord changes, and even lyrics can define the overall genre impression. These sorts of systemic genre influences can't be eradicated through production. They can, however be significantly reduced.

I recently produced a song that was systemically a folk/country song, and outside of my vision for the band. Frankly, I found the song demo boring and one-dimensional, particularly within the context of the group as a whole. Still, there was a subtle ska thread contained within the demo, and ska would certainly change the vibe considerably. So we pulled on that thread, and made it a feature rather than an influence. This made the song infinitely more compelling. It also made it more appropriate for the insanely eclectic nature of the band.

I worked with an Australian band called Mammal some years ago, who were a gamble for me that didn't quite pay off, seeing as they broke up just before they fully reached the mainstream. Welcome to the music biz! In the course of our initial interview, one band member asked me what kind of album I was going to make with them. It was a rather ambiguous question, one that would be difficult to answer if there was a lack of vision. Given that, it certainly wasn't an unfair question. "I want to make an R&B album with you guys, but everyone else is going to listen to it and think you're hard rock."

Well, that shut him up. Apparently, it's also what won me the gig.

There were a ton of R&B influences in the vocals. The singer was singing in a hard-rock style, but seemed to take an R&B approach to his melodic phrasing. Frankly, those particular influences are what made the band special to me. I'm not sure whether any of those influences will come out on the album to anyone other than myself at this point. My goal wasn't actually to make the band sound more R&B, or R&B at all. The balance was already there as far as I was concerned. I just had no desire to eradicate those influences. It's what I found compelling about the band. The bottom line is that the concept made sense to me, and it clearly made sense to the band. The best part of all? I didn't come up with it out of the blue. They did. All I did was recognize that element in their music, and chose to utilize the influence so as to avoid making a purely conventional hard-rock album.

It's not good enough to act as an organizational force for a project or band. You must be a creative force too, as that is what makes you valuable as their leader. The band (or even the artist) is so mired in being themselves that they have no perspective. They can't pore through their music and determine what they are. That's what you bring to the party. As an outsider you not only have the ability to evaluate a band and help them discover their true strengths and uniqueness, but you also show that to them in the form of their recordings. By the time you're done with a project, the recordings act as a mirror for your group. They will see themselves clearly as a band, and what their roles are, because you will have spelled it out for them in such a way that they can't help but understand it.

Sonic Landscape

The overall sonic landscape is critical to the production and should be a significant part of your vision. It's a mistake to believe that this part of the vision should be left in the hands of the recordist. The sound of a record has considerable influence on the listener; as such, it is wholly within your purview.

Tight, dead, Al Green–style drums recorded in a veritable anechoic chamber are not likely the best sonic choice for a huge rock track. That's not to say that you wouldn't or couldn't choose an Al Green drum tone for your rock track, so long as you choose it purposely. But when we're using words like "huge" to describe a drum sound, an ambient room seems a more appropriate choice, since dry tones tend to make you feel as though you are in a more intimate setting.

Many of you reading this book probably have your own recording space. When operating merely as Default Producer, it's reasonable to make your space work as best as you can for your client. As the legitimate and named producer, your room should only act as one viable option. If you need a big drum sound and your room is insufficient for such treatment, then you should consider renting an appropriate studio for tracking, even if that means less money in your pocket for the short term.

The other option is to record in your room and add space later in the form of reverbs and delays. While this works in a pinch, it has its own particular sound, which could very well prove a somewhat illogical sound. While plenty of recordings employ the use of large digital reverbs, if the telltale markings of a small room are contained within the individual tracks themselves, this treatment doesn't work particularly well. It is nearly impossible to keep the reflections from a small space out of a recording, even using close-miking techniques, especially on drums.

Even if you somehow just adore that '80s sound (and at the time I'm writing this, it's back in fashion), and your plans include the use of digital reverbs to create the illusion of a stadium-size space, then you certainly don't need an excessively large room. That doesn't mean you don't need a reasonable amount of space for the job. Even the smallest kits take up quite a bit of real estate, but more important, they require some space for a decent recording. Drums don't sound good in small rooms with parallel walls and eight-foot ceilings (although this can be totally appropriate for a punk rock album). They can get quite strident, among other issues, when the reflections return too quickly to the microphones.

Sometimes things don't work out exactly as you planned. If you record drums in a medium to small room, and decide later that you really want a bigger room sound, you can always re-amp the drums and record the room as a chamber. Houses with hardwood floors are great for this. If that's not possible, you can always rent a large studio for a few hours to perform the re-amp. Gross over-compression on the room mics with a fast attack/fast release can serve to make your room sound bigger.

More important than anything else regarding sound is how your tones work together. All the tones need to blend to create one sound. If you're recording a stylized track, then you need tones that fit the style appropriately and are consistent with each other. When I recorded Ben Harper's "Steal My Kisses" with J. P. Plunier, he didn't like my initial tones. We were well into the recording of the album, and this was our first hitch, but my vision clearly didn't match his on this particular song. As the producer, his vision trumped mine, but I can't go with a vision if I'm not brought in to it in the first place. After two failed attempts to come up with something useful, I asked in exasperation, "Can you give me an adjective that I can use to understand what you're looking for?"

"New Orleans," he replied.

And while, on the face of it, "New Orleans" is hardly an adjective, having been there, it was a term I could understand. I changed out Dean's kik drum for something a bit rounder. We swapped out the snare drum for one that was tighter and less rock. I swapped out Juan Nelson's five-string bass for a Hoffner (I won't lie, he wasn't happy, but he is so fucking good it didn't matter).

Now, you'll notice I didn't use EQ and compression to change the tones. I swapped out source instruments. And the only instruments I needed to touch (in this case) were the bass and drums. In most cases, the bass and drums dictate the sound of the record. I know that sounds crazy, but it's true. Just changing out a snare drum can completely change how a song makes you feel. Furthermore, once players hear the drums and bass, they typically adjust their sound to match. I didn't have to touch Ben's guitar tone. He changed it the moment he heard the new drum tones.

The use of electronic processing to create a tone should be a last resort. If you can get the instruments sounding right in the room, then they will sound right on the recording. J. P. wanted New Orleans, so I made the necessary adjustments on the instruments themselves. With the band now on board with the sound, they adjusted what they were playing to match, and we had New Orleans. Everyone was now on the same page where his vision was concerned.

I can't tell you how glad I was for J. P. to say "New Orleans," because that record wouldn't have been nearly as compelling produced as a straight folk/country track.

Eclectic Albums

In the '70s and '80s, and even in the '90s to some extent, it was typical for a band or artist to have a particular sound, and to stick with that sound. Beginning in the '90s, and continuing until the present, it has become more and more common for artists to create rather eclectic albums that jump styles and genres seemingly from song to song. I call this an eclectic album.

In the '70s, bands typically put out an album every year. These days, it often takes three years before an artist puts out new product. If you listen to each of the Led Zeppelin albums, they all contain a collection of songs that fit the same general vibe of the album. If you compare the first Led Zeppelin album through their last, you can hear how they progressed. When you listen to a Led Zeppelin greatest hits album, it comes off as an eclectic album.

Give an entire generation a steady diet of "Best of" records, or radio music marathons, and it will have an effect on music-making. The effect, from what I can tell, is the eclectic album, although I admit I have absolutely no scientific evidence to back this up. Still, I'm not actually trying to convince you of my somewhat random theory on this. I'm merely pointing out the existence of this kind of project.

Eclectic albums are a ton of fun. They also tend to require more work, more overdubs, and make an overall vision and identifiable sound more difficult. Therefore, the sonic landscape must be dealt with on a song-by-song basis. Given the current buying habits where music is concerned, album continuity isn't anywhere near as much of a concern as it once was. Besides, the singer will provide some semblance of continuity. Of course, if you're recording one of those bands that has more than one lead singer, then all bets are off anyway.

I like to actually visualize music. If I'm working with a band that's tough, then I want the record to sound tough. If they're pop, I want the record to have a sheen about it. If the group falls within the indie genre, I might want a rattier, less polished sound. But sound is a major part of producing, and if you as the producer hone the sound at the source, you'll need hardly any engineering experience to pull it off.

The source is the instrument you're recording, be it organic or electronic. If the kik drum sounds like shit, and moving the mic doesn't seem to improve its prospects much, then you are best advised to adjust the kik drum itself. Sometimes that means replacing it completely, sometimes that means tuning it, dampening it, changing the heads, or any number of physical fixes. The more you fix your problems at the source, the better in general your recordings are going to be. Some recordists ignore the source, preferring to manhandle poor tones through processing. While sometimes this is necessary, particularly with mediocre band musicians, it's typically not the best option in a studio setting.

I *always* listen to the source instrument in the room before I listen to it in the control room. This way I have some idea of how the sound is translating in the control room. While this may seem to be more in the purview of the recordist, it's good for you to know what an instrument sounds like in the room. If the source sounds bad, then it's quite possible its physical location in the room has something to do with it. This is especially true with instruments that take up a large swath of real estate, like drum kits.

Whether you're the recordist or you hired one for your session, I find it's always good to have a plethora of mics set up and distributed around the room. If you have a variety of mics—large-diaphragm condensers, small-diaphragm condensers, dynamics, and ribbons— all set up and ready to go, then you can quickly grab one for any overdub. This has the added advantage of providing you a near-instantaneous room mic at any moment. Multiple mics set up in the room is a massive time-saver. It allows you to quickly listen to multiple mics on a source without having to think. Of course, if the player is seated and ready to go, forget it. Grab the nearest mic, get in the control room, and press Record. Once your talent is in position, there's no more fucking around. Start recording. If that's not acceptable to you, then get the talent out of the room until you're actually ready to compare a few mics. There is nothing worse than allowing your talent to sit and rot in a room, wondering when the hell you're going to start recording.

The beauty of placing multiple mics throughout the room is that it's easy to bus and combine them, particularly when a console is involved in the process. Speed in this regard is more important than choosing between mic A and mic B. If you're ready the moment the artist is, then you have a better chance at a great take. Whatever you do, don't spend half an hour seeking the perfect mic for a fucking woodblock. I can already tell you, it sounds fine.

On the other hand, it's probably worth a little extra time exploring different microphones with a vocalist. This has as much to do with sonics as with the singer herself. If she doesn't like how her vocal sounds in the headphones, then she will lack the necessary inspiration. That said, you don't want to waste 20 minutes testing out different mics on your vocalist either. You risk frustrating her. So, consider trying out different mics as you track, especially if a high percentage of those vocals are going to end up as scratch vocals. This allows you and your artist to hear how she sounds on various mics in advance of an actual vocal session. Some songs call for a particular kind of mic. Sometimes the broad sound of a large-diaphragm condenser microphone isn't the best option. Sometimes a dynamic will sound best on a particular track.

Clearly, when you test your microphones throughout the tracking phase, there will be occasions when your artist delivers an undeniable vocal on a less than optimum mic. Your engineer might feel like you threw him under the bus if you insist on that vocal, but your instinct to put performance over sound considerations is correct. Believe me, I've had some wretched-sounding vocals delivered to me as a mixer, but unless they've been shattered by the pumping effect of an abused cheap compressor, they can be salvaged. Don't let your recordist convince you to re-record a great performance unless it's somehow unusable, and the only way that can happen is if there is some artifact that can actually hurt people (this has happened).

Market Considerations

Whenever you set out to make an album, or a single track, you should consider the target market. For instance, if your act will appeal mostly to jazz lovers, and you put an outrageously distorted, balls-out electric rock guitar in your production, you will likely alienate your intended market. When you first listen to the demos, you should think about who the music is meant to attract. Young tweens? Angry 20-somethings? 30-somethings? Will it appeal to girls more than guys, or vice versa? What region of the country will this product appeal to most? Is the goal radio airplay? To tour the festival circuit? Is this an established band or a new band? Established bands have a legacy and an identifiable sound that should be taken into consideration. A new band or artist needs to establish a sound, one unique to them.

Of course, you can always just copy what everyone else is doing, and certainly fashion has a place in music production. It just tends to date your material. If you follow a fashion on your artist's record, and they have a massive hit, you could find yourself with a one-hit wonder. The song "It's Raining Men" is basically a disco song that hit as disco was exiting stage left, and The Weather Girls never recovered.

Personally, I'm disgusted when I hear a total copycat production. There's a big difference between alluding to a great song or past production technique and completely ripping it off. As much as I live by the mantra "amateurs borrow, professionals steal," it's pretty lame to completely rip off every aspect of another production. I'm not going to name any names, because my purpose here isn't to call out peers who might have been under pressures they couldn't overcome, but the temptation to rip off another production will occasionally rear its ugly head, and I'm here to advise you to avoid this nonsense at all costs.

If you want to make your production familiar and generic in the hopes of capitalizing on a musical trend, you risk presenting your band in a manner so lacking in specialness that their likelihood of failure increases. If you create a production that makes a band sound unique without coming totally from left field, you have a far better chance of being a trendsetter rather than a trend follower. Trendsetters make the big money in this world, and then all the little trend followers capitalize on that trend until a new one comes along. If you're a trendsetter, thank me at the Grammys. If you're a trend follower, thank the band and producer you totally ripped off.

We have such a long and rich history of recorded music that there really are no conventions you can implement without coming off as unoriginal. A modern track does not require modern techniques. The reverberant guitar was big in the '60s, and came back in vogue in the '80s (everything was reverberant in the '80s), but just because you used a reverberant guitar doesn't mean you've made a '60s production, unless you create a production that's supposed to sound like it came from that era. In that case, copying those production techniques is almost essential to give the track the appropriate sound. This is especially true if you're producing a song for a period movie.

Gated reverb on drums was big in the '80s, and was so overused that it's tough to put that into a production without completely dating your music to the wrong era. If you want to make a song feel like it's from the '80s, that's fine, but if you're going to use gated reverb, you probably want to make sure that everything else sounds as modern as possible. Perhaps this would be the time to insert that lovely T-Pain Auto-Tune artifact we all love so much. Of course, in a few years, you'll have managed to date your track to the early '10s.

You see the risk here, right? If you use a production technique that will soon fall out of fashion, you could very well kill your track before it's even had a chance. So, choose your trendy production techniques carefully.

Sweating What's Important

Far be it from me to dictate to you what's important to a hypothetical production, but let's face it, as much as you need to sweat the details, you don't want to do so in a debilitating manner. You have to pick and choose your battles, not only with the band, but also with yourself.

I frequently have internal debates with myself as I work through decisions. I don't involve the artist in every debate, and sometimes I table debates until I have more information. There are several reasons for not involving your artist in every internal consideration. For starters, if you spit out everything you're thinking at any given moment, it won't be long before your artist is convinced that you're an absolute lunatic. Bad ideas are far more prevalent than good ones, and you should give yourself the opportunity to filter your thoughts before presenting them. The idea here isn't to hide your bad ideas. You'll reveal plenty of those. The point is to avoid spewing out seemingly contradictory and particularly stupid ideas. You have permission to come up with bad ideas, even stupid ones. But many of your thoughts can be rejected without involving anyone else. As long as no one else is required to try out an idea, work it out on your own first.

There's another reason to keep your ideas close to the vest. You want to give the artist an opportunity to confirm your thoughts independently. If you *know* a keyboard part isn't helping the song much, there's no reason to waste time beating around the bush. Kill the part and go in a new direction. If you merely have *concerns* that a keyboard part isn't helping the song, and your artist expresses similar thoughts without prompting, that serves as a clear confirmation that you should look for other alternatives. If I'm really struggling with a decision on the keyboard part, then I present my struggle directly to the talent in the hope that we can solve the problem together. Sometimes the best way to prove the overall worth of any given part is to try to improve upon it.

Of course, the most compelling reason for reserving your thoughts is the sheer volume of them. If I were to mention every thought or idea that came into my head while producing a record, I'd never shut up. It's impossible to listen if you're talking, and despite the incredibly obvious nature of that statement, there are plenty of people on this earth who have yet to learn that lesson.

Even in a smooth-running love fest of a session, there can be plenty of room for disagreement. And while ultimately it's the band's record, you have a responsibility to the entire band, not just the brainchild. You have a responsibility to make an album that can achieve the stated goals, and sometimes that requires more assertiveness and stubbornness than you're likely comfortable with. The biggest trick in producing is convincing your band, who is hiring you and paying you for your consultation, to believe that you actually have some power of veto. We already know that the artist has veto power over you as the producer. You must acquire a similar power, but don't abuse it, and remember to keep it within the limitations of the plan.

If the plan is to get a major label record deal, then you have to make an album that sounds like a major label record. I leave you to decide what that is, but if your artist is forcing you into a place that runs counter to your goals and vision, it's time to consider pulling out your veto pen.

Believe me, when you veto a band or artist's idea, they will often be quite pissed. It's best to avoid saying "no" to your client, but let's face it, if you don't have the budget flexibility to change the overall plan, then you're going to have to deny the request. Many problems can be dealt with by being creative. A Science Experiment of epic proportions is best worked on outside of the studio. You can put your brainchild in another room with the assistant, or you can send her home with the session to work on it later. What you can't allow is for your band to dictate how to spend the session time. They aren't the ones responsible for staying under budget and delivering the product on time.

You are in charge. You run the session. Your client has given you that power, and you will need to use it to keep the session running the way you know best. Even if you're somewhat inexperienced in this regard, or if you're not completely competent in running a session, there's no better way to learn than by gathering this coveted and all-important record-making experience.

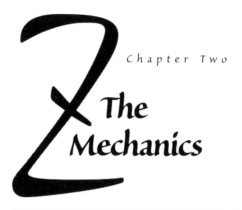

The Mechanics

Choosing a Winner

Producing requires a high degree of selectivity on your part. You should never, ever accept a producing job that you're not convinced is a winner. In other words, if you can't envision listening to the album yourself, then you shouldn't even discuss taking the gig.

"Yeah, but Mixerman—I need to make money, dude!"

Of course you do. But if you start accepting projects purely for the money and not for their potential, you risk reducing your perceived value, if not your actual value. If all you have is a discography full of mediocre material that even *you* don't fully believe in, then how are you ever going to break out from that position? Granted, there is such a thing as paying your dues, but at least pay them on material that you would buy yourself.

There are basically three cardinal rules for choosing a project. They are, in order: the songs, the songs, and the songs.

Now, clearly you could love the songs and despise the voice. You might even find the band generally atrocious, and those are perfectly acceptable reasons for *passing* on a project. But there's only one reason to *accept* a project, and that's the songs. I can promise you this: if the songs are great, you can make a production that works for even the most novice band. If the songs suck, even your favorite famous band will prove to be nothing short of a disaster. The difference being you're not going to take my advice when it's your favorite famous band.

Let me put it this way: it is always better to produce a shit band with great songs than a great band with shit songs. Some of my favorite albums are by bands that are almost infantile in their playing abilities. The 1983 Violent Femmes eponymous release comes to mind. U2's 1980 release of *Boy*. Neither of these bands were technically great at the time those albums were made, yet to me (and many others) they're magical albums. Why? Because I love the songs!

You'll notice I said that *I* love the songs. Pardon my stating the obvious, but the overall quality of a band's songs is purely subjective. Even if you hate those albums, that has no relevance to my point. If, in a parallel universe, a young U2 comes to you with songs that you hate, you should pass on the album.

So, what do you do if you find an absolutely compelling artist with awful songs? You convince her to perform other songs. Whether you write them with her, bring in writers, or get songs from a publisher, you need to replace those awful songs. With a band? You've got to pass. Bands don't perform songs written by professionals. None that I've ever come across.

Don't let some A&R guy or band manager convince you that the band's songs are great. Either you like the band or you don't, and no amount of hype should sway your opinion, or allow you to consider going against your gut in that regard. The further up the food chain you get in this business, the more likely you'll have some schmuck blowing smoke up your ass, telling you what a hot commodity his band is, and how you'd be a fool to pass on the project. For starters, there is a 99.9 percent chance that the pitch is utter bullshit. Second, who the fuck cares? Again, if *you* don't love the songs, you can't do a good job of producing the project. Period. Yes, you can do a stellar job of recording it, if you know how. You can do a killer job of arranging it, if you have the skills. But you can't have vision if you don't love the songs. It's impossible. And even if you could, you're going to put your name on a product in which you think the songs are pure shit? Seriously? When you put it on your reel, are you going to tell everyone you can that it was pure shit when you got it, and now it's just partly shit?

I realize I'm hammering this point relentlessly. My apologies. I just happen to know and understand the underdeveloped ego of a young producer. While reading this book is a good indicator that you're willing to avoid the usual delusions that go with youthful exuberance, I worry that it's not enough to save you from making this one major mistake despite my warnings. Right. So you must love the songs. I won't bring it up again.

Selecting a project is the first point of failure. Be picky.

Evaluating Demos

Producing opportunities present themselves in a number of ways. If you're particularly aggressive (and not very busy), you can actively seek out acts you wish to produce, both on the Internet and in person. Sometimes talent will find you through a former client or the buzz generated by your good work. Regardless of who finds whom, descriptive hype can only go so far. In fact, whether showered upon you by others or self-generated, hype is useless information and should be avoided.

You will hear all sorts of claims about record company interest, multi-platinum producer interest, celebrity interest, etcetera, etcetera, blah, blah, blah. Not only will most of that hype be overblown, but it would seem to preclude you from involvement unless you're in a position to pick up that kind of gig. Hey, even if the hype is true—and it rarely is—you still need to make your decisions based on the music. Believe me, when you or anyone else has an act that is undeniable, no words are necessary. You'll know it the moment you hear it. So, just set aside those Grammy visions for a moment, and focus your emotional response on where it counts: the music.

Nearly every act has recordings and videos of themselves available on the Internet. Frankly, if the first three tracks cause you to hit the Skip button, you're wasting your time listening to more. In fact, most acts can be rejected in a matter of seconds. They might not even be bad. They could just be outside of your position or preferences, in which case, there's not much point in sifting through more material.

When you come across an act with little or even no recorded material, you're getting involved too early. Bands and artists need time to find themselves. If you bring your influence in too early, they lose out on an important growth process—both musically and interpersonally—and you lose out on a great indicator of longevity. A high percentage of acts will fail and disband before they're anywhere close to generating a worthwhile product. If you get involved too early, you give yourself similar odds.

You can spend as much time as you like listening to available demos, but once you find yourself interested in or excited by a project, you should probably have a conversation with the artist.

The Interview

Your initial conversation with the brainchild is basically the first step in the courting process, and it's very similar in nature to dating. Just as you're judging the brainchild, he is judging you, and at the end of that initial conversation, you will both have determined whether you're interested in taking the next logical step. Like on any first date, everyone is typically on his or her best behavior.

Your greatest tool in the courting process is enthusiasm. Generally, there's no point in playing coy. You're not trying to sign them to a record deal here, so there's no point in trying to gain some negotiating advantage through feigned disinterest. Therefore, it's best to tell the brainchild exactly what you love about the band, and in full detail, based on what you've heard so far. Let him know specifically what it is that interests you about the group.

That said, do everyone a favor and avoid offering false or overbearing praise. You want to reveal your enthusiasm, but you also must establish trust, and if you go on and on about how they're the next big thing, and any other trite producer bullshit line you've heard on television, you'll lose the gig. At least you should. Either the band will think you're completely full of shit, which you are, or they will think you're out of their league.

It's also fair game to express your concerns. If you think the band has a weakness that needs to be addressed, there's no reason to withhold that information. This is especially true if you have a clear vision for the artist. How aggressive or pointed you are with your criticism really depends on the dynamics of the interview and the amount of material you've heard before the interview. Some acts have an unrealistic view of themselves, and if you get that sense, it can be a worthwhile strategy to knock the brainchild down a peg or two. Such an aggressive stance serves two main purposes. One, it lets the band know you're not coming just to hit Record and be awed by their genius. Two, it gives you an indication as to whether the band can be produced in the first place.

Yes, it's possible that ego-checking will cost you the gig, especially if you're too aggressive, but if it's evident that the artist is completely delusional, and you're not in a position right off the bat to counterbalance those delusions, what's the point in trying to win the gig? Sure, with a little effort, you might be able to win the act over, but the moment anyone of any stature comes into the picture, you'll be out. While criticism for the purposes of shock value can be a useful tool, it's basically a line in the sand, one that should be drawn only when you're fully prepared to walk.

Overall, the interview process is not meant to be a contentious one. Quite the opposite, really. Your goal is to get as accurate a picture as you can of the act, the lineup, their history, their goals, and most important of all, their personalities. You're going to spend hundreds of hours with this band. You need to know what you're getting yourself into. Your questions will vary based on the band and their demos, but I can certainly give you some idea of the kinds of questions you might ask.

Who writes the songs (is it a collaborative effort, or is there a brainchild responsible for all the songwriting)? How many members are in the band (if any)?

These are usually my first questions, mostly because the answers tell me whether I'm talking to the right person. The songwriter in the band is almost always the person with the most power. If it's a collaborative effort, or if everyone in the band writes the songs together, then you need to figure out who the leader is. You want to deal directly with the power player as early as possible in the process. If you align yourself with the least important member of the band, you're wasting your time. Your main connection must be with the brainchild or true bandleader.

On those occasions when you find yourself talking to the brainchild in a band made up of sidemen, you want to determine whether the band is a relatively tight-knit group who play together frequently, or a loosely formed group with little to no actual stake in the project. The stake a brainchild's band has in the product is important information. An artist with a static band of sidemen could be perilously close to becoming a band entity, and the politics of that kind of record can get a bit shaky, particularly when a legitimate producer gets involved. When a project begins to look promising, sidemen begin to want a stake in the product, and rightly so. Such a situation is ripe for a blowout, resulting either in a new band entity or an artist in desperate need of a new band entirely. Neither bodes well for completing an album.

It's also important to assess the overall commitment of everyone in the band. It's one thing for a band member to dream of living the life of a touring musician. It's another for him to actually face that prospect. Believe it or not, the idea of success can cause some to fold entirely, and if the presence of a bona fide producer makes the whole dream thing a bit too real, it can result in the loss of a band mate at best, and a complete breakup at worst. Unfortunately, the latter is the more likely scenario, since the only thing worse than ditching your dream is being reminded of it later. This means you'll be dealing with a saboteur, and you will likely be unable to prevent their tactics from bringing down the entire project. This is yet another reason why you must be careful about how early you get involved with a band.

Make sure you know the band's full history, including its personnel history. You need to know exactly how long this particular band lineup has been in existence. You're going to be listening to fully produced demos, which could very well have been performed by a significantly different lineup. This can yield some rather surprising results come your first rehearsal, and while it won't be too late to back out, you will have wasted considerable time. The whole point of the interview process is to prevent you from wasting your time.

Where are you from? What kind of following do you have? How far from home do you perform, and how often? How long have you been performing with this particular group?

By the time you get to the interview stage, you likely know where the act is based. The size and scope of their fan following is only moderately important, as it shouldn't necessarily affect your desire to take on the project. Still, the answers to these questions will give you some insight into how far along in the process your potential band is. As we have established more than once, it's inadvisable to take on a project for a band that's been together a month, has no following, and no experience playing together. In that particular case, the band is far more in need of demos for the purposes of booking club dates than an actual record.

Remember, if your goal is to become a professional record producer, you want to involve yourself in projects that have potential. As it is, you can expect an unfortunately high ratio of projects to crash and burn beyond your involvement. This is especially true if you get involved too early in the process. The best way for an act to prove its level of commitment is through the size and nature of its following.

Now, if you find a band that shows so much potential talent and musical skill that you just *have* to get involved in the embryonic stages, then you'll be as much their manager as their producer. This means that you'll be putting in quite a bit of time and effort with one group, which will negatively affect your ability to work on other projects. If you think it's worthwhile to spend one or two years developing and nurturing a single group on the side, then be my guest. But keep in mind that you can do everything right and it can still completely implode on you. Band members can have babies (with each other, even). Singers can lose their fucking minds. Irreconcilable differences can occur. And not everyone is replaceable. In fact, the less time a band has been together, the less likely it is that a replacement player will work out. There is too little infrastructure to withstand such a huge blow, and one could argue the band didn't ever really exist in the first place if it couldn't stay together long enough to build even a small following.

Developing bands is something that interests many fledgling producers. After all, if you don't have a discography and you wait until a band is actually in a position to hire a professional, you could lose out on a gig entirely. This alone is a reasonable argument for getting yourself in on the ground floor with an act. Just keep in mind that many more things can go wrong with a band than with an artist, and when there's no track record of the band's work ethic or seriousness of purpose, you're taking an exceptionally large risk involving yourself too early in the process.

Have I beaten this point to death yet? Good.

What are your goals?

You can ask this question early on or reserve it for later, as the information you acquire throughout the conversation should give you a rather clear indication of the band's goals. Still, it's good to get your brainchild to state the band's goals. Typically, the answer won't be as clear-cut as you might think. That's because you're dealing with artists, not businessmen, although these days artists must be somewhat adept at business too.

"I just want to make a living playing music, man."

That's a common answer to the above question, and while we can probably all understand the sentiment, the goal is rather broad. There's a grimy Elvis impersonator who busks on my local pier who technically makes a living "playing music, man." Hopefully, that's not what your potential client has in mind. Perhaps you should ask.

"I just want to make music that I can be proud of, man."

This is another rather broad and useless goal. What exactly does that mean? Frankly, this sort of statement scares me because there is absolutely no expectation of monetary success mentioned. As much as we all produce records because we love music, this is a business, and we can't eat if we don't make money from the records we produce. If an artist is under the delusion that a successful record won't make her proud, then "Houston, we have a problem."

"I want to be rich beyond my wildest dreams with my killer songs."

Here we have the other end of the spectrum. This is someone willing to sell his musical soul to make money. While we all want a salable product, there *is* a middle ground.

None of the above statements really count as goals. Businesses must have goals. When there is a band bank account used to save money for the purposes of making a product, then the band is a business. What are the goals for the business, both short-term and long-term? What are the goals for the album? Is the goal to get radio play? Is the goal to acquire a distribution deal? Is the goal to hit the road, and play 250 dates a year? Is the goal to make an album and license the songs for commercials and movies? Is the goal to create a product that the artist can sell at her shows? To parlay a record into a television career? To deliver a record that their major label can promote? Who is the market? Who likes the act now, and who will like them in the future?

Often the band's goals are undefined. In such cases, you should have a discussion that not only defines the band's goals, but also prepares them for the steps needed to accomplish them. If the goal is to pick up major distribution, we could be talking about an entirely different record from one where the goal is merely to tour and deliver music to an already existing and hopefully reasonably sized following.

How were the demos recorded? Was there heavy editing involved?

Once you've determined where your act is on the trajectory of success, you want to provide yourself with information regarding the demo recordings. This is especially true if the band is of significant distance from you. Frankly, you probably shouldn't even consider a nonlocal act until you have a track record. While personal connections are what will ultimately win you the gig, it's your discography that provides you the respect necessary to make that connection in the first place. If a band has to wait a month before they even get to meet you, then they pretty much need some indication that you're the real deal. No one is going to spend money flying out an unproven commodity. I don't care how good a salesman you are.

If you can't go and see the act live, then you need to have some idea of how enhanced their recordings are. This information is critical for proper budgeting. A band that requires excessive computer enhancement also requires more overall time. Personally, I have no interest in working with a band in need of a Gridiron

Producer, and it's best for all parties involved if we determine this need early on. Otherwise, we're all wasting time and money just so I can ultimately pass.

How many previous albums were there? How many songs do you have written as a band? How many do you have in demo form? How many of these do you perform regularly?

Here's a hint: If you're calling back The Rolling Stones or some other known entity because they want you to produce their next album, don't ask how many albums they've previously recorded. Look it up. Otherwise, these are good questions that should give you an idea of how prolific your act is. The more songs that exist, the better, even if half the songs are no longer performed. This shows a clear track record, and will give you some indication as to whether the band is ready for a producer.

What kind of a budget do you have?

If you're feeling good about the act, and you think you can help, you might as well figure out whether you can take the gig or not. Without a budget, you can't even begin to determine whether you can take on the project. If you discover early on that a band is completely delusional in regard to what they can accomplish and for how much, and if the budget turns out to be an immovable number, then there's not much point spending hours poring through all of their tracks. Unless you're planning on developing the band on a speculative basis, you can't take the gig if the budget isn't large enough to make the record you envision.

After a while, you get a pretty good sense of whether there's a reasonable amount of money available for a project. Still, this question must be broached directly. Whatever you do, however, don't open with it. Not only does that make you appear more interested in money than anything else (like the music), but the money isn't fully relevant until you have a basic idea of what will be involved in making the album. A $25,000 budget can be minuscule for one project and enormous for another. Until you know what the project will entail, it's difficult to judge whether the budget is reasonable.

I'll warn you now, bringing up the budget can be somewhat shocking and slightly uncomfortable for an act. Some clients might not want to reveal their budget to you, but there is absolutely no justification for such a reaction. While it's true that the bigger the budget, the more money you're going to get paid up front, everything is relative. If there's a $100,000 budget, your client won't stand for you getting paid $90K as you all slum it in a bullshit studio for the remaining $10K. Conversely, you won't stand for spending months in the finest and most expensive studio around only to work for pennies. The budget is the budget, and you need to make the best record you can within it. This includes your fees and/or advances.

The difference between an album that costs $1,000,000 to make and one that costs $10,000 to make is time and personnel. The million-dollar album can afford a full orchestra, a top engineer, a caterer, a cartage crew, a guitar tech, and yes, a highly in-demand producer. But none of those things is a requirement for making an album. In fact, the only real requirement is a recording space that has some modicum of isolation and an adequate collection of recording gear.

It takes a great many days to spend a million dollars in the studio. Even with a burn rate of $4K per day, it would take 200 days in the studio to reach $800K. When you have 200 days to make an album, you can spend an entire day fucking around on a Science Experiment of little to no actual consequence. When your budget is $25,000, such experiments are prohibitive.

No one needs 200 days of top-dollar studio time to make an album. I'm not saying that no one uses it. I'm saying no one *needs* it. Furthermore, whether you're paid a $10,000 or $100,000 advance, a record that sells 10 million copies will pay out the same. The advance is recouped first, then you're paid royalties. In other words, the $100,000 advance protects you against failure, not success.

If you find yourself considering a project that is in your estimation underfunded, you can always attempt to expand the budget. Unfortunately, it's difficult to expand a budget before you've established some trust. Furthermore, a band can't possibly perceive your value without working with you first. Sometimes it makes sense to invest some time into a project in the hopes of expanding the budget, but you shouldn't bother unless you're willing to make the album for the proposed budget. Whether you take a project based on an insufficient budget is dependent on how much you love the project, how you think producing the project will benefit your career, how much time you can devote to a project that offers no upfront funding, and how effective you are at the beg, borrow, and steal game.

Equally important to knowing the budget is your control over the funds. Typically, a label or band isn't just going to hand over their budgeted money to you, so that's not to be taken literally. Control over the budget merely means you're in a position to designate and authorize all expenditures. If you don't have that kind of control, you will surely go over budget. Every time. There's no point in your potential client withholding this information from you, and there's no way you can possibly commit to a project or even plan for one without knowing and controlling the budget. So ask the question, and if there's any hesitation, then explain the realities. No matter what the budget, your decision and ultimately your fees will be based on that number.

When dealing with a major label, you will occasionally be asked to submit a budget based on the needs of the project. In some cases this is slightly trickier than working within an established budget; in others it's easier. In this situation, you're charging a per track price, and you're setting the budget. If you're highly in demand, that price will be high, and so will the cost of the album. Typically, labels don't ask you for a budget unless they have every intention of hiring you, and they probably have a good idea of what you charge and what to expect in a budget. That said, you could submit a budget of $100,000 only to be told you must halve it. No worries—you just managed to acquire the maximum allowable budget for your record. Aren't you glad you didn't say $40K? Personally, I wouldn't worry too much about overbidding. Major labels are institutions full of superstitious people. The more you cost, the more they think they made the right decision.

Whew! All that for one simple little question. Money always complicates things, doesn't it? But it also simplifies things, because once you know your budget, you can use your experience to make the numbers work. If the budget is low, you can schedule a short amount of time in an expensive room, and a large amount of time in a relatively inexpensive overdub room. If paying for an editor is prohibitive, you can track the band, then take a week off and tighten the tracks at your house. If you don't have enough days to track 15 songs, you can reduce that number to 12 or even 10 songs if you must. If there's not enough money for an engineer, you can use the studio assistant. There are plenty of places where you can cut costs to make a budget work.

The interview process is your best defense against wasting copious amounts of time. You will only treat this part of the process as unimportant once in your career. Upon completing the initial interview, you will begin to invest significant time and energy into the project, and you still might pass or lose out on it. As you become more experienced you will come across scenarios that are deal breakers. These are usually born from bad experiences. When a record blows up on you because the singer is dating the bass player, you may start asking whether any of the band members are dating each other. This is natural. Your deal breakers are not necessarily mine. Either way, you want to use the interview to flush out any and all worrisome situations. Knowledge is power, and even if you choose to overlook a particular problem, at least you're in a position to monitor it. So, make sure to use the interview to find out everything you possibly can about your future clients.

Give Me Everything You've Got

Once you've determined that everyone's goals are in alignment and there's a sufficient budget, you need to get your hands on every piece of music the band has ever recorded and played. This includes past albums, reject tracks from past albums, reject demos, and current demos.

Honestly, I can't tell you how many times I have expressed my desire to hear *everything*—to emphasize the definition of "everything" as I've laid it out for you here—only to get some paltry collection of tracks that barely amounts to "some," let alone "everything." I can't explain it, nor will I ever understand why "everything" is such a difficult concept to grasp. If the band has it on disk, tape, CD, or any other delivery medium known to man or not yet invented, I want it. Period. Sure, the band can label the tracks however they want. They could very well give me a folder of songs called "songs we hate and if you ask us to play them we will fire you on the spot." Whatever. I want the fucking songs!

So do you.

I can't advise you on how to get "everything" from a band, because no matter what, they will withhold songs from you, either because the word *everything* confuses the leader, or because he completely forgot about certain songs. Either way, you likely won't discover the band's most compelling song until the very last day of recording, at which point it's too fucking late. If you can figure out some way to adequately get across the meaning of *everything* to your potential clients, and in a consistent manner, then I would very much like to know your secret. To date, I'm still trying to figure this one out.

Right. So, once you're reasonably convinced that you have *everything*, you can pore through all of your talent's music—past, present, and unfinished. This information paints a picture of the band, their capabilities, their likes, their strengths, their weaknesses, their focus, and their overall progression. This bodes well for vision.

When it comes to evaluating previously recorded material, pay attention to overall patterns and trends rather than the specific details of any given song. There's no point in tearing apart a record that's long been complete. It's a snapshot in time, but one that can provide great insight into how to approach the band's next body of work. For example, if you find the bass parts (and playing) are weak on the first album and strong on the second, it would be good to know why. Is that because the bass player improved? Or is it because another producer worked out the parts with her? Whatever the reason, this information will be valuable for budgeting recording time. If you know you're going to have to teach the bass player all the bass parts for the album by rote, you need to budget for that event accordingly.

Previously recorded material is a treasure trove of your artist's own past lessons, many of them yet unlearned by your artist. Let me give you a few examples: If the singer tends to sing outside of her effective range, you can make the necessary adjustments to the new material in preproduction, either by selecting the songs that best fit her range, or by changing keys. Perhaps the band's previous recordings are generally too slow across the board. Past arrangements could be excessively busy and distracting to the vocal. Whatever the issues, make note of them.

Make note of your band's strengths, too. If the singer sounds best in his lower register, this could explain why some performances pop more than others. The band could be considerably more exciting when performing off click. Anything that you notice on the recordings as a whole is information that can and should be used to both sell the band on your vision and prepare them for recording.

Depending on the band's physical distance from you, a shortage of material could require some travel on your part. Unless you're considering signing the act to a production deal, they should pay your travel costs, at which point you're only risking your time. I mean, if there's a budget to make a record, then part of that budget should be spent by the talent to find the right producer. If the talent isn't willing to pay for that, then they aren't serious about hiring you in the first place. Pass. Of course, if the band's local, this is hardly an issue. Set up a rehearsal.

Rehearsals

First things first: bring beer.

At least a 6-pack, if not a 12-pack. And pull it out the moment you walk in the room. This nominal act of gift giving is such an effective softener it can actually mean the difference between winning and losing the project. As much as your purpose here is all business, you want to create a relaxed atmosphere, one in which defenses are lowered. A couple of beers per person will serve you well in this regard. Even if you don't drink, you should bring beer, preferably at a level of quality the band can't usually afford.

Once beverages have been adequately dispensed, take a moment to work the crowd. Remember, enthusiasm sells. Tell the band everything that you love about them. Be specific. Explain what each member brings to the band as you hear it. Just don't get carried away and start making shit up. The band will listen intently to your every utterance, and you will most certainly be caught in a lie if you allow yourself to start blowing smoke. If you're always forthright with your opinions, this can never happen.

Your first meeting with a band is your best chance to sell yourself, and first impressions matter. Why the hell do you think I always bring beer to the first meeting? Frankly, the best place to get to know the band is to join them in a rehearsal. It gives them a chance to showcase their abilities and you yours. In fact, you should actively engage in preproduction on at least one song, even if you're just there for a meet and greet.

There's not much point in getting all protectionist about your ideas. If the band loves what you bring to the party, they're probably going to hire you. It's highly unlikely that they're going to invite you in so they can take all your great ideas and hire someone else. That wouldn't make a whole lot of sense. So, if you're coming in as a dark horse, or if you feel you're against some stiff competition, then you might as well go for it in as bold and convincing a manner as possible. This is really the best way to win the gig anyway, so there's no point in being cautious with your ideas. You always want to approach the band with absolute confidence. Don't even think about losing the gig. It's irrelevant. If you're the right producer for the job, everyone in the room will know it.

When you can provide the talent with instant and clear-cut improvements to their music in a short period of time, this always bodes well for winning them over. If the band hates your ideas, you'll lose the gig, but who cares? Do you want to produce a band that completely disagrees with your vision? It doesn't matter whether your vision is right. It doesn't matter what the prospects of the band are. If they don't buy into your vision, you're done. You can't produce them, nor would you want to produce them. Don't waste your time or theirs.

Whether you're the dark horse or the wily veteran, the first rehearsal gives you the opportunity to wow the artists and gather information. Really, you either wow them or you don't, based on how you run the rehearsal in conjunction with the quality of your ideas. The information gathering happens concurrently with the wowing. "Information" is basically anything that will be useful to you when it comes to the process or the politics of making the record. Basically, that means just about everything that happens.

A rehearsal with the band allows you to hear them without edits, sweetening, or overdubs. It's just you in a room with the core band. Everything is stripped down to its most basic form, and the comparison between the live rehearsal and past recordings will be quite telling. Not only can you more accurately evaluate individual playing abilities, but you can also evaluate the arrangement without the distraction of a full production (demo or otherwise). This comparison can reveal both strengths and weaknesses you didn't know existed from the recordings alone. It can also provide you with that final bit of inspiration that solidifies your vision. Most important, you can make your first adjustments and evaluations without the pressure of studio time.

Sussing out the politics requires paying attention. Is there a clear leader? How quickly does the band kowtow to the leader? Is there an irritant in the band? Is there any kind of power struggle going on? Does the power shift based on who wrote a particular song? Does anyone seem like an outsider to the band? If so, why? Is there an apparent partnership in the band? Who runs the band business?

Any and all information regarding how the band members interact with each other or how the duties are distributed is critically important. This is somewhat more complicated than the musical evaluations, because most of this political information must be inferred through the interactions of the band. This means you must be paying attention at all times to everything that's going on. Every stolen glance, every verbal jab, every action and reaction should tell you something about the band and its members. This information must be gathered and considered as you move forward with your suggestions.

You don't need, nor should you perform, preproduction on the entire album in a first rehearsal. All you want to do is get across your overall vision, and that can be done in just a few songs at the most. The rest of the time should be spent discussing the project, including your goals, impressions, and vision. You must put into words how you hear the album, how you wish to approach the album, and precisely why you've come to these determinations. You want to discuss the songs, including the collection that you feel will best represent the band and your vision for them. Essentially, this is a sales call, and you are there to sell the band on who they are, who you are, and why you should work together. The best way to accomplish that goal is through effective communication, and by the end of the rehearsal, both the band and you should have some idea of how you wish to proceed. The next step is to schedule a full and proper preproduction session.

Preproduction

Preproduction is the process in which you prepare for a recording. You might hear it referred to as "prepro" for short. This is the time when you work out the song tempos, keys, basic parts, form, and anything else that can be done before entering the studio.

Preproduction is without a doubt the most critical phase of making a record. Yes, more critical than mixing and most certainly more critical than mastering. This is when you set up your vision. All the major decisions are made now. It's the framework for your record—the foundation. Everything that follows this process builds upon it. Not only is this the time when you get to try out your ideas, but it's also the time when you get to fully solidify your vision.

Before you set foot in the studio, you want to relieve as much pressure as possible from the process. The best way to achieve this is to make sure your artist and band fully understand your vision, wholly buy into your vision, and are completely prepared to implement the vision.

Before you begin, you probably want to set some ground rules.

1. **No matter how wacky an idea may seem, it can't be shot down until it's been tried.**

Honestly, there is nothing dumber than arguing over an idea in the abstract when you have the tools necessary to demonstrate. It drives me crazy.

"I don't think that's gonna work."

"Yeah? Well I'd like to know it doesn't work before we scrap the idea."

Presenting ideas to a band for the first time can be an awkward experience at best. Certainly, if your very first suggestion causes the band to recoil in disgust, you could have a problem. It's always best to save your more controversial suggestions for later in the process. Attempting to convince a hardcore punk band to open their album with a string quartet is a poor maneuver, no matter how brilliant the idea. I'm not suggesting that you shy away from your convictions, just that you time them well. A radical change will likely freak the band out significantly. Unless your goal is to cause a freak-out (and who knows, there might be a time when that's a good play), I would recommend starting with your less controversial changes.

Your best bet is to begin with a track that you feel is in reasonably good shape but that you can significantly improve with some relatively minor musical or conceptual changes. If you think that changing the kik drum pattern can greatly improve the feel of the track, that would be a good place to start. If you feel the band missed a rather obvious musical opportunity, that would also be a contender. By the time the preproduction session is over, the band should be open to your more radical ideas.

When presenting a radical idea, it's always good to couch it in such a way that prepares your act. "So, I had this idea, and frankly, it's a rather crazy idea, and it could be the worst idea I've ever had in my life, or it could be brilliant. I'd like to try the idea, but I need you guys to give it a chance before you decide to shoot it down, and I promise, if you hate it, that will be the last time I ever bring it up."

Playing coy like this does several things. It prepares the band to accept your idea no matter how outside the box. This little speech tends to open the band to just about any idea. It also gives them permission to agree that it's probably the worst idea you've ever had, and the fact that you're willing to accept such criticism reduces any angst on their end. Lastly, you've let them know that you view the concept as a long shot, and have no intention of spending time defending it if it falls flat.

Even after I've fully established trust with a band in the recording process, I will still couch edgy ideas as potentially awful or brilliant. I never want a band thinking they can't shoot down an idea, just so long as they're willing to try it in the first place. Of course, it doesn't do you much good to try out an idea with the band if they're not giving you their full-on effort. When this happens, feel free to remind them of rule #1 in order to reestablish it as the modus operandi.

The fear every band or artist will have is that your purpose is to change them. While it's true you'll be making changes, your goal isn't to change *them*. It's to present them in the most effective manner possible. Any changes that you make are based on your vision and the songs. Ultimately, you're there to help them make the most effective record possible—preferably, one they adore.

Not everyone will agree with every decision. A band producing themselves wouldn't be able to accomplish that, so why should you be held to such an unrealistic standard? It certainly doesn't do you any good to make an album that the band hates. That's why I prescribe such a careful courting dance before you jump into the studio, and believe me, you're still courting come preproduction. I mean, we haven't discussed a contract yet, right? Besides, there are almost always multiple solutions to any musical problem, so any particular idea that makes the band uncomfortable can be followed up with numerous other ideas that accomplish something similar.

Frankly, if you're paying attention and you're sensitive to the overall dynamic of the band, it's unlikely that you're going to pull the band so far outside of their comfort zone that you'll have to deal with an all-out mutiny. There might be specific instances or songs when it's a good idea to take the band out of its comfort zone, but in general, you're working with a group that has an identity, so that is clearly not going to be your modus operandi. You know this and I know this, but they don't necessarily know this. Do everyone a favor and ease their fears in this regard, repeatedly and as often as you must. Tell the band straight up that your goal is to make the best record for *them*, not turn them into something they're not. This goes a long way toward easing legitimate fears.

2. Once we make and agree to a plan, we're going to stick with the plan until the track is done.

If you trust yourself, you should trust your vision. I'm not saying there won't be occasions when you'll discover a brilliant missed opportunity that completely changes how you might approach a particular record. But that should be a somewhat rare occurrence, and the band needs to be willing to take that journey with you. They also must trust your vision, and once the band signs off on it, they must agree that there's no turning back. In reality, there *is* turning back, at least until the CD is pressed and selling like hotcakes. But the argument for abandoning the initial plan must be so compelling that there can be little debate as to the merits of the new plan.

There's a very good reason for sticking to your vision. You may not always be perfectly clear-headed during the recording process. If you don't treat your original vision as set in stone, you run the risk of changing your mind at a time when your judgment is impaired by exhaustion. Making a record and an album requires discipline and focus. There are many ways to make any given record. Once you pick one, you need to stick with it until you're absolutely convinced that you completely fucked up, and even then it's probably too late, so what's the point? Dump the track.

Throughout the record-making process, you can and will be tempted to change course. Doubts will come into play, both from you and from your artist or band. While there's certainly nothing wrong with doubts, if you allow every minor struggle to force you into an overcorrection, you're never going to finish the record, and even if you do, your production will come off equally as unfocused as you. Go figure.

This rule also serves as a very nice protection. If your band is unfocused, it's easier to hold the line. That's the beauty of stating a rule like this. Embrace it.

Lastly, make sure you document all the changes you make to a song in rehearsals and preproduction. This is why I record these sessions, but I don't rely purely on the recording. I write down every change that we make, and there's a very good reason for that. Invariably, your band will forget the changes. You might too, so protect yourself against having to fix things twice. Document.

3. Only one person runs the session at a time (and that's usually me).

This may seem rather obvious, but inexplicably, some people have a difficult time understanding the concept. This isn't about who is capable of running a session. This is about how many people are running a session at any given time, and that can never be more than one. If you are stepping out of the room for a moment, then you should pass the metaphorical producing baton to someone else in the room—whomever you trust the most to take care of the job. If you have a close relationship with your recordist, then have him take over the producing session. If your brainchild is working out an idea with another band member, hand the responsibility to her. But someone must have clear control of the session at all times.

I go so far as to announce who is in charge at any given moment.

"Jimmy is producing this triangle part," I might say.

That may seem silly, but if you don't do that, you could come back to a clusterfuck of a session, with some poor soul in the room absolutely frustrated because he's getting four different sets of opposing instructions. I even go so far as to designate a producer for meals.

"Jimmy is producing dinner tonight!"

Even sillier, I know. But putting one person in charge of something as important as dinner means it's likely to get done. This is also a good strategy for dealing with someone who is getting in your way, although I do prefer to delegate the dinner detail to the band member with the best taste in food.

There's nothing wrong with allowing the brainchild to take the producing controls every now and then. This can give you a much deserved break from the room, and allow you to step back and evaluate a more complete idea. Such a strategy is especially effective during mundane tasks like waiting for the guitar player to work out a part he forgot. It's also a great technique to use for those ideas you're just not buying. Just be sure you're not handing off the producer controls as an act of petulance. That's not the purpose of such a maneuver. There can be many reasons why you're not buying a part. Handing over the controls allows a band member the opportunity to fully develop and present her idea. This is in keeping with rule #1, and you have a responsibility to give the band the opportunity to try out their wacky ideas too. Within reason, that is.

Once your ground rules have been set, you'll have gone a long way toward easing some of your artist's fears. At this point, you should have softened her up sufficiently that she'll allow you to mold her like clay. As long as you aren't too aggressive at the start, you'll be able to build up a nice cache of trust in your first preproduction session.

If you like, you can record the preproduction session. I wouldn't get any more fancy than just a single mic in the middle of the room. This recording is purely for reference, and is particularly useful if some time elapses between the prepro and the recording session. Personally, I like to schedule preproduction as close as possible to the actual recording session. That's not always possible, and there are reasonable arguments for giving the band some time after prepro, the most obvious being rehearsal. Unfortunately, they can also forget the changes, and I assure you, they almost always do. Regardless of whether or not you record the prepro session, you want to take copious notes of any and all changes. This way, when you go into your day of rehearsal before the session, you can reinstall any forgotten changes.

Tempo

Any given tempo, in conjunction with the internal rhythms of a track, will cause a certain physical reaction from the listener. Done well, a track can virtually force a receptive listener to move a certain way. Clearly we can't overcome free will, but any track that forces you to move will force others to move in a similar manner. I'm sure some of you are thinking that it would be nice to have a chart that maps tempo to physical movement, but the rhythmic characteristics of the production itself will have far too much influence over people's physical reactions. In other words, there's no simple formula for this.

Rhythm and tempo are just as responsible for how a track makes a listener feel as the melody and lyrics. They're all supposed to work together. If the lyrical content of a song is upbeat and happy, the rhythm is generally going to match that feeling. A brisk, skippy beat would match an upbeat message. A slow, brooding eighth-note pedal pattern would go with a somewhat darker message. The overall rhythmic feeling and tempo you settle on should take the content of the song into account. Most songwriters will do this innately. You should be conscious of it as the producer.

While rhythmic pattern and song content will often dictate the general tempo, performance considerations are paramount to the precise bpm (beats per minute) of the song. That's true whether or not you're using a click. One beat per minute can be the difference between an undeniable groove and an unsettled performance. It doesn't do you much good to record a song at 120 bpm if your band plays it best at 121 bpm. Further complicating matters are the needs of the vocalist. If your singer can't perform the song comfortably, then your tempo is unusable. Typically this isn't a problem unless you've radically altered the tempo, but you should always be conscious of the singer's needs. Believe it or not, the singer will not necessarily protest until it's too late to engage in anything other than damage control.

To put this as plainly as I can, never lock a tempo in stone without first checking with, and listening to, the singer. You must find an adequate compromise that allows the track to cause the physical reaction you seek while serving the performance needs of your vocalist and band. Typically, that isn't a difficult compromise to reach, but occasionally it can become an issue. When in doubt, the vocalist wins. If that means you have to change the groove to accommodate the singer's needs, so be it.

You'll probably want to have a click track available even if you don't intend to use a click on the record. At the very least you want to have a metronome, an app, or a stopwatch so that you can adequately determine the tempo any time the band hits the right groove. Any tempo you come up with in prepro is nothing more than a starting point, albeit a rather accurate one. Really, you should be within 4 bpm, and frankly, that's an enormous margin of error. That said, it's far easier to determine the best tempo when you have killer tones coming out of studio monitors than it is in a living-room-size rehearsal space listening through a subpar PA system.

Tempo can, at times, be a bit of a headfuck. How you're feeling, or what you were listening to previously, can affect how a certain tempo hits you. On more than one occasion I have been convinced that I recorded a track at the wrong tempo, only to realize the next day that everything was fine. Just as you need your team to trust you, you also need to trust yourself. Even if you did record a song at a less than ideal tempo, there are all sorts of ways to deal with it through technology and arrangement technique. You can speed up or slow down the overall feeling of a track through internal rhythms alone. In fact, if you're second-guessing a tempo decision, the arrangement could be the main culprit. So, don't beat yourself up unnecessarily. First, trust yourself, then figure out how to solve the problem—but only after you're certain it's a problem in the first place. Whew!

Key

Honestly, it should be pretty rare that you change the key of a song, and there's really only one usual reason to do it—for the sake of the singer. As I stated earlier, the singer's range is what she can sing on any given day, not what she can sing on her best day. If she's even remotely struggling to hit the top notes of a song, you're far better off bringing down the key to where she can consistently hit the top notes. Just be careful not to pull the song down beyond her lower register in the process.

Changing key is a drastic move, something that should be performed only when necessary. You also want to be sure you don't undermine your singer's confidence in the process.

Song Form

There's an old adage in the music business: "Don't bore us. Get to the chorus." You should live by this credo.

Modern songs can be broken down into sections, such as the verse and the chorus. Each section has a specific role in a song, but it's how these sections work together that promotes forward motion. The most effective songs push the listener forward through the song, providing several payoffs along the way. This is achieved through a number of musical and lyrical techniques. Many songwriters do this instinctively, which means they will falter at times. That's where we come in. Making song-form adjustments can be one of the simplest and most effective ways to improve a song. You could conceivably turn a good song into a great one with a single change to its form.

Most popular songs hit the chorus in under 40 seconds. You don't have to pull out your stopwatch—it's just a rule of thumb, but one that seems to preclude such things as two-minute intros. Of course, like anything in music, there are exceptions to every rule, and a long intro is not necessarily a bad one.

Take the Stones' "You Can't Always Get What You Want." The song has an exceptionally long intro, which functions as an operatic interpretation of the chorus. I remember the first time I heard the full production of the song (a decade after it was released), and even as a lad I was absolutely mesmerized by the operatic opener. What was even better was the lone guitar and the soulful vocal that followed. What a setup! That intro draws you in as a listener and pushes you to the verse. Imagine that production without the intro. It wouldn't have been nearly as effective.

I could easily insist you keep your intro short, and in most cases that would be good advice. I can tell you to get to the chorus in under 40 seconds, and that will would be a good suggestion in general. In reality, there's no set time to get to the chorus, and if you can keep the listener's attention for two minutes, that's a fine length for the intro. Given this, you have but one goal when it comes to song form. Keep pushing the listener forward.

The difficult part about evaluating a song, its form, and its overall effectiveness at pushing the listener forward is the subjective nature of the task. I would argue that it's not nearly as subjective as you might think. If you produce a song, and you play it for a focus group (and I'm not suggesting that you do), and 75 out of 100 people shut the song off before the intro is over, guess what? The intro is undoubtedly too long. So, it's actually not all that subjective; we just like to think of it that way.

Your only reasonable measure is to put yourself in the place of the listener—the first-time listener in particular. Now, I type that with a rather knowing smile, because I'm aware that it's impossible to listen to a production that you know like the back of your hand as if you're a first-time listener. Still, you must do the best you can to consider the production from that perspective, even if you can't experience it. If you were hearing this song for the first time, would it draw you in and hold your attention? If not, where does it lose your attention? When you make your evaluation in this manner, it becomes quite easy to cut an intro or an exceptionally long verse in half. Of course, the verse has lyrics, so cutting the verses can be tricky, since this can alter the perceived meaning of the song.

Lyrics are part of the song's forward motion. It's not just the music. Rap music can have long, drawn-out verses with very little musical deviation; that doesn't mean there's no forward motion. A great rap with a compelling lyric is plenty to push the listener forward. The whole operating principle of hip-hop music is the use of flow, rhyme, and content to carry the listener forward to the payoff. The more effectively the song is at pushing the listener forward, the less you should have to alter the song form.

This is a crucial point, one that we shouldn't merely gloss over. If the verse feels too long, and you're considering cutting it in half, it's a songwriting problem. There are many ways to fix a songwriting problem, and cutting out sections of the song is only one possible solution. It just happens to be the simplest, and often the easiest to implement. That doesn't change the fact that there's a songwriting issue preventing the necessary forward motion.

Inexperienced songwriters tend to write in block format. Melodies and lyrics are typically set in blocks of two or four spread across an even number of bars. Combine a blocked melody with mundane lyrics that seemingly go on ad nauseam, and you have absolutely no forward motion whatsoever. If you can't manage to push the listener through the first verse, it doesn't matter how great a payoff you have, the listener has already moved on to the next song. Besides, a disappointing verse that goes into an exceptionally strong chorus doesn't provide a payoff, but rather a relief.

As a producer, you need to evaluate and understand the short-comings of every song. Not all shortcomings will be fixed or nixed. There are such things as album tracks, and just because a song doesn't have hit potential doesn't mean it's not an enjoyable song. Not every song on an album needs to be some fast-paced, forward-pushing machine. If you like a song, then it's likely that others will like the song. However, on those occasions when you find yourself working on a song where a slightly better lyric or melody in the verse would make the difference between a possible hit and an album track, it's within your job description to attempt to fix it.

You may or may not want to get involved with the songwriting. That depends on your skills in that regard, and the willingness of your artist to involve you in that particular arena. At the very least, you can point out the problem you're having with the song, and challenge the songwriter to come up with something stronger. The best time to bring this up is in prepro.

Getting involved in songwriting can be touchy. You most certainly don't want to start with a song that you think is broken. But if your band really trusts you, they'll be far more open to songwriting suggestions. If you're a Songwriter Producer, they likely got involved with you because of your writing skills. If you're coming from any other position, you need to approach songwriting issues with a modicum of sensitivity and finesse.

While the best place to fix a song problem is at the song itself, we can certainly use arrangement and production to relieve some forward-motion issues. Ideally, the arrangement should enhance the overall forward motion of a track, but if the lyric and the melody are falling short, we can use other elements to pick up the slack. Harmonic and rhythmic variations can be effective for this, but countermelody and response are often the best ways to enhance musical forward motion. An uninspiring melody can be given a whole new life with a well-constructed countermelody. And the whole point of a response part is to momentarily take the musical focus off the melody and put it right back on the vocal, seamlessly perpetuating forward motion. So, song-form adjustments are but one option when it comes to solving forward-motion issues.

Preparing for Basic Tracks

How deep you get into working out specific parts in a preproduction session is up to you and depends on the lineup and skill as a band. The more parts you can nail down during prepro, the more parts you can keep during the tracking session. If you can record the band all at once, that's ideal, but you must have the space, the isolation (if necessary), and the quality of musicianship to pull it off. For instance, if you have a lineup composed of drums, bass, electric guitar, acoustic guitar, keys, percussion, background vocals, lead vocal, and horns, you're going to need an exceptionally large space, and likely some isolation. The less isolation you use, the more skilled your band and recordist must be.

Recording a sizable band all at once takes considerable practice, and you should get a veteran recordist to help you pull it off. Frankly, most young recordists aren't skilled enough, mostly because people don't tend to record like this any longer. The only reason I have this skill set is because it's how I learned to record in the first place.

It's doubtful that you'll be recording an 11-piece band in one sitting unless it's for a movie or a live performance. Still, the more you can capture in the basic tracks, the better, although it's not uncommon to walk out of a basic tracking session with nothing more than the drums and bass, and even then you're happy to have a bass track. Such is the nature of recording these days, but you don't have to lock yourself into that methodology if it doesn't work for you, or the record.

How far you microscope beyond the drums in preproduction has to do with what you're hoping to achieve during the basic tracks. If you're looking to keep the bass and drums, then you're going to need to suss out the bass parts during the preproduction session. This is not a reasonable course of action if your bass player is weak or in need of some serious rewrites. There's not much point in putting the entire band through a bass part over-haul when you can accomplish that in the studio. Granted, it costs more to work parts out in the studio, but it's a bit tough on a player to make him work out parts with the band acting like some sort of live looping mechanism. You're far better off honing this kind of part in the studio. Of course, if any player accidentally comes up with something brilliant in prepro, you should stop and figure out the part right then and there; otherwise, it will surely be lost. Frankly, if you're not recording at the time, the part will likely be lost anyway, as performers often don't always realize what they're playing at the time.

If you intend to use your own recording space for the tracking session, an argument can be made to perform preproduction in your studio. I mean, if it's not going to add to the budget, then why not? Of course, if you're charging top dollar for your own studio, then there's really no justification for doing prepro there. As far as I'm concerned, if you're producing an act, you shouldn't be charging top dollar for your studio anyway; in fact, you should even make it part of the deal. You're the producer. As such, you're in charge of making the best product possible. If your room assists you in that goal, then it should be part of the benefit of working with you. It should not be a line item in the budget.

Now, there are cases where it's totally legit to charge for your room as part of the package price, but not if your room is insufficient for the task at hand. In other words, if you have a small overdub room, one that is completely ineffective for the band's basic tracks, then you shouldn't be recording them there, as it will appear as if you're bilking your client. Notice I used the word "appear." Well, appearances matter, particularly when your band is pissed off at you because you're using digital reverb to make them sound like they're performing in a large concrete room.

If you own a multi-room shop, which is a veritable production house, then you're likely putting together a package price for all services rendered. Fair enough. But if you're a freelance producer with an overdub room, you have no business charging anything more than a nominal fee for it. Ultimately, your budget is going to determine how much can reasonably go into your pocket anyway. Why take risk bad feelings over what appears to be unscrupulous billing?

If you need a big room for rock drums, and your own room is sufficient for everything else, including bass, then really all you need to walk out of a basic tracking session with are the drums. The budget will dictate the way you work as much as production considerations, but as far as I'm concerned, how you wish to record trumps any budget considerations. In other words, if you think the production is better served by capturing the entire band in a large room, and that's going to require two more days of an expensive room, then you should probably cut costs elsewhere in the process to make that work—even if the cost-cutting comes out of your own front end. If you're in this business to make money on the front end, get out now. If your goal is to become a successful producer, then the back end is of far greater value and should be your main consideration.

Song Selection

As we discussed earlier, you will enter preproduction with a list of available songs in order of priority. Remember to keep your specific prioritizations to yourself. Everyone knows that people have favorites, and some songs are better than others. You're not trying to hide your overall preferences. You just don't want to put undue pressure on specific songs by foolishly labeling them "hit singles." A hit song is not defined by the high hopes of a few, but rather the undeniable reaction of the many. You also don't want the band thinking that the lower-priority songs aren't worth their full effort. Believe me, everyone will have their own priority list, and you need to figure out how your list relates to the band's without revealing your detailed priorities.

Think of yourself as a parent in this regard. Sometimes our children do things that require discipline, even if they somehow make us proud. When your son comes home with a hickey, as a dad you might be thinking, "Right on." But you don't pat him on the back for fear of sending him the wrong message. You tell him that the next time he comes home with a hickey he's in big trouble, and then you ignore the fact that he's taken a shine to turtlenecks. When the band's favorite song is also your favorite song, you don't tell them this. It will undercut what you're trying to accomplish with the album. You let them know it's a top contender, but no more so than some of the other top contenders. Don't commit to a favorite until the album is done—not out loud, anyway. Besides, some of those priorities will undoubtedly change.

You can use your preproduction session to evaluate the songs lacking demos. I recommend you avoid getting involved in songs that haven't been worked out beyond a basic sketch. Of course, if you find a song in the embryonic stages that is undeniably compelling, then you always have the option of preparing it for recording. Tracking a fresh song can increase the excitement level of a session considerably, partly because there are no preconceptions, given the lack of a demo. There's nothing quite like recording a song for the first time, and if the song is great, then why not?

Between recording new songs and making improvements to old ones, it's highly likely that your priority list will change throughout the course of preproduction. This is especially true if the band has a cache of relatively strong songs that haven't reached the demo stage. Your priority list will likely change throughout the recording process too, although it's unlikely that a song will go from a high priority to a low one. As far as I'm concerned, there's not much difference between the top five songs. They're all in the top five, and number one is somewhat irrelevant when they're all supposed to make the album.

Since you're prioritizing, you should have a goal in mind where final track counts are concerned. Personally, I like 10-song albums. It's far better to release 10 killer songs and leave the fans wanting more than to include 5 weak and uninspiring songs. Given the current online buying habits of consumers, there's really no point in keeping any of the fat. In fact, an argument can be made that an album laden with subpar tracks gives the consumer an incentive to purchase your band's songs individually. In other words, the consumer is far more likely to spring for the entire album if there is a high percentage of quality tracks. Given this, you want to maximize the overall quality of your album based on the budget. If the band only has enough money to record five songs properly, you should convince them to put out an EP, as that would serve them better in both the short and the long run.

As you record, be sure to keep your budget in mind. When you find yourself behind and unable to catch up, then you must be prepared to abandon songs. You most certainly don't want to blow your budget on song number 15 before you nail the top 10 contenders. That may seem like basic math, but bands can be exceptionally unfocused and free-spirited in this regard. As they should be. This is a major reason why the band needs a producer in the first place. They need someone who can keep the project on course and prevent wild shifts in the plan. Bands in the studio can be like mobs, and mobs can be unpredictable in their course. This is why you're the leader: to keep that from happening. So, don't become part of the mob. Stick to the plan.

I've worked with producers who are highly unfocused, to the point of being a one-man mob. When this happens it forces someone else on the team to step up and be the voice of reason. Sometimes that voice will come from the band, sometimes from the recording team. I suppose if the producer is making creative improvements to the project and the team is somehow able to prevent mayhem, then all is good. The clusterfuck happens when the unfocused producer ends up with the free-spirited band. Not only will the album most assuredly go over budget, it will be a complete disaster if it ever gets finished at all.

Someone needs to keep to the plan, and an inherent inability to focus does not mean that you're somehow lacking in creativity. It *only* means you lack basic organizational skills and focus. This is not a virtue, especially in a producer. There is nothing creative about lacking discipline. Creativity is most effective within the confines of a definitive and proven structure. That's a basic law of art, if not life in general.

The Contract

Some of you are probably wondering why I'd wait this long to even think about a contract. Surely, if you feel strongly about it, you can work out a contract before you go into preproduction. You can even work out a contract before your first rehearsal. Hell, you could command a contract before you even listen to demos, if you think you're in high enough demand. Unfortunately, that's not reasonable, nor is it how things work in this business for anyone other than perhaps the most super of superproducers (and not even for them).

Let's think about this logically for a moment. You're going to demand and pay to have contracts drawn up for a project you're not fully convinced you should take? And you're going to insist that a band or artist sign this contract, with a veritable stranger?

A contract is an agreement, and an agreement can't be made until all parties understand the expectations. How could you possibly enter into an agreement if you don't even know what you're getting yourself into? What if you have the band sign the contract only to realize they're unproduceable?

There's no point in drawing up a contract until all the parties are ready. If you're a veteran producer, you most certainly want to keep your options open. If you're a young producer, you want to increase your perceived value before you negotiate a price. Besides, as I've already explained, the budget is the budget, and your fees are going to be based on that budget, whether you're a veteran or otherwise. Sure, if you're a superproducer in high demand, you can name your price and turn down any record that can't meet it. But what happens when you find a band that you're in love with, that you think is going to make some noise, and with a budget that can only pay you half of your normal advance fees? Are you going to turn it down?

The answer is a definitive no! Producer rates are almost always negotiable. Again, the advance only protects you against failure. The real money is made on the back end, not the front. The front end is your guaranteed payday, regardless of how successful the album is. Your back end is where you make your money, and if you think a group is going to sell millions of records worldwide, you're going to turn down the record because the advance is lower than your usual fee?

That said, I totally buy into standing firm with an established act. That's different, because there are sales expectations at that point. We can make accurate sales projections for a band with a large fan base. It's only reasonable that you demand an advance that's in line with those projections, because otherwise the record company is merely attempting to defer payment for what amounts to over a year. But on an untried act? If you honestly believe you can make an album that will be an enormous sales and radio success, and you adore the music, you'd be crazy to turn it down based on a low advance.

All that said, the only reliable indicator you have of a label's commitment to the project is their willingness to put up money. If you feel that you're in such a strong position for an album that they will pay your full advance, then by all means demand it. Just be prepared to lose the gig if they don't meet your number, and understand that a great many records have been shelved because they cost too much to make. I realize that sounds counterintuitive, but the label must release the albums it believes will sell best.

How Producers Are Paid

On any given project, the producer's advance is part of the overall budget. It is an advance on future royalties, so if you get paid a large sum of money in advance, then you will have to recoup that before you get paid any royalties. As we've already established, if you take a small advance and recoup early, you'll make the same amount of money as taking a large advance and recouping later. It's just that you'll get paid later, sometimes up to a year or more later, based on major label release and accounting timelines.

As the engineer on a project, you're "work for hire" and you don't collect royalties; therefore, your payments are not considered advances. Sometimes you can get points as the mixer, but unless you're a hot commodity, squeezing out an extra point for mixing can prove difficult. Therefore, it is worthwhile to pay yourself less in producer's advances and more in engineering fees. This is a negotiating point, so don't be surprised if the other side balks at this.

Let's say you've worked very hard to make a name for yourself, and you get the opportunity to record a successful artist. From your perspective, you want to base your advance on the sales of the last record. The band management will do all they can to reduce that advance, and will argue that there are no guarantees of similar success. I find this line of argument amusing, because if you're hiring me to produce the album, then you're hiring me because you think I can make it successful. Who the hell hires a producer for a successful artist purely to save money? No one does, and you shouldn't be bashful in pointing this out.

If the artist sold 500,000 copies of her last album, then you should work out your advance based on those numbers. The standard fare for a producer in the United States is 3 points on the manufacturer's suggested retail list price (MSRLP). So if the list price of the CD is $17, that means you would get paid 3 percent of that $17 for every album sold, regardless of what the store price of the CD is. Based on those numbers, that comes to about $0.50 per album. Of course, labels don't like paying money, so they have all sorts of clauses in artist contracts that tend to reduce that number substantially, and you're more likely to get paid somewhere in the neighborhood of half that. That means an album that sells 500,000 units amounts to anywhere from $125,000 and $250,000, depending on the terms of your contract.

The typical producer of a known artist can collect anywhere from $3,000 to $5,000 per track in advance money. The hotter a commodity you are as a producer, the more you can charge for your advance. If the expectation is for the second album to do as well as the first, then there isn't much danger in charging $50,000 to record the album. You would recoup at about 166,000 albums sold, but there are ways to reduce the number of albums needed to recoup by charging for other services.

If you're also the engineer and the mixer on the album, then you can charge for those services, and reduce your advance while getting paid the same amount. Given the same $50,000 fee in the example above, if you charge $10,000 for engineering services, and $15,000 for mixing services, you will only have to recoup $25,000 in advance money. Those engineering fees aren't advances; they're part of the recording costs that must be recouped by the band. It doesn't matter if you normally charge $25,000 to mix an album. Those are arbitrary numbers that are negotiated purely for recoupment purposes. You make more money if you have to recoup less in advances. Let me explain.

The band pays you out of their points. If they have 16 points in their deal, then they are paying you with 3 of their points, and the label is instructed through a letter of direction to pay both you and the artist directly. This way you don't have to chase the artist for your money. Your producer's advance is recouped by you. The artist must recoup the rest of the budget, including engineering fees. This means you'll get paid $25,000 in producer's fees and $25,000 in engineering fees, and once the band sells 166,000 units, you'll be due another $25,000 in royalties. So instead of having earned $50,000 at the point of recoupment, you'll have earned $75,000.

I would go into considerably more detail if this wasn't currently an archaic model. The fact is that records don't sell like they used to, and many artist deals are now structured so that the label has a piece of everything that generates money for the artist, including their live shows. This is called a 360 deal. To date, producers weren't paid for revenues earned outside of record sales, but the way deals are being structured now, record sales aren't a reasonable place for producers to take their cut. It seems as though the industry has all but given up on making money on the records themselves, and tends to treat them as a loss leader for the other revenue centers. This means an advance on record sales is basically a farce. There are no record sales.

Not like there used to be. So, there's really only one place where a producer can profit-share now, and that's publishing monies.

The big money in record-making is publishing. The songwriters make the lion's share of the money in this business. It's not uncommon for the writing member of a successful band to be a multimillionaire while the others struggle to make their house payments. Therefore, the argument against paying a producer out of publishing royalties is that it will often unfairly cost one member of the band more than the others. Of course, if the song is such a hit that it gets massive radio play, is re-recorded several times by other high-profile artists, or ends up in a Microsoft commercial down the line, your role in making that a hit in the first place should be rewarded from this particular revenue stream.

Producing is big business, but not if the producer doesn't get paid while everyone else does. If that trend continues, it won't be long before the pool of good producers shrinks to nothing. It's not unreasonable for a producer to take 10 percent of the publishing, and I'm not the only one thinking along these lines. It may take years before there are any standards in this regard, which makes this kind of structure a heavy lift for young producers lacking juice. It also makes offering advice on how to structure a contract difficult at best.

The entire game has changed in recent years. Until it all shakes out, you might find yourself agreeing to points on sales. You probably won't make much money on your first successful album, but at least it will put you in a position to demand a back end that's worth a damn. As the producer, you are an important component of a successful album, and as such you should be rewarded through profit-sharing. A band can make millions on touring, merch, and publishing revenues while bringing in pennies on the dollar for the recording itself. There are some acts that still sell records, but they are currently few and far between, and the likelihood of a decades-long career selling records is low. This means catalog album sales for the artist are likely to be nonexistent.

Just to be clear, when I say to you that "there are no record sales," that's not a literal statement. It's a relative one, based on the fact that there is not enough of a major label industry to support the number of producers. Sales have been on the decline for many years, and that trend is an indication that the business is changing. We must change with the business.

For a great many years, radio was the loss leader for record sales as far as the label was concerned. Only the publisher and the songwriter made (and make) direct money from radio spins. The label made money on the record sales that were generated by the radio. With declining record sales, the labels have dipped into other revenue streams. Now with streaming sites like Pandora and Spotify, the user can choose what to listen to without even owning the music. The likelihood of a consumer buying a track they can stream any time they like is dismally low.

Further complicating matters, the only sales of any significance currently come in the form of singles. This makes amassing back end money of any real value difficult, if not impossible. It's unreasonable for a producer to get paid from a revenue stream that for all intents and purposes no longer exists. I would argue that streaming is the new sales; therefore, the producer should get a piece of the publishing. No matter what your position as producer, this should be your basic argument to the band when you're negotiating a straight producer's deal.

The Production Contract

There will be times when you will have a band with no deal, no money, and no prospects. On the surface, that doesn't sound particularly appealing, but if you find them compelling and you have a clear vision, then it could make sense to fund their record. Much of that funding can be accomplished through sweat equity. Given that you normally charge for your production services anyway, that's still technically funding. Typically, the goal is to make the album and seek a record deal. This is an exceptionally difficult road to take, one that will require many hours of perseverance upon completing the record, but if you really believe in a project, it can be a worthwhile venture on your part.

With risk should come reward, and if you're going to fund an album, then you need an agreement with the band that spells out the terms of this relationship. This kind of agreement is called a Production Contract, and it's made between you, as a production company, and the band as an entity. Typically, a production contract makes you a 50-50 partner with the band for multiple albums, and can include a significant percentage of publishing as part of the deal.

As a production company, an eventual record deal is made with you, and you act as a liaison between the record company and the band. If the label prefers to sign the artist directly, you'll probably be leveraged to let her go (although you don't have to), but there should be contingencies for this in your contract through overrides.

Of all producer contracts, the production contract is the most involved, and requires an attorney. Frankly, given the current state of the music business, this may not be your best option. The main reason to do a production company contract is because it gives you a large stake in multiple albums for minimal risk if you're well connected or if you have an act that's so undeniable it's a slam dunk. I'm not sure that such a thing exists anymore, at least not in its embryonic stages. A band that is successful enough to be its own business does not need to sign a production company contract, and frankly, it has always been the choice of last resort for a band, given how much they give up. But hey, 100 percent of nothing is still nothing, and that was always the argument from the production company's perspective.

I've done production company contracts, and as a freelancer without a room, I lost large sums of money in the process. As a result, I'm not too keen on production company deals, and would rather help a band find some funding that will pay me for my services than take that kind of risk again. If you want to shop the band, you can always make up a separate agreement for those services in the form of points or publishing, but unless you're well connected, you will likely need to use a portion of your points and publishing to incentivize an attorney or manager to shop the act.

As in flux as the music business is today, a band is in a better position than ever before to operate as a self-sufficient business. With record sales a distant memory, and distribution channels rendered valueless by the Internet, a record deal is not necessarily a measure of success. This makes the argument for acquiring publishing points on your back end even more compelling. A band without a label can sell 100,000 albums and bring in $1,000,000 in revenue, of which you would get about $30,000 in points after "breakage" and all the other bullshit their lawyer puts in the contract, since they are technically the "label." Going after that $30K is prohibitive other than in small claims court, particularly after you subtract your advance from that sum. But publishing monies are paid directly to the parties with a stake in them, which means you don't even have to go after your money. If the same band that sold 100,000 units has a song that is being streamed or spun regularly, or was licensed for a national commercial, or was re-recorded by a major artist, in the long run you could potentially get a nice payday for your efforts without the artist ever having to write you a check.

Preparing the Budget

Now that you've picked out your songs, gone through preproduction and rehearsals with the band, and come to a contractual agreement with them, it's time to put together the budget. I realize we discussed budget earlier in the book, but now it's time to actually make an imaginary budget, one that has every line item I can think of thrown in. That's going to make this a rather expensive album to make on an independent level, particularly by today's standards. Don't get bogged down by the numbers. This list is designed to give you an idea of the kind of line items you might find on a budget. Consider this a list of possible inclusions:

Studios

Rehearsal Room	$50 per day	3 days	$150
Tracking Room	$1,000 per day	5 days	$5,000
Overdub Room	$400 per day	20 days	$8,000
Mix Room	$1,000 per day	5 days	$5,000
			$18,150

Side Musicians

Union Fiddle	$640 per session	1 session	$640
Union Piano	$360 per session	1 session	$360
Church Choir	$200 donation	Flat fee	$200
Union Washboard	$360 per session	1 session	$360
Didgeridoo	$300 per session	5 sessions	$1,500
			$3,060

Rentals

U-Haul/Cartage			$300
Hammond B3	$100 per day	1 day	$100
Marshall Cab	$50 per day	3 days	$150
Distressor	$50 per day	5 days	$250
Black Beauty Snare	$50 per day	5 days	$250
			$1,050

Tape and Drives

ATR ½" Tape	$90 per reel	10 reels	$900
ATR 2" Tape	$300 per reel	5 reels	$1,500
500 GB Hard Drive	$100 per drive	2 drives	$200
CDs	$20 per 100 pack	1 pack	$20
			$2,620

Miscellaneous

Drum Heads	Ambassador White	$200
Drum Sticks		$40
Guitar Strings		$100
Bass Strings	Flat Wound	$40
Bass Strings	Round Wound	$40
Drum Tech		$200
Guitar Tech		$200
		$820

Travel Costs

Producer Airfare			$350
Producer Hotel	$100 per night	25 nights	$2,500
Didgeridoo Player Airfare			$2,500

Didgeridoo Player Hotel	$100 per night	2 nights	$200
			$5,550

Per Diems

Recordist	$30 per day	25 days	$750
Didgeridoo Player	$30 per day	3 days	$90
			$840

Sustenance

Food	$75 per day	25 days	$1,875
Alcohol	$25 per day	25 days	$625
			$2,500

Producer and Engineer Fees

Producer's Fee	$2,000 per track	12 tracks	$24,000
Engineering Fees	$500 per day	25 days	$12,500
Mixer's Fees	$1,000 per track	12 tracks	$12,000
			$48,500
		TOTAL:	$83,090

I've included everything I can think of in this budget, and we're just over $83,000. Depending on who this budget is for, you might need to massage the numbers a bit. If it's for a major label, and you have a $100,000 budget (good for you!), then you've still got nearly $17K to play with. This is good, because you can almost always expect to go 15 percent over budget. So, now you want to pad the budget with that remaining $17K so that you hit the $100,000 mark. This budget is actually going to go to the label for approval, and you don't want to screw yourself out of that extra $17K in resources. Believe me, you'll use every penny of it, so make sure it's in the budget from the beginning.

Adding money to a budget is easy. Just add more days of recording time, which adds more days of personnel costs, travel costs, and sustenance. Just work the numbers until you've hit the target cost of the album. You won't be held accountable for under-shooting any given line item. All the label cares about is that you don't go over budget, and they won't be comparing your budget to the bills they pay unless there's a problem. Besides, I've never had to add money to a budget. I wish! No, the far more likely scenario is you're going to have to cut costs.

Suppose you only have a $50K budget to make the album. That would put you about $30K over budget at the moment. Whoops! You have some serious cutting to do. Budget slashing is the ultimate exercise in compromise. What makes it so difficult is that some expenses can't be removed. Getting rid of your sustenance line item might seem like a no-brainer. It would instantly save you $2,500 on your budget. Unfortunately, your band and personnel still need to eat, so all you're doing is shifting that item from the budget to the pockets of everyone on the session. Besides, unless you're working on an album for an already successful band, if you don't put the food in the budget, you're often going to end up buying food for everyone anyway, and then you'll start eating badly, because the record is costing you a fortune. Take it from me: sustenance should be the last line item you touch.

There's not much we can do about travel costs. My ticket is only $350, so it's not like I'm flying first class here. But the didgeridoo player? He lives in Australia, and it's a $2,500 ticket to get him out here, $200 to put him up in a hotel, $1,500 in session fees, and $90 in per diems. That's $4,290 for a didgeridoo player on what should be a $50K budget. Ten percent of the budget for a sideman is pretty outrageous. Besides, if there's going to be didgeridoo on nearly half the album, why doesn't the band have its own didgeridoo player?

Regardless, either we need to get someone a bit more local (maybe she can join the band!), or we need to have our authentic Australian player record his parts in Oz unattended. If the didgeridoo player is someone I've worked with before, and I feel comfortable sending tracks and giving direction remotely, then that's a reasonable option. If that's not going to work (and if you've ever met a didgeridoo player, you know it won't), then we could always attempt to set up a remote session with an Australian studio, but keep in mind that that will cost us some of our recovered $2,790. So, let's hire someone local and put him in the band.

Clearly, it was my desire to record this album analog. But that's just not a reasonable option given our budget constraints, so let's use just one reel of 2" tape and transfer our takes into the DAW before reusing it again. That will save us $1,200. Let's do the same with the ½" tape. That will save us another $810.

So far we've cut $2,790 in travel costs and $2,010 in tape costs. That brings us down to just over $78,000. We're still $28K over budget.

There aren't many more places to cut. We could kill some of the miscellaneous line items, but that merely shifts the string and head costs to the individuals in the band. We could hire a mixer who doesn't require a $1,000 per day room on top of a $1,000 per track fee—someone willing to give us a package deal for the whole project. We could get rid of the engineer, and rely on the studio assistant to help with that function. That's not ideal, but you've done enough albums now to do it in a pinch. You could also mix it yourself, but unless you're a bona fide mixer, don't.

Clearly, the more jobs you can perform, the easier it'll be to bring this budget down to $50K. If this were my budget, I could knock off about $25K in engineering and mixing fees and $5K for the mix room, which would put me right under $50K. If you have your own overdub room, you can immediately cut that $8K for the overdub room. I realize you'd prefer to charge for your room, but if you're going to make a small budget work, you can't reasonably put 65 percent of it in your own pocket, no matter how you couch it.

Unfortunately, there will come a point where there's just no more fat to cut from the budget without cutting your own producer's fee, and that just might be what's required here. Let's cut where we can, assuming that you're not an engineer and you don't own your own room, so those line items must remain.

First things first: we're going to hire a mixer who can work within our budget, and an analog mix room is not going to work. That cuts $5,000 right there. We'll deal with the mixer's line item when we get to it.

Studios

Rehearsal Room	$50 per day	3 days	$150
Tracking Room	$1,000 per day	5 days	$5,000
Overdub Room	$400 per day	20 days	$8,000
~~Mix Room~~	~~$1,000 per day~~	~~5 days~~	~~$5,000~~
			$13,150

Everyone please welcome our newest band member! Mr. Didgeridoo himself!

Side Musicians

Union Fiddle	$640 per session	1 session	$640
Union Piano	$360 per session	1 session	$360
Church Choir	$200 donation	Flat fee	$200

Union Washboard	$360 per session	1 session	$360
~~Didgeridoo~~	~~$300 per session~~	~~5 sessions~~	~~$1,500~~
			$1,560

I've decided we'll ask the drummer to borrow some snare drums from his buddies, and we'll get the guitar player to borrow the Marshall cab. Our engineer is just going to have to live without the Distressor, and we can borrow a van from the keyboard player's uncle.

Rentals

~~U-Haul/Cartage~~			~~$300~~
Hammond B3	$100 per day	1 day	$100
~~Marshall Cab~~	~~$50 per day~~	~~3 days~~	~~$150~~
~~Distressor~~	~~$50 per day~~	~~5 days~~	~~$250~~
~~Black Beauty Snare~~	~~$50 per day~~	~~5 days~~	~~$250~~
			$100

We'll record takes onto tape, and then transfer them to the DAW. Same with the mixes.

Tape and Drives

~~ATR ½" Tape~~	~~$90 per reel~~	~~10 reels~~	~~$900~~
~~ATR 2" Tape~~	~~$300 per reel~~	~~5 reel~~	~~$1,500~~
ATR ½" Tape	$90 per reel	1 reel	$90
ATR 2" Tape	$300 per reel	1 reel	$300
500 GB Hard Drive	$100 per drive	2 drives	$200
CDs	$20 per 100 pack	1 pack	$20
			$610

I'd rather not get rid of the techs, as we could easily save $400 in studio time with well-tuned drums and intonated guitars. Don't be penny wise and pound foolish.

Miscellaneous

Drum Heads	Ambassador White	$200
Drum Sticks		$40
Guitar Strings		$100
Bass Strings	Flat Wound	$40
Bass Strings	Round Wound	$40
Drum Tech		$200
Guitar Tech		$200
		$820

I'd rather stay in a less expensive hotel if that's what's required. Hell, I'll sleep in someone's guest room if that's what needs to happen to make the album.

Travel Costs

Producer Airfare			$350
~~Producer Hotel~~	~~$100 per night~~	~~25 nights~~	~~$2,500~~
Producer Hotel	$75 per night	25 nights	$1,875
~~Didgeridoo Player Airfare~~			~~$2,500~~
~~Didgeridoo Player Hotel~~	~~$100 per night~~	~~2 nights~~	~~$200~~
			$2,225

We no longer need the per diems for the didgeridoo player. And we're now going to use a local recordist, so there will be no need for any per diems on this project.

~~Per Diems~~

~~Recordist~~	~~$30 per day~~	~~25 days~~	~~$750~~
~~Didgeridoo Player~~	~~$30 per day~~	~~3 days~~	~~$90~~
			$0

Much to my chagrin, we've reduced the sustenance per diem, which means that by like day 20 we'll be out of that money, and somehow I'll find myself paying for three out of every four meals. Oh well.

Sustenance

~~Food~~	~~$75 per day~~	~~25 days~~	~~$1,875~~
~~Alcohol~~	~~$25 per day~~	~~25 days~~	~~$625~~
Food	$50 per day	25 days	$1,250
Alcohol	$20 per day	25 days	$500
			$1,750

I've reduced my rate to a project rate of $20K. I figure I can get the engineer and the mixer to help me out, given my budget constraints and because I'm a regular client.

Producer and Engineer Fees

~~Producer's Fee~~	~~$2,000 per track~~	~~12 tracks~~	~~$24,000~~
Producer's Fee	Project Rate		$20,000
~~Engineering Fees~~	~~$500 per day~~	~~25 days~~	~~$12,500~~
Engineering Fees	Project Rate		$10,000
~~Mixer's Fees~~	~~$1,000 per track~~	~~12 tracks~~	~~$12,000~~
Mixer's Fees	Project Rate		$10,000
			$40,000
		TOTAL:	$60,215

Right. So the budget is $50K for this record, and we've just cut across the board only to find ourselves still more than $10K over budget.

Even if we cut out Sustenance and Miscellaneous completely, we're still almost $7,000 over, and we've already cut my fee by $4K.

Therefore, either I'm going to have to ask my engineers and studios to take less, I'm going to have to take less, or a combination of the three. At some point though, the only remaining line item available for adjustment is going to be your producer's fee. When that happens, you have a limited number of viable options.

Record the album yourself using the studio assistant.

Be forewarned: if you don't have skills as a recordist, you'll very likely reduce the overall quality of the product. If you can hire a young studio assistant whom you're familiar with, and who has the skill set necessary to accomplish your goals, that's reasonable. If not, this is a very risky decision, particularly if you end up with a uselessly green assistant.

Mix the album yourself.

I put this as an option purely to dissuade you from it. Unless you have had some success as a mixer, don't do it.

Reduce the amount of time scheduled to make the album, and/or completely change the recording plan.

This is not an ideal solution, and you will very likely go over budget if you try it. A budget isn't an exercise in wishful thinking. It's a projection that should be as accurate as possible. You have budgeted your studio time based on information. Unless that information has changed somehow, hoping you can record the album faster is likely a pipe dream. The only way you could really reduce your studio time is by changing the overall vision from a relatively polished album to a rather raw one. Your vision should be based on the music and the band, not on the money needed. Otherwise, you're just going to make the wrong album for too much money, no matter what the budget is.

Pass.

Come on. You're going to pass at this point? You love the music, and you knew the budget going in. Unless the available budget was slashed for some reason, you should be pretty much committed at this point.

Work for a reduced advance on the strength that you'll make it up later on the back end.

This is probably the most likely scenario. However, if you find yourself having to cut your rate in half like this, you might consider charging it as something other than an advance. If you're going to give up that much, then the artist or band should be willing to recoup your fees. If it's an advance, you have to recoup, as it's an advance on your future earnings. If it's a fee, the band has to recoup, and in theory you'll make royalties from dollar one (based on the archaic business model).

Attempt to expand the budget.

Depending on the real numbers (rather than these hypothetical ones), if I find that I'm really taking a drastic hit on my advance due to expenses out of my control (such as if the band insisted on working in a $1,500-per-day room for the duration of the project), then I will most definitely attempt to expand the budget. This puts the onus on the band to reconsider their demands. Your success at expanding the budget depends partly on your ability to sell the concept. Really, what's another $9K if it's going to be the difference between greatness and mediocrity?

If you were a slightly less scrupulous person, you could purposely underestimate the time required to make the album in order to hit your mark on paper, knowing you'll go over in reality. Going over budget happens on occasion. Setting aside the moral issues, technically if you go over budget, the money comes out of your advance monies. In other words, you pay for it. In my experience, that's an uncommon event, but it can and will happen, especially if it's your fault you went over budget. Blatantly underbudgeting the time needed to record will likely be perceived as just that— your fault.

Of course, collecting a $20K advance on a $50K budget might be a bit steep. There's no rule of thumb regarding what percentage of any given budget should go to the producer—not that I can figure. But in this example, that's 40 percent of the budget going into my pocket, and I'm not performing any of the engineering functions.

I can't tell you how much you should charge, or how much of the budget you're worth. Only you and the market can make those determinations. But if you make a budget that is so heavily weighted toward your own enrichment, in combination with an impossibly short recording schedule, you will look like a pig. You're better off passing.

All of your decisions, budgetary and otherwise, must be made on the basis of creating the best product you possibly can, within reason. When you find yourself with a budget that makes your vision impossible, then you must either expand it, pass on it, or work on a speculative basis. But as much as this is a business, it's one in which the final results are actually more important than how much you made in the process. If you make great albums, the payoff will come. If you make mediocre albums, you will always be nothing more than a second-rate work-for-hire. So in terms of the big picture, you're better off choosing wisely and making less in the hopes of putting yourself in a position of demand.

The records you make create the brand. If you want your brand to say "quality," then don't do anything to undermine that goal.

Renting Studios

So, now that we have a $60K budget in place (I have successfully pleaded our case for an extra $10K or so), it's time to book some rooms. According to our hypothetical budget, we have $1,000 per day for a tracking room. I can certainly find an adequate room for less than that.

If there are only a few proper tracking rooms in your area, booking rooms can be a relatively simple process. In a place like Los Angeles, it can be a major undertaking, given the sheer volume of studios around. If there are particular rooms that I'm interested in, I might be inclined to call them myself. But usually, I'd much rather have someone else perform that particular legwork for me. In fact, that can be quite advantageous.

There is a company called Studio Referral Service here in Los Angeles. All you have to do is provide them with a list of your requirements, and a maximum price. Like magic, Ellis will provide you with a list of available rooms that meet your needs in the time frame needed. Studio Referral is like having a production assistant at your disposal. Not only is this free for you and your clients, but he can perform this service for you well beyond the confines of Los Angeles. If you like calling multiple studios to find an adequate place that's willing to accept your price, then you should most definitely ignore my advice on this.

When it comes to selecting a room, one of the more important considerations is acoustic space—mainly the size and nature of the main room and the number of isolation spaces available. After that, I evaluate equipment—musical instruments in particular. There are certain consoles that I prefer as a recordist, and that also comes into play. If you're hiring a recordist, then you should involve her in that process. In fact, you should probably work directly with her to find the right room for your goals. Otherwise, you might discover that you've forgotten something rather important. Since so many decisions are engineering ones, you might even be better off allowing your engineer to choose a few rooms and provide you with some options. If your recordist has relationships with these studios, you might want to have her negotiate the rate for you as well.

When renting a room, you want to be sure that you fully understand the terms. Will there be charges for going over 12 hours, and if so, how much? Is everything on the website and/or the equipment list available, in working order, and included as part of the price? Do the musical instruments come with the room as part of the deal? What amenities come with the room? Some studios put out food every day. Others provide a runner for the entire day, or part of the day. The formula is rather simple: the more you pay for the room, the more amenities you get as part of the deal.

Your overdub room doesn't need to have nearly as much space as your tracking room. For the most part you'll be recording one part at a time during overdubs, although acoustics still matter. You want to avoid recording in an overdub room that's so small and poorly treated that it makes everything you record sound boxy. If this describes your own overdub room, you might want to fix that sooner rather than later. Horn sections and percussion are best recorded in a slightly larger acoustic space than your average overdub room, and this should not be forgotten. You might choose a multi-room complex, and see if you can slide into a bigger room for a few hours when you need more space.

Aside from the recording room itself, the next most important consideration is the control room. If you end up in a control room where the monitoring is skewed, nothing you do will translate in the real world. If there are frequencies in the control room that you can't hear, you could have quite the surprise when you get the tracks out of the room. This is yet another argument for getting involved with a professional veteran engineer early on in your career.

How soon after your tracking session you schedule your overdub sessions is up to you. Personally, I don't like to take breaks between sessions. I want to record an album top to bottom as quickly as possible, and I recommend this method. For starters, you don't want to be bogged down for months on what amounts to 21 days of recording, mostly because it puts you out of commission for any other records that might come up. Secondly, if you continually allow your artists time to go home and listen endlessly to the tracks, or worse yet, to fuck with them in their own DAWs at home, that three months will turn into a year.

I find that many young producers and engineers are willing to take a year to make an album. Many even prefer it. That's all well and good when you don't have a mortgage, a family, or responsibilities. It's all but impossible if you actually wish to maintain a career.

If you want to take a few days between tracking and overdubs so you can get some editing done, that makes sense. But unless you have a logistical reason for delaying the overdubs, you should probably schedule them soon, if not immediately, after tracking. Even if you plan on taking some time off between sessions, you should at least schedule overdubs so your personnel can plan. When you're the producer, you're responsible for everyone on the project, so you can't just think about yourself. If you do, you will never have a loyal team.

Preparing and Organizing Your Session

As you can see, there is an immense amount of organization required to prep for a session, and that work doesn't stop once recording begins. In fact, it gets considerably more difficult, given that you're working 12 hours a day on the recording. That leaves only a few hours each day to take care of business, lest we forget unwinding and sleep. The better organized you are, the less you'll have to deal with your own fuck-ups in the studio. There are a few things you can do to help with the organizational aspects of producing.

First, you want to make sure to keep a document on your computer with your thoughts throughout the process. It should have your prioritized list of songs, what you think about the songs, a documented list of changes you made to the arrangements in preproduction, the tentative tempos, the keys, their priority, and an overall description of your vision (which can be as simple as one word, as long as you understand what it means).

Before you go into a tracking session, you want to have a basic schedule, particularly when it comes to sidemen. Obviously, if all of your players are for hire, you need to nail down their schedules before you book a studio. This can be more difficult than you might think, particularly if they're really good, as you must often deal with touring schedules and competing sessions.

There's not a whole lot of point in hard-scheduling your sidemen for the overdub process, certainly not before you've begun tracking. For starters, your basic plan can change significantly. You could end up dropping songs, which in turn could conceivably change your sideman requirements. You will also often have plenty of work to do during your overdub sessions, so you can schedule your sidemen a bit more loosely, although I prefer to book them for the first part of the day.

When you're dealing with the band, and they're just as tired as you are, it's easy to fritter away the first few hours. But when a guest comes, all of a sudden everyone is on their best behavior where productivity is concerned. Even if a guest does little to light a fire under your band's ass, at least you can keep the session moving by bringing in someone fresh.

The best argument for scheduling a sideman for hour one as opposed to hour six is timing. In general, you don't want to abandon a creative task, as that is an exceptionally inefficient way to work. Can you imagine starting a vocal an hour before your guest is due to arrive? What are you going to do? Stop? Or are you going to make your guest sit there for two hours waiting for you to finish something you shouldn't have started in the first place? Not only would that be unfair, but in the case of a union musician, it would be a significant expense. If you schedule someone for a session, don't be so unprofessional as to be unprepared to work when they arrive.

As much as it's usually best to schedule a sideman for the beginning of your day, there are certain performers who do better in the evening. Many singers prefer that time period, so unless your sessions start at 7 p.m., scheduling of the night-owl performer for the beginning of your session will be undesirable, as any efficiency you hoped to gain will be lost in the process.

Then, of course, you will come across a sideman who has no earthly shot at ever making a session before 11 p.m., and will need an hour before commencing to roll an immense blunt full of the most potent marijuana one can find. The Blunt Sideman is often highly efficient once you've got him in front of the microphone. The problem is getting him there in the first place. The best procedure is to schedule your Blunt Sideman for the end of your session. Please be advised, this is a very loose and tentative engagement. In all likelihood, you will have to make several attempts to get the Blunt Sideman there, and he will ultimately require a ride. Save yourself some time and make the necessary transportation arrangements in advance.

The Whiteboard

Scheduling isn't the only organizational element you must be concerned about during your session. When making an album, you're juggling anywhere from 10 to 20 songs, all of which have potentially different arrangements and requirements. As effective as computers are for organization, sometimes you just want to have your basic checklist right there in front of you, easily seen by anyone and everyone involved in the project. For this, you need The Whiteboard.

I didn't come up with this. I can assure you, it's as old a technique as the whiteboard itself. The bigger the board, the better (within reason). You want to be able to see the board from anywhere in the room. On the left side of the board, list all of the songs on the album with a dry-erase marker. Across the top of the board, list all of your instruments. Then you can make a grid and keep track of where you are in the recording process.

If you turn your book or e-reader to landscape view when you get to the next page (not yet!), you can peruse and explore an example of a whiteboard and how it might look on one of my sessions. I'll explain things further when we meet up on the subsequent page.

You may now turn your reading device.

[Music plays]

	Drums	Bass	E Gtr	Ac Gtr	Keys	Vocal	BGs	Horns	Strings	Perc
Mixerman Theme	x	x	x	x	N/A	x	x	N/A	N/A	?
Mixerman Song	x	x			x			N/A	N/A	
Like a Mixerman	E					***		N/A	N/A	
Mix It Like a Man	N/A	N/A						x	x	

There are all sorts of codes that you can come up with for marking the whiteboard. In the example above, we're recording four songs. Any box with an "x" means we have a take of that particular part. The "E" means the part is recorded, but in need of some editing. The "N/A" means that part or instrumentation doesn't exist in the production (that can change, at which point you will simply erase the "N/A" and replace it with something else). The "?" indicates some question as to whether that particular instrumentation will be on the track, or it could mean you're not sure about the performance (although you should probably have a discussion with that player before rudely inserting a question mark there). The "***" is the equivalent of a gold star.

The whiteboard serves a number of purposes. For starters, it prevents you from forgetting a part. When you have many songs, and you're working 12 hours a day for weeks straight, it's pretty easy to forget something. Let's say you had a brilliant idea at the end of a long day to record a trumpet part on a song. With a whiteboard, you can erase the N/A and write "TPT?" in the box as a reminder. This way, when horn session day rolls around, you won't forget to take a stab at the horn part.

Now you could easily enter this information into your computer as well. Far be it from me to tell you how to remind yourself of late-night ideas. But there are other, more important, reasons for using the whiteboard. It lets everyone else know where you're at on the session too.

As much as you're the producer and you have the trust of the band, you will on occasion have ideas that are treated with disdain. Clearly that breaks one of our rules of engagement, but there will be times when this is an expected reaction. Marking a concept you wish to try on the whiteboard serves to give notice of that to everyone. There will be a trumpet part recorded. It's on the board, and remains on the board until the horn session is complete. The question mark tells the band there is some doubt in your mind as to whether that trumpet part is a good idea. This relieves any angst that the pending horn part might be causing the group.

Lastly, the whiteboard is a powerful visual organizational tool that involves everyone on your project. When you're ahead, it helps to boost morale. And although the board can also illuminate how far behind you are, this is not something to fear. It's far better for the session overall if your entire team can view the board and plan around it. You will find that when you get behind, your team will often step up to the occasion and serve up a kick-ass day. Furthermore, you can use the board to acknowledge an exceptional individual or even a group performance. Kudos can go a long way toward inspiring your team, and you should use the board to give praise on regular occasion.

Setup

Your main organizational task before your first tracking day is the setup. Much of this falls within the purview of your trusted recordist. Whether you're using a staff engineer or your own freelance recordist, you should probably get together with him to discuss your goals and vision. If you invited your recordist to the preproduction session, this discussion has already taken place. If not, this conversation can't be put off any longer.

The setup for a session can take anywhere from a few hours to a full day. How long it takes depends on many factors, including the size of the band and their skills as musicians. There's really no reason to rush the setup process, particularly if you're going to be camped out in the room for an extended period of time. It's well worth it to burn a day to get the right tones and create a recording environment that's comfortable, as this will save you countless hours later. Disorganization slows the process down considerably, and when you're trying to capture magic you can't afford to fuck around.

I like to create comfortable little "apartments" for the musicians—a designated space that each musician can call his own. Every instrument that has been brought to the session should be out and ready to record at a moment's notice. Guitars should be on stands, acclimating to the room. Extra snare drums should be laid out behind the drummer. Pedalboards should be hooked up, plugged in, and neat. Every musician should have a headphone box, a music stand with pencil and paper, an appropriate and comfortable chair, and creature comforts. Cases and junk should be removed from the recording space entirely. The goal is to create an environment where the transition from idea to implementation is as short and simple as humanly possible. If you think this sounds silly, try it once. I promise, you'll never tolerate a disorganized session again.

You want to work closely with your recordist when it comes to setting up the session. Your needs will often diverge from those of your recordist, at least on the surface. As the producer, your main concern is comfortable musicians who are able to perform to the best of their abilities. Sight lines are often a producer's main concern, since eye contact is useful between musicians. Your recordist will want to place instruments in a manner and location that is beneficial to the recording over other considerations. In reality, all of it matters, and there must be a compromise. You don't want to put your recordist in a position of failure because you value sight lines over acoustic considerations, and your recordist should understand that a good performance makes for good sound. You must find a solution that works for everyone on the team.

Most studios have a to-scale map of their room that you can use to mark where you'd like your players. If you can physically go to the room, that's always best, but you most definitely want to put together a mic and instrument placement plan *before* tracking day. Otherwise, you're in for a very long first day in which nothing other than setup gets accomplished. Now, some producers like to take the first day purely for setup, regardless of how long the process takes. While setting up gear is physically exhausting and getting tones is mentally so, unless you're working with a crew of dainty flowers, I don't think a designated setup day buys you much. Besides, the band is excited. I say try to make some takes.

Your recordist should put together a setup sheet listing the source, the mics, the mic pre, and the processing gear. This list may change as you and your recordist work on tones. Frankly, you really shouldn't worry too much about the mic selection. Even if you're skilled in such matters, it's best to allow your recordist to work with what he is comfortable with. For starters, that's what you hired him for, and if you undercut his preferences at every turn, he's not going to be happy, or effective. You'll also slow him down. What you need to be concerned about is the recordist's approach to the recording. Not his tools.

I've spent a portion of my career as a recordist, and I can promise you this: I am quite capable of placing a part in a sonic box from which it has no chance of being extricated, short of re-recording. I know, I did it on regular occasions. Not to the producer, mind you. I always announced my intentions to the producer along with my reasoning. It was the eventual mixer whom I wanted to put in a box, for the purposes of protecting the producer.

You have to understand, when you got into the $500,000 budget range, the politics changed considerably with major labels. I say this to you in the past tense mostly because a $500,000 record budget is currently rare at best, and has been for several years now. At the height of the madness in the early '00s, I worked on several albums with this kind of budget. Back then, it was not atypical for the label to take away all power from the producer come mix time. Overpriced mixers were cherished for their ability to make everything sound the same. The best way to protect a producer in this circumstance was to record the band in a manner that prevented the homogenization of your hard work. I did that through highly aggressive recording techniques. Instead of giving the mixer 12 tracks of drums that could be easily manipulated, I would give the mixer just 6 highly processed tracks that were essentially locked in. There was very little the mixer could do to alter the sound—not without completely fucking it up, that is.

Now, you can view that any way you like. I don't tell you this for you to make any kind of judgment, but just as a warning. The same way that I could purposely tie the hands of the mixer, so too can your recordist, and they might not even do it on purpose. As far as I'm concerned, this kind of ultra-commitment is a good modus operandi for both producer and recordist alike. As a producer, you should know what you want, so why not try to make it sound exactly like you want it to from the start? Granted, this doesn't leave you much room to change your mind, but it also prevents such foolishness. You're going to second-guess the early decisions you made fresh and with laser-like purpose at a time when you're tired, oversaturated, and hypersensitive? How often do you think that's going to work out for you? I'll answer: rarely.

There's another equally compelling reason for aggressive recording techniques: you will have access to gear at the recording stage that may not be available come mix time. Analog compressors, limiters, and EQs don't react the same as their digital counterparts.

If you're likely to end up in a computer come mix time, you can gain enormous benefit from analog processing.

Now, aggressive recording doesn't necessarily mean you're pushing compressors to the point of breathing. It means you're recording in a manner in which the tones are fully realized as you record. The goal is to avoid excessive processing of the tracks come mix time. The beauty of this method is that everyone knows where they are in the record at all times. There are no surprises. The words "We'll be able to fix it in the mix" are never uttered. Your band feels comfortable because they're hearing the record as it develops.

A passive recording approach is one in which you leave yourself as much wiggle room as possible. The point is to get the tracks down in a manner that allows you to process them later. Compressors are often used on playback to give the band an idea of what the record is going to sound like. This is a fine way to work if you're locked into the same room from start to finish and have plenty of outboard gear available. The thinking is, why lock yourself in when you can do all your processing on playback and make adjustments as you go along? That's a reasonable argument in this scenario. But if the plan is to record in more than one place, you might want to lock in your tones.

Here's the problem. Regardless of which recording philosophy you find more alluring, should you find yourself on a session with a recordist who is unskilled at aggressive recording, it would be inadvisable to work in this manner. Worse yet, if you're not paying close attention to the tones yourself, you could find yourself unpleasantly surprised later. Given this, I recommend you hire someone who is highly skilled and flexible to your needs as a producer.

As you go over your setup with your recordist, you want to be sure that the project is being recorded in the manner that you're expecting, whether that's passive, aggressive, or somewhere in the middle. If you see only four drum mics on the setup list, and an outboard compressor on every mic channel, you probably have a rather aggressive recordist. At the very least, you need to have a conversation with your recordist regarding her recording philosophy, and the kind of flexibility you're looking for come mix time.

Tracking

It's the big day!

The musicians are ready. You're ready. Your artist is ready. You have a vision and a master plan. Your team knows and understands your vision and master plan. You have the band prepped. You have your tempos mapped out. Your song forms sorted. What more do we need to talk about? Know the plan. Implement the plan. That's it!

Ahem.

Plans can be somewhat fickle when it comes to creativity. Oh, I realize I've told you repeatedly that you must stick to the plan where vision is concerned, and I'm not going to back away from that now. But let's not confuse the end with the means by which we get there. While you can use the process of recording to assist in your goals, there are far too many variables outside of your control to rigidly depend on a plan. You can't hear the record you're about to make in your head exactly as you intend it to turn out. You can only envision the feeling you wish to evoke. There are a great many ways to get there, and you must be flexible in your approach.

We are wholly dependent on the talent when it comes to making a record. If you want total control over the project, then I would suggest programming your tracks. When you're dealing with humans, acoustics, and art, it's more like herding cats in a general direction than walking a leashed dog to a specific spot.

It's all well and good to budget six hours to get tones, but that's nothing more than an estimate. A high-quality, experienced studio drummer like Adam Topol (Jack Johnson's drummer) requires all of 10 minutes of my time when it comes to pulling tones. Your average band drummer, even a decent one, could require hours. The difference is consistency in tone. Great players have a knack for pulling consistent and compelling tones from their instrument. Where any given player is lacking in this, we must pick up the slack on the technology side.

As much as microphones will color the tone of an instrument, whether the resonances "sing" in a compelling manner, or merely "sound" in a rather uncompelling one, *all* microphones pick this up with marked accuracy. Sure, if you record the same tone with two different microphones in two different positions, one will be more appropriate than, if not superior to, the other, but both will capture the *performance* with absolute accuracy. When the performance is lacking, the tone is lacking, at which point you must maximize the tone as best you can. While much of this is in the recordist's purview, you can help.

The most effective way to deal with tone starts at the source, which includes both the instrument and the player. The very first thing a great drummer is going to do when he sits down at a kit is adjust the drums themselves. In order to pull the best tone from an instrument, you must tune it, and when I use the term "tune" here, I mean both pitch as well as tone. A snare drum with a nasty over-tone ring that beats with the first tom is a problem that can't be fixed with any kind of mic placement or processing. A kik drum that rattles at the rim will be picked up by every mic in the room.

You have only one way to deal with these kinds of issues, and that's to adjust the source.

The idea that you must fix a rattle in the room is rather obvious, and I don't mean to insult your intelligence. What seems more difficult to grasp by many in this business is that *all* tone issues are most effectively fixed at the source. As the producer, it's up to you to get the instruments sounding appropriately in the room first. If you want a clicky kik drum, and there's no hole in the front head, you're never going to get the tone you seek—not organically, that is. Sure, you could sample-replace it later, but that doesn't deal with the sound of the kik in your aggregate mics, like the overheads or rooms. A sound of a clicky kik drum is organically achieved with a hard beater head and a hole cut into the resonant head in conjunction with the aggressive foot of the player.

When working on electric guitar tones, your first instinct should be to adjust the tone of the amp in the room. After that, it's a function of mic placement, and then processing. Compressors and limiters are exceptionally useful tools for players with incon-sistent tone and dynamics, but only after you've gotten the source close. There is nothing your recordist can do to make a Les Paul Jr. into a Marshall amp sound like a Tele into a Supro. That must be achieved at the source.

Once you have the right instrument, the player is responsible for the quality of the tone. As I pointed out earlier, a great player makes an instrument sing, with a marked consistency of tone. This tone translates easily into the control room by simply sticking a mic in the proximity of the instrument. At that point, how far the mic is from the source affects how much acoustic ambience you get from the room. A weak player does not have nearly the same command of instrument, and mic placement can help tremendously toward maximizing his tone. The worse the player, the more significant a change in mic placement is, to the point that a one-millimeter adjustment can be the difference between a good tone and a bad one. This is especially true on instruments in which there are many mics in close proximity to one another, like drums. The best way to find the sweet spot on a source is by moving the mic.

In order to understand the benefits of mic placement, send your assistant out into the room to slowly move a mic on a source instrument. As he moves the mic, you will literally be able to hear the sound go in and out of sonic focus. Often, there will be a sweet spot, in which the mic sounds best. The better the player, the larger the sweet spot. If you take my advice on this, you will save yourself hundreds of hours over the course of your career.

Compressors and limiters are highly useful tools, ones that tend to even the playing field somewhat when it comes to tone. Their purpose is to reduce dynamic range and balance tone. Used ultra-aggressively, they can "breathe" and lop off transients. Used aggressively, they can be used to shape tone, and help a somewhat anemic tone sing. These are your recordist's tools, and just as I've suggested with microphones, it is best to stay out of your recordist's way unless there's a specific problem. It's fair to tell your recordist that you would like an ultra-aggressive sound, but you should allow her to arrive at that sound of her own accord.

Finding the right tone for the production is your job. Surely, you can delegate it to your recordist, but you will no longer be in control of your vision if you do. If acting as Overseer-in-Chief is the role you wish to play, then you'd better make sure to get an exceptionally talented and experienced recordist on the session. Just keep in mind that you usually get what you pay for in life, and when you pay peanuts, you get monkeys. When you accept peanuts, you're the monkey. So, unless you have the kind of money that brings in a top-flight recordist to your session, you better be willing to involve yourself in the sound of your record. That said, you must also be willing to give your recordist room to maneuver.

Historically, the producer is the person who can walk the line between the technology and the music. You're most effective as a producer when you can make the technology nearly invisible to your band or artists. The best way to achieve this is to make the band sound the way you want in the room, so that your recordist can capture and shape the tone appropriately. As much as you want a fast recordist who is able to think ahead and keep you from leaving the producer's head space, setup is not the time to rush her. If she needs an entire day to get tones, it's probably because of the band, not her.

You may be the boss, but that doesn't mean you can't pitch in to accelerate the setup procedure. Move instruments, move headphone boxes, do whatever you have to in order to get the session going. But don't put pressure on your recordist to get fast tones over good ones on setup day, even if you're the recordist. Take the time that's needed in this part of the process. Recording is a building process, and if you don't a form a rock-solid foundation, your house of cards will ultimately crumble.

At the very least, you want to get one song cut, if not two—but again, if all you accomplish is the ability to hit Record the moment you walk in on day two, then you're fine. Keep this in mind when you're budgeting time. In fact, you should just budget the entire first day purely as setup even if you intend to start making takes. This provides you with a built-in pad, and prevents you from falling behind before you've even gotten started.

If you know for certain that there are parts from your initial tracking session that are merely for scratch, try to resist sloughing off those particular tones. You want the recordist to have a decent depiction of what the record will sound like; otherwise, it becomes more difficult to judge the track. Besides, you never know when a part or performance might be so magical that you just have to use it. If you pay little attention to the sonic character of the guitars, you could find yourself with a great performance and terrible tones. That can work out great, depending on the type of band and music, but typically not. At the very least, you will torture yourself endlessly for not having paid just a little more attention to the rest of the band before making takes. Learn this lesson now, and make sure that even your scratch tracks are at the very least usable—particularly the vocal.

There is one final consideration when it comes to tone, and while I bring it up last, it's without a doubt the single most important reason to take your time on setup day: you must wow your band.

The more trust your band has in you, the easier it is to produce them. When you blow your band away on the very first day of the session, you set yourself up for the remainder of the project. You send the message to your entire team that you're looking to accomplish something special, and not only will they appreciate you for this, they will never worry about it again so long as you don't do anything to erode that trust. There is nothing quite as effective as removing all doubt from your band, and no matter how much they trust you before your tracking session, this is the time that they verify that trust.

Happy and excited players are good players. The more excited you can get your team, the easier your job will be. This is true at all times in a session, but a poor job on tones right from the beginning of your session can be unrecoverable. Job number one on the first day is to solidify the band's trust in you. If you can do that, then when things go awry, they will trust you to deal with the problem. If you fail to impress, they will begin to second-guess all of your decisions, and you will completely lose control of your session.

When the band listens to their first legitimate take of the first song, you want them grinning ear to ear. You want them inspired. You can only accomplish this if you blow them away, and you'll only blow them away if you take the time necessary to do so in the first place.

Making Takes (Tracking)

When making takes with a band (for hire or otherwise), the basic parts are worked out in preproduction and rehearsals, which we'll discuss in detail later. What you want from your band more than anything else is an inspiring performance, one that can be built upon in the overdub phase (if there is one). There will be times when a band's very first take is magic, and there will be times when they will require 20 takes (although you'll likely edit takes together before that happens). The number of takes a band needs depends on a great many factors, and the fewer takes necessary, the better for both morale and time. Fortunately, there are strategies to reduce the number of lackluster performances.

In general, it's best to limit your takes to no more than three at a time. This is usually true in any phase of recording, but particularly so in tracking. Even if those takes are abominable and unusable, it's good to let your band get off their instruments and out of the recording room to regroup. Playback provides your players with a connection between the physical act of playing and the reproduction of their work, and you should not underestimate the power of this comparison. Sure, their bad playing could very well disgust them, but it's far better for your band to come to that harsh conclusion on their own, when possible. Not that they won't already know from your muted reaction. Of course, there's no point in stopping to listen if your band can't even get through a full take.

There are times to abandon the three takes suggestion. The problem is that you will put yourself and your band into complete and total oversaturation if you attempt to evaluate too many takes. Oversaturation is a common malady in recording, one that will make you unable to discern even not-so-subtle differences in such things as timing, tuning, expression, musicality, and balances. That's not a good state of mind to be in when it comes to picking takes.

Occasionally, your band will need to rehearse a particular track in the studio. This isn't ideal, but it shouldn't bust your budget. When this happens, you need to stop the recording process in order to transition back to the rehearsal process. The difference between this rehearsal and one executed outside the studio is that you have the ability to capture a take at any moment. You're all set up! Therefore, your recordist should keep the deck in Record at all times, just in case. In all likelihood, you and the band will work on sections and transitions before you actually start making takes again, but you never know. Recording a rehearsal in the studio could capture magic when you least expect it—if not in the form of a take, then in the form of a brilliant mistake. I can't tell you how often it happens, but it's quite common for musicians to make a mistake that they are unable to repeat. Recording solves this problem.

I'm sure some of you are thinking that this would be a fantastic way to record. Bring the rehearsal into the studio. This is certainly *one* way of recording, and it works great with a group of high-caliber professional sidemen. It's a rather risky strategy to take with a band entity. Studio musicians are coming in without any preconceptions, and bands have to relearn their parts once you make changes. Besides, rehearsals are for you too. The designated rehearsal is the time that you can work and experiment without concern for the clock or budget.

Everyone performs poorly sometimes. When a band is struggling with a take, they could still be thinking about their parts. Let your band struggle for a while, but before they get completely frustrated, insist upon a break. The brain has this remarkable way of working on things while it's seemingly at rest. I'm not sure how that works, but I can promise you, a break can have the remarkable effect of solidifying parts, and often leads to a killer take. If you have any experience with video games, you know this to be true.

Once your band nails that amazing take (or what you believe to be amazing at that moment), it's not unreasonable to let them make another take right then and there. No matter how unlikely it is that they'll do better, at least you give yourself a take to harvest from for edits (if necessary), and more important, you set aside all doubt that they've peaked. Don't underestimate the value of setting aside doubt. Besides, it's not uncommon for a band to walk out of the room convinced they pooched a great take. They certainly aren't going to complain about recording another.

I almost always make my way into the room to greet my band so as to personally discuss a take. There are a number of reasons for this. For starters, you boost morale by getting off your ass and communicating face to face with the band. Secondly, talkback through headphones sucks. It's a necessary evil at times, but for complex instructions, I prefer to deliver my notes personally. Lastly, and most important, you get a chance to look around the room.

You would think that with several people in a room, someone might notice a microphone drastically out of place, but you can't rely on that, particularly with an unseasoned band. Equally problematic is a room littered with unused and blaringly loud headphones. This is a fantastic way to get that click track (among other things) burned into several takes, rendering them unusable. While it's certainly within the purview of your recordist to check the room, the buck ultimately stops with you. Even if you think it's your band's stupid fault, you're the one that must deal with the ramifications of the error, and scolding your band doesn't help your cause much. If your band didn't notice something out of place, it's probably because you didn't ask them to watch out for it in the first place.

There's nothing worse than having a perfect performance in which the recording is fucked up because a mic got bumped, especially one of the drum overheads. This puts you in an exceptionally awkward position. Do you keep the performance and deal with the recording mistake as best you can? Or do you attempt to beat the performance? It's catastrophically disheartening to everyone on the session to try and beat a killer performance, all because you weren't on top of your session. And don't even think about trying to sweep the mistake under the rug. Deal with it while you can—otherwise you could have an unhappy artist at a point in the session when it's too late to do anything about it.

At the very least, you must determine if a problem track is salvageable before you decide to move on to something else. If the recording mistake can't be overcome, then you're going to have to explain what happened to your band and bring them into the decision-making process. Your morale (and possibly trust) will take a severe hit when this happens. But that's better than waiting until mix time for your band to realize they have a rather compromised recording. At least if your band has the opportunity to consider the options, they're invested in the decision.

Judging Takes

Sound and performance are inextricably attached. When the sound comes into focus—and I mean that term literally for sound as you might for sight—you're usually getting a killer performance. For whatever reason, a player in a groove often translates into a consistent and compelling tone. Given that I often record the albums I produce, I have to split my time between listening as the producer and listening as the recordist, and sometimes it's difficult to switch at will between the recordist's left brain and the producer's right. On those occasions when I find myself mesmerized by tone (or lack thereof), I can at least make an initial judgment on a take with reasonable accuracy.

It's not a given that a good-sounding take is the best take. It's also not a given that a poor-sounding take is a bad one. It really depends on the music. Sometimes a trashy sound is perfect for the music at hand, in which case the trashy sound is a good sound. So don't get bogged down on the concept of good tone. That's subjective and program dependent. It's the consistency of sonic focus that happens sonically on a good take. This can be a rather handy tool, particularly when you're listening to a take go down live.

Playing back a take is an entirely different experience from listening to a take as it goes down. The mild anxiety that comes with a live take unfolding is enough to color your evaluation of it, and your initial judgment must be verified. Your first impressions regarding a take can be completely shattered upon playback. For this reason, you want to evaluate each set of takes with the band. You will find that it's rare to get a split opinion regarding a keeper take. One player may be unhappy with one moment of their performance (that's why overdubbing and editing were invented), but if everyone is on the same page where the overall vision is concerned, there shouldn't be much debate regarding the keeper take.

Drums

Drums require space. They're acoustically loud instruments that cover the entire frequency range, and lack of physical space in combination with many microphones within a few feet of one another can be problematic. When recording a band, drums are often the first part that you'll keep, and there's a very good reason for this. Not only do they take up a large swath of real estate, but they often eat up a significant portion of your recording resources.

Typically, you want to record all of the drums for all of the songs during your tracking sessions, even if that's the only thing that you keep in the process. The other option is to record one song at a time, but this is a far more expensive way to record, since you must camp out in a proper tracking room. It's also a logistical nightmare, given that so much gear is locked down and unavailable for recording other parts.

If you can get more than just drums down, that's best, but if all you get during the tracking session are the drums, then you should be in good shape. Of course, if the bass parts are well defined and worked out, and the difference between walking away with bass and drums on any given track is 20 minutes of punching in on the bass to repair some mistakes, then you'd be crazy not to do it. You're all set up!

As we discussed earlier, it's best to record the drums within the kind of space you're seeking. The closer your room mics are to the source, the less ambient they will be. If you find yourself in a room of insufficient size and building material for your desired ambience, then you will be forced to either re-amp the drums later in a larger room (which is essentially a chamber), or simulate the space through the use of digital reverbs. There are certain styles of music and production where a digital reverb is actually desirable, but if you're hoping for organic tones, digital reverbs are a less than ideal alternative.

When your drums are located in an overly reverberant room, you can easily attenuate the perceived space with baffles. This is especially so where the close mics are concerned. In fact, you can completely choke the drum recording if you're too aggressive with your baffling. As much as I'm a proponent of commitment when it comes to tones, it's not a bad idea to leave yourself some wiggle room. By putting your room mics outside of the baffle zone, you can add as much room as you like. This is especially useful if you have a limited context in which to evaluate the drums in the first place. In other words, if all you're listening to is bass and drums, it becomes difficult to judge your drums.

It's not a bad idea to subtly switch up your drum tones on different songs. Changing the snare drum alone will make a tremendous difference in the drum presentation, as will how much room you use in the drum mix. I try to have several choices of snare drum on hand for any given album. The tone of the snare can completely change the impact of a track, particularly if you seek to accentuate other genre influences. For instance, if the goal is to bring out a bit of ska from a hard-rock track, then a wide-open, high-pitched, ringy snare works brilliantly. If you want an old-school '70s-style R&B tone, a deep snare with a wallet on the head will do the trick (although you'll probably want to dampen the other drum heads in that case).

Bass

The bass is often both the musical and sonic foundation of a track. Musically, it defines the root of the chord, performs an important rhythmic duty, and anchors the bottom of the record from a frequency standpoint. If you get the bass right, your chances of getting the record right increase a thousandfold, and I'm not being hyperbolic in the least. The weaker the bass part, the weaker the production. The weaker the player, the less your track will groove. You should make special note of the bass player when budgeting your time.

I spend an inordinate amount of time making sure the bass part is great. There's a very good reason for this: it allows me to place it prominently and audibly in the mix. Low end is critical to a mix, and if the bass part is sloppy and unfocused, this will affect the impact of the track. Think of the bass as the foundation of your house. Without a solid, concrete foundation, the integrity of your house will be weak. That's how important the low end is in music.

Honestly, there's nothing more disappointing than a bass part that is merely taking up low-end space. Even the simplest of bass parts should mean something to your production. Clearly you don't want your bass part so prominent that it distracts from the mix, but it should most certainly be an audible part. On those rare occasions when I find myself in the room with a weak or uninventive bass player, I'll write the part from scratch if I must.

Bass is often well served with distortion, especially on rather dense productions. You can distort the living shit out of a bass, and that distortion can be nearly inaudible within the context of the track. Distortion is useful because it tends to affect the upper harmonics most, which makes the notes audible without losing a robust low end. A good mixer knows how to deal with bass, but make sure you give him a strong part.

Of course, you can always hire a sideman bass player if you must, but that is quite a risky move with a band, no matter what the instrument. Any time you mess with the structure of a band, you risk blowing it up completely. A band is a delicate combination of personalities, and one change can affect the dynamic dramatically. When you usurp the trust within the band by bringing in outside help, you create a nearly irreparable fissure. Even if you're producing a band for a major label, you should be loath to replace a player. Any improvement will almost always be overshadowed by the tremendous hit to morale and enthusiasm. Keep this in mind.

Electric Guitars

There are literally hundreds of guitar–amp combinations. Obviously, that number is reduced considerably based on what's available. When recording a rock band, or any band with electric guitars, it's helpful to have a reasonable supply of useful amps. Of course, the genre makes a difference when choosing the right amp. If you're recording an R&B record, a Mesa/Boogie amp isn't likely to be very useful.

Learning the basic characteristics of guitar–amp combos is similar to learning about wine. You need to taste a whole lot of wine before you begin to recognize good wine–food pairings. Unfortunately, when you're green in the guitar–amp world, you're relegated to using adjectives and reference material to describe what you're looking for in tone. On those occasions when you have no reference for what's in your head, hit-or-miss techniques seem to be the best option.

It's not uncommon for a band to have a rather limited supply of amps and guitars. In fact, it's not unusual for the guitar player to have only one useful combination. When your supply of good instruments is limited, you should probably rent and borrow some alternatives, or seek out a room that has a supply of good guitars and amps.

Sometimes, one amp and one guitar—even lousy ones—will suffice. It really depends on your overall vision, the band, and the genre. It's not a requirement to have 10 guitars and 5 amps at your disposal at every session (although it don't hurt!). Of course, many of you reading this are probably thinking, "What the fuck is this guy talking about with five amps? I've got unlimited amps!" No, you have unlimited *virtual* amps, and that's not the same thing.

For some genres, particularly ones where the electric guitar is not an important sonic force in the arrangement, a virtual amp is probably acceptable. But if you're recording a real rock album, or any part where the electric guitar has some prominence or importance in the musicality of the track, I'm afraid I cannot give you my blessing to use virtual alternatives to electric guitar. Real amplifiers move air and allow a precise interaction between the player's hands and the tone of the amplifier. The difference between playing through a virtual amp and a real one is the difference between playing notes and music. And while there are plenty of guitar players who have not yet made the jump from playing notes to playing music in general, you're not doing these players any favors by putting a virtual governor on them.

Regardless of amplifier availability, the use of adjectives like *grittier, overdistorted, sustain, broken up*, or *thicker* will likely give your team enough information to help you find the desired tone. I suppose you could spend some time trying out virtual amps, and then try to match tones with the available analog amps, but you must realize this will ultimately result in the virtual amp making the record. Hey, if the virtual amp is better for the production than any of your available analog amps, then you should use it. Just be sure you're taking into account the overall importance of the part. If it's critical to the production, this is probably not an advisable corner to cut. Only you can make that determination.

The best solution is to provide concrete examples of the tone you're seeking through reference material. You're never going to match any particular tone exactly, nor would you want to, but there are so many possibilities that it's critical to narrow it down for your team. Clearly, if there's a signature tone you're looking for on the whole record, you should address this well before tracking day. This way the guitar player has some time to put together an acceptable guitar rig before you're on the clock.

As you proceed in any given session, you'll start to get an idea of what available guitar–amp combinations you like and what they sound like. This will speed up the process considerably, and as you gain more experience, you'll have a pretty good idea of what you want when. In the meantime, you might consider hiring a recordist who is knowledgeable about guitar tone.

Now, some of you are probably content with recording the direct signal from the guitar, with the intention of finding the best virtual amp you can as you get further into the production. I've saved this scenario for last as we have to take a break to get into a bit of a philosophical discussion about the virtues of commitment in a production.

Commitment

DAWs, while useful tools and reasonable recording platforms, allow the producer and artist to work in a rather noncommittal fashion. Between playlists that allow one to keep every take of every part throughout the process, and virtual amps, which allow one to change the overall guitar tones at any time, the temptation to leave your options entirely open is a powerful one.

So why should you commit to a guitar tone if you can change it any time you like? Why should you commit to destroying a part that absolutely doesn't work, when it very well could work tomorrow, or come mix time even?

If you find these questions reasonable and deserving of an answer, I have a question for you: Do you really have a vision for your recording if you're unable to commit to parts and tones?

If you keep every part that you record, regardless of how it works with your track, you're not committing to a vision. I have worked with producers who are loath to remove parts from a session under any circumstances, even after it's been determined by everyone on the team that there is no use for the part. Every bad violin take, every poor guitar solo, every stupid attempt at a bad idea not only remains available, but also fair game until the day the CD is released (if not beyond). This combination of data collection and total lack of commitment is not a philosophy of recording, but rather a disease. One in which the final results are nearly as random as the collection of material in the first place. Not only will your band have no idea what their record is until it's too late, they'll likely hate the final product.

Making a record requires discipline—today more than at any other time in the history of recording. In fact, the progression of recording technology has been one that consistently shifts commitment to later in the process, to the point that producerless bands find themselves mixing in mastering sessions with stems. The ease with which you can change your mind, while seemingly a positive technological advance, is nothing short of a hindrance where effective record-making is concerned.

With only 24 tracks available in the early '70s, you didn't have the option of keeping every part. You didn't have the option of changing guitar tones, not without performing the part again with a different guitar amp. The idea that you would have to muster up a second high-caliber performance was enough of an incentive to get the tone right in the first place. At the very least the hurdle of making another take to replace an already great one was enough to give a producer pause.

Hey, don't get me wrong. I'm not saying you should never use the technology available to you. As a mixer, I make radical changes to tracks on a regular basis, but never when the vision is clear. When you find yourself with a track that is not coming off the way you planned, the power of the DAW can come in handy, and can certainly salvage a production gone awry—*salvage* being the operative word here. No one ever goes into a fresh production in the hopes of "salvaging" a record. The goal is to create music so undeniable that it ultimately touches millions of people as it makes its way into human consciousness.

You made a plan. Stick to the plan, until you're sure it's no longer working. Frankly, that decision can't be made until after it's been mixed. I mean, if the original plan really isn't working, you'd probably know that in preproduction. So, if you find yourself giving up on a track before you've seen it through to the end, that probably has far more to do with an overall lack of discipline than anything else.

Tuning and timing issues are so easily fixed in the computer that young producers are often content, if not downright comfortable, with accepting a less-than-stellar performance. This method provides results that are neither artistic nor musical. Personally, I hold the aggressive Gridiron Producer in low regard, mostly because he operates with profound mediocrity under the guise of professionalism. In other words, there is absolutely no talent required on either side of the glass to create a product that's in perfect tune and perfect time, and if you disagree, then I suggest you make a record without a DAW before you decide I'm wrong.

I'm not suggesting you avoid editing drums, or forever reject the grid. There are times and situations when this is the best course of action, and doesn't automatically mean that you lack commitment. Nor does it mean that you or your band are mediocre. A track on a grid has a certain monotonous and trancelike feel to it. For some genres, this is a good thing, although those genres are typically programmed. As long as putting your band to grid is a production decision made for the benefit of the song, then I can't possibly criticize you for it. Sadly, in most cases, it is nothing more than a rationalization by a producer who lacks the skills to inspire a good performance.

This is what I mean when I say that making a record requires discipline. The DAW doesn't have the built-in limitations of tape machines and consoles, and while this flexibility allows for new creative forms of musical genres, it doesn't necessarily make the process better for our more mature genres—particularly rock music.

The idea of recording a direct guitar so that you have the ability to constantly change the tone of the record is downright debilitating to the process. Just as you want to move the listener forward with your arrangement, you also need to move your band forward in the record-making process, culminating in a brilliant vocal performance. If your production inspires your singer, she will, at the very least, perform to the best of her abilities. I'm not sure you can ask for more than that.

As much as you *can* change your mind, alter direction, or go back to a part that should have long been deleted, in general it's an inadvisable way to work. Your band will not have confidence in you if they feel lost in the process. They're not hiring you to stumble your way through the record and hope it all comes out all right. They could have done *that* on their own. They're hiring you to provide vision and leadership, and if you rarely commit, you're providing neither. This will result in a band that doesn't trust you, and rightly so.

You have a responsibility to your artist to make a record with purpose and forethought. This doesn't mean you can't change your mind. It doesn't mean you can't completely alter your original vision if the creative process has all but forced that decision. It doesn't mean you can't keep parts and use them if they serve an unexpected purpose later. You should use all the tools available to you when appropriate. But if you go to enormous lengths to make your performance as a producer of greater importance than that of your band, your record will sound like it.

The power of producing is not contained within a computer. The power lies within you. Music is a soulful and personal experience, and if you can recognize and accentuate what is musically compelling and record it, computer editing will only manage to fuck it up. When you spend your session hoping to find the musical genius in a track, then clearly you couldn't see the musical genius that was there to begin with. Just sayin'.

Acoustic Guitars

Acoustic guitars pose a number of challenges. For starters, depending on how it's recorded, an acoustic guitar is a rather broad instrument that takes up an immense amount of frequency space in the sound field. This isn't a problem on a production consisting of acoustic guitar and a vocal, given the sparseness of production. It's drums that are easily dwarfed by a broad acoustic guitar.

Most recordists are reticent to record acoustic guitars, or any instrument, in a manner that doesn't hold up in isolation. This is understandable from the perspective of the recordist, although I don't subscribe to it myself. As the producer, however, if your vision is that of a small and dusty acoustic guitar (just as an example), then you should record it that way. Like everything else, the tonal quality of the acoustic guitar starts with the source and the player. So, if your guitar player is strumming a big Taylor, and you're looking for a much smaller, trashier sound, then you should get the right instrument for the job.

There are times when it's best to record a performer who plays acoustic guitar as she sings. This requires a bit of finesse, as two microphones in such close proximity are fraught with phase-coherency issues. Even the slightest movement from your performer will cause the vocal to momentarily shift within the stereo field. This will also cause select frequencies to cancel out in a seemingly random fashion. This is called comb filtering, and in combination with the phase shifts, it will cause a vocal to sound downright swirly.

The fact is that some people sing better when they play, and sometimes play better when they sing. If we are to put performance above all else, and we are, then it's best to record them simultaneously, regardless of the sonic issues. Fortunately, there are ways to reduce the swirliness.

My preferred solution is to use Seymour Duncan's Mag Mic, a modular guitar pickup that is half mic, half actual pickup. The device clamps right into the sound hole, and features a wire terminating in a $\frac{1}{4}$-inch output for the pickup, and an XLR output for the mic. There is a thumbwheel on the device that lets you adjust the ratio of mic to pickup. This combination allows you to reduce the awful plucky sound of most pickups and the phase-coherency issues caused by an external microphone. It is a handy device, and if you tend to record singer-songwriters, it's one you should consider investing in.

If you don't have a Mag Mic, you might try using a dynamic microphone for the vocal. The most common dynamic is the Shure SM57. All dynamic mics tend to have good rejection patterns. The problem with dynamics is that they're terrible on moving targets, and you will have significant tonal changes if the singer is somewhat animated and doesn't stay squarely on mic. There's nothing wrong with an active singer, but once you know this to be the case, you'll probably want to rethink this option.

The last solution is to use one mic for both the acoustic and the vocal. This technique is highly dependent on mic placement, and you'd better tape your marks in case you decide to punch in on a take. I'm talking a square around the feet of the stool, "X" marks where the singer's feet should go, and a mic with a pop screen to mark exactly where his mouth should be. Even taking these precautions, you could find it difficult to match the tone between takes. This technique also relegates your vocal and acoustic guitar combination to mono, which is why I typically don't use it.

Many recordists and producers think it's a good idea to record acoustic guitars in stereo. It's not. Stereo acoustic guitars will wrap around the listener's head unnaturally due to phase-coherency issues. You cannot get a proper and coherent stereo image without a reasonable distance between two microphones. A stereo representation of a pinpoint source requires a time differential between two mics. To achieve that differential, there must be distance. There is no possible way to get enough distance between two *close* mics on a single acoustic guitar. All you will accomplish is what I call faux stereo, which is both distracting to the listener and problematic in mono.

The number of people who will defend this way of recording an acoustic guitar on the Internet is simultaneously horrifying and hilarious. The inability to pinpoint the directionality of a sound is disconcerting to the listener. Placing an acoustic guitar within the sound field that comes from no particular place is distracting and will cause the listener to feel uncomfortable. Just think how uncomfortable you would feel in the jungle if you were unable to pinpoint the sound of a vicious man-eating predator. I would imagine this is instinctually similar, although I have no scientific evidence to back that statement up. It just seems logical to me.

The use of faux stereo guitar has everything to do with one's own hang-up with asymmetrical mixes. There's nothing wrong with having a single acoustic guitar on the left, and only the left. There is overwhelming precedent for this, both on records and in real life in general. If you're unwilling to accept some asymmetry in your music, then you will at all times use symmetry, which is boring and lacking in contrast.

Piano and Keyboards

Stereo pianos pose many problems for a producer. You may not have noticed, but they're rather large instruments, and every single one of them has unique sonic characteristics. Given budgetary and logistical constraints, finding the right piano for your production can, at times, be challenging.

If the piano is meant to be a lead instrument in your production, then the piano itself and how you record it will have a profound effect on the production. A nine-foot Steinway recorded in a giant hall and miked from distance sounds entirely different from a seven-foot Yamaha with the mics directly above the hammers. Combine that with the vast differences between pianos of the same make and size, and finding the right piano can be a daunting task.

If you have all the time and money in the world, this is not a problem. Take the time, and spend the money necessary to get the right piano on your session. If you have a budget like the rest of us, you're just going to have to do the best you can with what you have available.

If you're recording someone like Elton John, then you're going to get a particular piano shipped in for that session—probably his own. That only makes sense for someone like Elton. If you're producing the local jazz pianist, then you not only need to find a piano he's comfortable with, but you also want to record him in the appropriate space for the record. Therefore, it might be worthwhile to invest a significant portion of the budget to get the right piano in the appropriate space. While I'm all for finding a precise tone for any given instrument on any given production, budget constraints will usually preclude perfection when it comes to instruments like pianos. Ultimately, if the piano takes a back seat to a vocal, "close" will likely be the reasonable goal.

How difficult it is to find the right piano in the right space depends on where you're located. If only two studios in your area have pianos, then you'll either have to use one of them or get a bit creative.

You can find pianos all over the place, and a little bit of cash (and the offer of a free tuning) can often give you access to instruments that aren't necessarily available to the public. You can find pianos in churches, schools, and even local bars and clubs. You might find that coveted detuned honky-tonk piano somewhere close by, and if you do, make note of it. If it's important that the piano player and band play at the same time, and a remote recording isn't an option, then you can always attempt to rent the piano and move it to the studio for your session.

You can also travel with the band to a studio in another city for an appropriate piano. You can record the band together with a scratch piano and then overdub the master piano part on location. You can record the piano on location and then record the band to that part. Now, on the face of it, you may not prefer any of these solutions. I know I wouldn't. I especially don't prefer to record lead instruments as an overdub. It's the *lead* instrument, after all. But sometimes plans must adhere to reality, regardless of preference. At the very least you must weigh the negative of a disconnected piano against that of a connected one that sounds inappropriate. I can't tell you which option is best. That's why you get the big bucks.

Keep in mind that a piano must be tuned before a session. As large as a piano is, it's a delicate instrument that will go out of tune when moved. So be sure to move it at least several hours (if not a full day) before your session and allow it time to acclimate to the recording space before having it tuned.

As with any instrument, mic placement makes an enormous difference. Two mics placed well off the piano will produce a far mellower tone than two mics over the hammers. How far you can pull the mics off has much to do with the amount of space surrounding the piano. If you're in a small room, then the sound doesn't really have time to blossom, and this will lead to all sorts of dead and overblown frequencies. So, if you're looking to mic the piano from a distance, make sure you have a room that can accommodate this.

In my estimation, recording a piano/vocal is even more challenging than recording an acoustic guitar/vocal. If you want any kind of isolation at all between mics, then you have to close up the piano and cover it with blankets to create a cocoon, which produces a highly unnatural sound. If it works, great! If not, you might have to get creative again.

If the studio has a large enough glass between the iso booth and the room, you can encase a grand piano in such a way that the keys are in the iso and the body of the piano is in the room. Depending on how crazy you want to get with this (and how long your talent can survive in the iso booth with no food or drink), you can get incredible isolation this way.

The default for many recordists is to record a piano stereo, with two mics in close enough proximity to the hammers that the piano takes up the entire stereo field. For many productions that's a reasonable way to record a piano. For many others, it's a ridiculous way to record the piano. On rock productions, particularly ones where the piano is the secondary instrument to the guitars, a stereo piano tends to take up too much space within the mix. This is true with just about any full range keyboard, particularly when the player is using the entire breadth of the instrument. Keyboards are space eaters, and you should carefully consider how much space you want a piano or keyboard to take up in your production. There are many cases in which a mono keyboard is a much better choice than a stereo one, and if you're going to use it in mono, then you should probably just record it in mono.

Hammond B3s and Rhodes keyboards offer movement and therefore record well in stereo. A B3's Leslie cabinet rotor distorts and spins the sound. This movement can be captured nicely by placing a mic on each side of the top rotor. The Rhodes suitcases have a stereo tremolo function, which acts as a panning effect when set to its widest setting. But just because you can record these instruments in stereo doesn't mean you should feel compelled to do so at all times. Ultimately, you should allow the track and the arrangement to dictate the best placement and use of the instrument, stereo effect notwithstanding.

Synthesizers, like all keyboards, can also take up the full breadth of frequency space in a production. They produce a rather subtle stereo spread, and for the most part occupy the middle of the stereo field. This means that a stereo synth pad can take up an inordinate amount of space in a production. If filling in the middle with a synth pad helps to glue the track together, then that's fine; otherwise, you might want to place the synth as a mono instrument within the stereo field, especially in a dense arrangement.

Horns and Strings

When you're recording a horn section of four (or fewer), you don't necessarily need charts. Horn stabs and unison parts are especially easy to work out on the spot with a good section. If, however, your arrangement calls for four-part harmony within the section (whether that's for horns, strings, or voices), you'd best have charts made. Writing four-part harmonies is called voice leading, and you can get yourself into a little trouble if you attempt this on the session.

Voice leading has very specific and stringent rules, all of which can be broken under the right circumstances. You just have to know when. Learning the rules is the easy part. Actually writing four parts that abide by the rules is difficult at best, and learning when to break them takes considerable practice and overall experience.

In voice leading, the goal is to create four discrete melodies that work together to create one harmonic part. If your horn section is composed of bari sax, trombone, alto sax, and trumpet, the bari sax (which has the lowest range within that lineup) should carry a melody that begins below the trombone and stays there. No part may cross lines with the other parts. You must avoid parallel fifths, unisons, or octaves in motion. And you should avoid large melodic jumps (although the bass voice can jump more than the others).

The stronger each individual melody, the better the voice leading, but as you'll learn, it's almost impossible to have four compelling and fully self-sustaining melodies within four parts that never cross. This is a basic description at best, and there's no possible way we can have a voice leading class in the middle of a book on producing. Besides, I haven't done a voice leading exercise since college. The point is, if something doesn't sound right in a four-part harmony, it's probably because a rule was broken.

While learning the rules of voice leading is a worthwhile endeavor, it's certainly not a prerequisite to producing (if you haven't figured it out by now, little is). Your horn section leader should know these rules, and you can always hire an arranger. If you have a very specific part in your head you can mock up the parts with a synth patch, but you will soon realize why voice leading is an actual college-level class. I'm not sure I would even try to score a four-part harmony at this stage. At the very least, if you provide the top notes or the melody line to an arranger, he can fill in the rest.

If you can't afford an arranger, go to your local music college or high school and see if someone there can help. If that doesn't work, go on the Internet. I could voice lead in high school, and my band teacher most certainly could voice lead. As with anything we discuss about producing, a little creativity in networking can go a long way to solve just about any problem. The sooner you start to think like this, the easier your life is going to be as an up-and-coming producer.

Sectional instruments like horns and strings are best recorded together—as a section. The recordist will likely give each player her own mic, and that's fine, but recording a section one part at a time is not only time-consuming, it's nowhere near as effective as recording them together. A good section will operate as one instrument, and recording each part individually would be similar to recording a synth chord one key at a time. Horn players play best when they're able to hear each other for tuning and timing purposes, and will often use only one ear of their headphones for this purpose. If you can record a section together, you should.

Orchestra

Recording an orchestra requires hiring a director, an arranger, a properly sized and outfitted studio, and a recordist who knows how to record an orchestra. There is no room for error on this kind of session. You will have anywhere from 30 to 120 players, each paid between $350 and $1,050 for every 3 hours of their time.

A 60-piece orchestra (which is typical for scores) will cost tens of thousands of dollars for one 3-hour session. If you're on a project that has the budget for that, you're on a project that has the budget to hire the personnel necessary to do it properly. Unless you're a legitimate orchestral arranger and director, your job at that point is as Overseer-in-Chief. You're in charge, but for everyone's sake, don't get in the way unless something is going down wrong in the first place.

The problem with recording an expensive string section is that you become stuck with the results no matter what they are. I wouldn't consider recording even a 10-person orchestra without a MIDI mock-up of the parts, and I'd likely live with the part before scheduling the orchestral session. Underdubbing a $25,000 string section is a political nightmare, one that will not win you any friends at the record label. So you'd better be sure you know what you want before your orchestra sets foot into the studio.

Percussion

The genre you're working in usually dictates the prominence of percussion. R&B and pop music, which are often programmed, typically rely on percussion parts to carry the internal rhythms of a track. In rock music, the drums carry most of the internal rhythms, and percussion is often used for lift and excitement. Tambourines are the odds-on favorite in a rock chorus, since the surge in high end and rhythm is exciting to the listener. The more integral the percussion is to the internal rhythm of the track, the earlier you should record it.

If the percussion isn't a critical part of the internal rhythms, I prefer to save it for last in the recording process, and I judge whether a percussion part is good by one simple criterion: Is the track better with it?

As much as it might seem like a good idea to capture a plethora of percussion parts and sort them out later, I'm afraid that is a highly inefficient way to work. It is far better to select your perc parts by how they improve the track than to throw perc parts up on the wall and hope they stick later. They won't.

When adding percussion parts, keep in mind the frequency needs of your track. If you have a track laden with high-end information from cymbals and shredding guitars, a tambourine could very well be overkill. Egg shakers should be used with caution in rock music, because they tend to cause the guitars to sound dull in comparison. You need to be highly attuned to how percussion affects the track. If a part provides a lift because it fills in a much-needed frequency and internal rhythm, then it's a winner. If not, try something else.

If all you're going to do is lay down some tambourine parts, and the band has someone with the skills necessary to do this (there's usually one member of the band that can play tambourine), then there's no point in hiring a percussion player. If you intend to have a plethora of percussion parts, then a professional player is recommended. Not only will a high-caliber percussion player have great rhythm, she will often play parts that work well within your production. The time you can save makes it well worth hiring a professional percussionist.

Any instrument that is percussive in nature does well with ambience. The short duration of a percussive hit not only excites the room nicely, but there is plenty of space and time between hits in which to hear the reverberation. That said, there is certainly precedent for bone-dry percussion parts.

Vocals

There's a reason why the vocal sits prominently in the middle of our most popular and enduring songs—the vocal is money. The lead vocal carries both the melody and the lyric, and as such, it carries the entire song. In fact, melody and lyric are the very definition of a song. This shouldn't denigrate the importance of a track or an arrangement. The functions of harmony, countermelody, response, and rhythm make a production considerably more interesting and compelling than a simple a cappella vocal.

In general, recording a killer vocal is simple, and I'm going to provide you with the key to success where this is concerned. If you deliver your singer a track that inspires her to perform, you will likely get an inspired performance. I don't mean to go all Yogi Berra on you with that statement, but it's true. This is the best argument of all for making arrangement decisions as you go along. If you make the record in a manner that inspires your singer, you've just set yourself up for success. Think about it. How on earth will you ever inspire your singer if you don't provide him with a concrete and compelling production?

You won't.

The goal is to get your singer to ask *you* if she can lay down a vocal. When she does, drop everything and let her sing immediately. Nothing is more beneficial to a production than an inspired singer delivering an undeniable performance, all because the music moves her.

Given the importance of an inspired and perhaps spontaneously performed vocal, you should be sure not to get caught flatfooted. Whether you're in a tracking or overdub session, you want to be sure you have two vocal mics ready: one in the recording room and one in the control room, each fully set and tested for your vocalist.

You might consider recording vocals in the control room. Not only does this make communication more efficient, but it also allows you to kick everyone out of the control room. Of course, if your singer prefers to perform in the live room, then that's where you should put her. All that really matters is that you're rolling the moment she's ready to sing. This is not the time to allow your recordist to go into anal mode. Make sure your singer isn't distorting the pre inappropriately (sometimes distorting the pre is a good thing), make sure she's not clipping into the DAW, and roll.

So much of recording is about keeping the process invisible to your band and artists. Performance is about being in the right headspace. When the technology gets in the way of headspace, you've failed as a producer. Hey, whatever—dust yourself off, and do better next time. Even the most veteran producer is going to be caught unprepared occasionally. But the more often you're ahead of your artists, the more successful recording moments you're going to have. If you manage to capture your artist as she delivers the best vocal of her life, you're worth your weight in gold as a producer.

When it comes to vocals, all rules go out the window, particularly singing rules. Open vowels are useful for keeping a singer on pitch, but proper singing pronunciation is rarely desired in modern music. It's one thing if you're Christina Aguilera or Adele, where incredible technique is combined with soulful singing. For these pure singers, technique is used as an asset. But most artists and singers, especially band singers, are not technicians by any stretch of the imagination. The only time to bring technique into the equation is if it will improve the singer's ability to perform. More often than not, it will only serve to fuck your singer up.

Proper posture isn't worth thinking about unless your singer is having an issue with breath control. It doesn't matter if the vocalist wants to stand on her fucking head—if she's convinced it's going to give her a better vocal, let her. In fact, sometimes it's best for your singer to perform in a manner well outside the norm. I had an artist recently who was so used to singing in bed that some songs were best performed on his back. If something makes your singer more comfortable, forget about convention—encourage her. Keep this in mind when you're recording vocals, especially when your singer is struggling.

Compiling and Punching

There are two basic ways to record a vocal as an overdub. You can record multiple takes of a track and compile a performance out of the best of them (a comp track), or you can record a track by section, punching in on problematic lines. Many times you'll need a combination of both.

Singers often have a natural quality curve that you should figure out as soon as possible. Some singers consistently deliver their best stuff on the first take and then drop off considerably in quality after that. Others need several takes before they begin to shine. Still others need a mark to beat before they deliver their "money" take.

If a singer kills it on the first take, record at least two more. She might surprise you and beat it. If the quality drops precipitously, there's really no point in beating her up. Have her take a break as you compile a take for her.

When comping a take, you want to find the best overall take, and go from there. The more takes you have available, the longer the process. Even if you have six tracks of vocals, three will likely make up the majority of your comp. As with tracking, it's best to record takes in sets of three. If the first three takes are less than inspiring, then let your singer hear some playback so she can make the necessary adjustments. If the next three takes are also unusable, then you probably need to rethink your strategy. This is where advice in the abstract gets particularly difficult, because there are many reasonable courses of action to take when this occurs.

You could have the singer listen again, and sing three more takes. You could tell the singer to spend some time warming up. You can have your singer perform in front of the monitors rather than using headphones or in-ears. You can put together a comp out of what you have, let her listen and get pissed, and record six more. You could move on to another song, although this is risky and should be avoided unless there's a physical issue with her vocal cords. You could move your singer from the control room to the recording room or vice versa. You could give your singer some specific direction, and start working by section.

Which option you choose has to do with the problem at hand, and what you believe the reaction will be. If moving on to something else is going to send your singer into a tailspin, then that would be a poor option, regardless of your reasoning. If your singer is normally a champ with headphones, then changing to monitors isn't likely to cure the problem. You must evaluate the personal and professional idiosyncrasies of your talent in order to determine the best course of action, and even then you're taking a veritable stab in the dark.

When an artist is really struggling, and it seems to be a mental problem rather than a physical one, putting together a comp for her to beat is a highly effective method. Not only does that give your singer 30 minutes of rest, it also provides her the opportunity to hear a comped vocal for herself. This will often inspire your singer to go beat the comp. Once a singer knows she has a take to fall back on, she will often loosen up and deliver the goods.

When your singer is struggling with a section, skip it and work on it separately. This is an especially good idea for parts that are hovering at the top of her range. Parts that cause your artist to push hard or even scream should be approached with caution. Letting loose on a screaming part can occasionally open a singer up, but is a risky move, as it could blow her out for the evening, if not longer. Screaming will also make a singer raspier than usual, and if that's an undesirable quality, then you most certainly want to save the screaming for the last part of the day, if not the session in general.

Punching in on sections is sometimes a necessity, one that you should reserve for those times when your singer is struggling. While the punching process can be exceptionally tedious, it's important to exhibit marked patience when dealing with a struggling singer. If you stress, they will stress. You should be the calming influence in her life, particularly at this juncture of it. For instance, if your artist wants you to loop a section in Record (a method I prefer to avoid), by all means do it, even if you've had bad results in the past. By the time you're producing an artist they've probably already been through the recording process more than a few times. While you certainly shouldn't allow an artist to revert to bad habits, she will likely know how to get herself out of a jam. A frustrated singer is a useless one. So, blocking her methods could very well prove counterproductive.

Many times producing is about giving your artist a little rope. Not so she can metaphorically hang herself with it—you do that with your enemies. More like a tether, one that can be gently tugged back when necessary. Even when you know that a proposed solution isn't going to work, if the price is 10 minutes of time, there's really no reason to block the idea. If your artist is convinced she knows the most effective approach, you'd best stay out of her way until she needs you. This is especially so if you're at a loss yourself. If her solution succeeds, great! Use it in the future with her. If her solution fails, then at least she won't feel as though you're holding her back. She'll also trust and appreciate you more since she'll know you're there as a collaborator and a guide, not as a dictator.

On those occasions when the track is proving to be just a bit out of your singer's range, you might want to save it for another day, but I'll warn you that it's unlikely she'll get stronger as the session goes on (although it does occasionally happen). You can put off the part for another day, when your singer is feeling up to it, but if she continues to have problems hitting the notes, then you'll have to slow down the track in order to bring down the pitch for the purposes of recording. Time compression is also a reasonable alternative.

A struggling vocalist can be the result of a bad cue mix. Many studios today have multi-channel headphone boxes. These can be handy when everyone on your tracking session wants a different mix, but they have their disadvantages. Singers are notorious for putting together skewed mixes, and the result is bad timing and bad tuning. It becomes difficult to focus on performance when your singer can't nail the basics.

Generally speaking, you shouldn't allow a singer to create her own headphone mix. It's far better to give her the mix that you're monitoring, and force her to request changes in the mix. This way, you know what she's monitoring as she sings. The beauty of controlling the monitor mix is that, well, you control it. This means you can protect against an artist's typically skewed cue mix, and you can make the necessary adjustments. When the vocal is over-bearingly loud in the cans, the singer will tend to go flat. When the vocal is too low, the singer tends to push sharp. So, if your singer is flat, you should give her more harmony instruments. If your singer is sharp, she may need to be louder in the cans. If your singer is out of time, then she needs more rhythm instruments in her mix. If she's out of tune *and* out of time, she's too loud in the cans.

Some singers like reverb in their headphones. This is generally inadvisable, as reverb can cause a singer to go sharp. If you must supply a singer with some 'verb, try using a 250 ms delay tail instead of a reverb, as it will make him less susceptible to tuning issues. If your artist insists on actual reverb, then you should give it to him until it proves to be a problem. It's more important for him to be comfortable. Besides, if he's consistently sharp after you warned him of this potential problem, the reverb usually doesn't last long.

Vocal Mic

There is no such thing as a magic mic, one that works on all singers and all songs. That is a myth. A fallacy.

Furthermore, no one can accurately predict what the best mic will be for any given singer. You may even choose different mics, depending on the song. The best way to pick a vocal mic is to select several, set them up, and have your vocalist perform briefly in front of each mic. Pick the best-sounding mic and move on. If you're going to be tracking for a while, and have no reasonable expectation of a keeper vocal, then you can audition mics as you track simply by swapping out the mic on each subsequent song. Of course, if your singer nails a take on a less-than-stellar mic pairing, you're stuck with it. As long as your recordist didn't excessively compress the vocal, this isn't too much of a problem for a good mixer.

Once you find a winner, there's not much reason to continue auditioning mics. Your purpose here is to find a mic that doesn't get in your way. It's not to audition every mic in the locker in pursuit of the perfect mic, forever amen. Once you find a good mic, keep it until a particular song and production dictate otherwise.

Limiters and compressors will also affect the color of your singer's vocals, so you want to be sure that your recordist has chosen a limiter that works well with your vocalist, preferably before you begin rejecting microphones. Sometimes you'll find a song doesn't work quite as well with your chosen mic. In those cases, it's fair game to explore other alternatives, but certainly not at the expense of an artist who is ready to perform. Of course, when your singer doesn't like how she sounds in the cans, that would be a good time to switch out the mic, too.

Background Vocals and Harmonies

Background vocals can range anywhere from a single vocal harmony to stacked harmonies in which each note is doubled or even tripled, to an entire choir of schoolchildren singing "We don't need no education."

Given that the vocal is the focal point of most songs, the way you treat it will have a huge effect on how the track is perceived. Any track in which all of the backing vocals are stacked as overdubs by the lead singer has a far less organic sound than harmonies performed by the band or sidemen. I'm not making a value judgment here. Organic doesn't equal better, it merely equals organic, in that it can be performed live as it was recorded. A single vocalist singing the leads and the harmonies breaks the bounds of realism, and is therefore perceived as a much more produced and polished sound, in which studio trickery is used to accomplish the record.

Harmonies in general are far less intimate when doubled and tripled, as they cause a natural chorusing effect. If the goal is to create the illusion of a highly polished pop record, then stacked vocals is a good effect. If the goal is to create a raw, heartfelt track, then any more than one background vocal would typically be counter to that goal.

The more precise you are in your vocal stacking, the more polished the record will seem. This is true whether it's harmonies or stacked unison vocals. It is not so true with sloppily stacked vocals. Near as I can tell, Jane's Addiction's Perry Farrell used upwards of six stacked unison lead vocals on his productions, but they were all sung with slightly different timings and inflections, and the effect is a thick vocal without sounding polished.

Before the advent of programs like Melodyne, doubling a lead vocal was a great way to deal with a weak singer, particularly one who didn't tend to use vibrato. But there's no reason to use this effect on any and every weak singer you come across. It depends on whether you're trying to hide the singer or expose him. If you expose a weak singer, you're counting on the listener being drawn in to the heartfelt nature of his vocals.

Some singers don't blend well together. Often the suggested solution is to have the lead singer perform the harmonies, but if that's not the sound you're looking for, then that's not a very good solution. You're far better off either hiring a sideman or having another band member sing the parts. Or you could do what I do: sing them yourself.

A harmony part will change the feeling of a track. If the proposed notes are creating the wrong feeling, then you should get in there and change them. Harmonies are basically voice leading, and as such, you should never allow parts to cross. It's exceptionally confusing to the listener, as they will have no idea where the melody is, and relative volume isn't really going to help matters.

When the harmony is in a higher register than the melody, you have to be careful about how you place the two in terms of relative volume. When two parts are identical in level, the higher vocal will appear to be the melody. Therefore, a harmony higher in pitch than the melody should be noticeably quieter than the lead, so that it blends in. Even in cases where you want the harmony to appear even with the lead in level, you must duck the harmony slightly; otherwise, the listener will have trouble focusing on the right part, which will make the parts seem like they're crossing. I realize that ultimately the vocal blends are the purview of your mixer, but if there's a problem, you should know how to fix it.

Even when you're dealing with a lead and two unique background parts, you should be aware that you are taking your production into a sweeter realm.

Didgeridoo, Dulcimer, and Bagpipes

Throughout the course of your producing career, you're going to come across all sorts of wacky instruments that you've never heard of, seen in person, or recorded, such as didgeridoo, dulcimer, and bagpipes. I've recorded all three of these instruments, and not a single one of them came with a "how to record" instruction manual. Go figure.

While I want to stay away from recording techniques as much as possible in this book, I can save you much agita when it comes to recording an instrument you've never seen before. The advice I am about to give you is not only ridiculously simple—it's the secret to recording in general. If the instrument sounds good in the room, no matter how exotic, mic placement is the key to capturing it in all its glory.

If you can find a location where all the important aspects and notes of the instrument are picked up evenly, you can successfully record the instrument. It's as simple as that. Listen to the instrument in the room. Find the spot by ear that seems to best capture the entire instrument. Place a mic there. If it's deficient, move it until you find a spot that works across the board. If it sounds right, start recording.

See? I told you it was simple. Okay, yes, yes—if you stick an SM57 mic 10 feet off of a dulcimer, you'll likely be disappointed. But even the greenest assistant is going to suggest you try a large- or small-diaphragm condenser instead. And it doesn't take very many sessions before you start to realize the basic characteristics of different microphones. This is why I suggest keeping a whole slew of mics set up during overdub sessions. It makes listening to different mics on a source as simple as moving them. It also allows you to quickly listen to mics that are distant from the source, in the hopes of finding one with an ambience worth recording.

Overdubs

The lion's share of modern record-making is accomplished during the overdub phase. Prior to the advent of multitrack recording, a producer recorded the full arrangement all at once. There was no such thing as an overdub. The full band, including the artist, performed the song until they had a perfect take, or one that could be edited together from different takes. Four-track recording became available in the late '60s, and proved to be so powerful that it was only a few years before producers had 24 tracks available to them.

Multitrack recording changed both the process of recording and the results significantly. Records were no longer a pure capture of a live performance; they were an artistic medium in their own right. Now a producer could concentrate on one part at time. A mistake by a single player no longer ruined a take. It could be fixed with a punch-in. Today, a producer isn't limited by track count, and a mistake doesn't even need to be replayed by the musician. A technician can manipulate it, move it, tune it, time it, stretch it, and even alter the tone beyond all recognition without ever getting up from her chair. What was once a musician-driven process, one in which all the performance power was in the hands of the band, became a technician-driven process in which much of the performance power lies in the hands of the producer.

So, why then am I hammering relentlessly on the importance of frontloading your decision-making as a producer? I mean, you have all of this technology available to you. Why bother spending time with the band working out the form? You could just record the sections and put them together any way you like. Why bother working out a tempo? All you need to do is get it close and use flex time to adjust it from there. Why take any time at all getting drum tones when you have sample replacement? Why bother with a vision? You have the tools available to make the record any way you like once you capture the band playing the track.

My response to that is: yes, you can! In fact, some producers have been making records like that for more than a decade now. If you like, you can completely remove all power from the band and place it in your own capable and predictable hands. Hey, maybe you could even put your picture on the album cover!

If you think the best way to make a record is by sampling the band and programming it, you have the ability to do so. If you honestly believe that is going to make the best record for your band, who am I to argue? But let's not kid ourselves here. Once you do this, you're no longer making the band's album. You're making your album. This will be a successful business model for about one out of every 50,000 of you, if that.

Given the power available in the DAW, producing a band takes discipline. I'm a nut about getting the musicians to play their parts. And while bands often find this technique amusing at first, by the time we're done, that amusement turns into appreciation. Why? Because the band feels like it's their record. The band will feel like they played their record, and even though there might be some edits, a little nip or tuck here or there doesn't cheapen the hard work of developing and *performing* their album. Nor should it. The confidence you will instill in a band by insisting that they perform should not be underestimated.

There is a difference between performing music and playing notes. Performing music moves people. One can't perform snippets of music. That's not music. That's a snippet. A snippet has no emotional impact on the listener. Therefore, to produce the music of a band, you must be willing to record their music, and that means you must be disciplined enough to demand and record their performances. In order for your band to perform, there must be a master plan. A vision, worked out ahead of the recording session.

Of course, the purist position would be to dump the overdub process completely. While, technically speaking, overdubbing is "cheating" (as if), it's been the modus operandi of record-making for the past 40 years. Overdubbing allows you to focus on one part at a time with your musicians. It prevents you from keeping all your personnel in the studio all the time. Overdubbing even gives you the time necessary to find the record. To create sonic textures that you wouldn't be able to otherwise.

Taken to its extreme, overdubbing can be just as detrimental to music as aggressive producer programming. There are all sorts of stories about certain bands and producers recording guitar chords one string at a time. I'm sure most of you reading this would think that's absolutely ridiculous, which it is, yet some of you have no problem capturing as much musical data as possible in the hopes of putting together something useful later.

There's nothing wrong with employing a hit-or-miss methodology on occasion. That is an absolutely reasonable way to record when you're having a problem finding the record, or implementing your vision. Where sessions go awry is when hit-or-miss recording replaces any and all semblance of decision-making. If all parts are in a constant state of flux until the mix, then you have no intent, and no idea, as to what kind of record you're making. If you lucked into a part, and you love what it does for the track, then you should lock it in and build from there. You might as well choose a direction and go, because you will never have the time or budget to exhaust every idea you have.

The beauty of the overdub process is that it gives you the ability to build upon your earlier work. Once you complete a part, you can give that player a rest and move on. If you treat the overdub process as a building process, one in which each part builds upon the next, you will create a record with purpose and forethought. And while there will be times when your record seems to be going in the wrong direction, at least you and your band will be aware of the problem, and more important, will be able to fix it. You can't fix a problem if you can't tell the problem is there in the first place.

Even working in such a disciplined manner won't prevent you from overproducing your record during the overdub process. Somehow that raw, stripped-down record you intended to make has become a veritable wall of sound. Shit happens. The good news is that the CD won't be released tomorrow in a state of incompletion, and you have time to correct it. All you need to do is take some time to sort through the mess. When you embrace overdubbing as a viable way to make a record—and I'd say most people do—then you must embrace underdubbing as well.

As a mixer, I engage in underdubbing on a regular basis. Nearly all producers, no matter how disciplined, can get carried away in the overdub process. On the rare occasions when there's little to no underdubbing required, it's usually because the producer took the time to sort through the tracks before he handed them off to me. This is a good habit to get into during the overdub process.

The best way to determine what's missing from a production is to mix it as you go along. When you try to make a track sound like a mix, it's easy to tell where it's lacking in terms of arrangement. If, for instance, you find the pre-chorus is lacking both rhythmically and in the lower midrange, you might solve both problems with a single part. Perhaps a rhythmic electric guitar part in its lower register will do the trick. If your chorus has plenty of rhythmic motion but somehow there's a glut of high-end information, your production might very well benefit from violins. Of course, if violins are the wrong call where your vision is concerned, there are plenty of other options. The point is, when you think about your production specifically in terms of what it seems to be missing, you'll be far less likely to go astray. That said, sometimes your production will head in an unintended direction.

The creative process is fraught with possibilities. As sure as you might be of your intentions, there will be times when a part or idea takes the record in a wholly unexpected direction. This can be somewhat disconcerting and confusing if it's clearly outside of your original concept. Sometimes this sort of left turn in your production can be a brilliant development, one that requires no debate whatsoever. Sometimes it leaves you sitting on a fence, unsure of which way to jump. You may even find yourself in love with the part, even though it also makes you feel downright uncomfortable. The best way to deal with this scenario is to live with the part before making a decision.

If you set the part aside and move forward with your production, you will most likely strand the part. As much as I have admonished you on regular occasion to stick to your vision, an exciting and compelling left turn on any given song or production should certainly be explored. The best way to explore a part is to build upon it until you're certain about it. The moment you determine you've taken a wrong turn, get rid of the part and any poisonous fruits that may have blossomed along the way.

Left turns can be worth exploring, but you must do so in moderation. If you find yourself easily distracted by new ideas that fall well outside of the original plan, you will not only go over budget, you will lose your way in the process. The setup of the record is in the preproduction phase. The foundation of the record comes during the tracking phase. The making of the record occurs in the overdub phase, and if you work with discipline and purpose, you will have your record the moment you complete the last overdub. Yes, even before it's been mixed.

The Mix

Mixing is such an important part of the recording process that I wrote a whole book on the subject. The mix is nothing more than the culmination of the producing process. It's a highly specialized job, one that requires the ability to deal with the big picture and the details alike. The mixer is essentially a temporary extension of you as the producer.

Simply put, the job of the mixer is to bring the production to its fullest potential. If you deliver an undeniably special and focused production, the mixer should follow suit. If you deliver a confused production, all the mixer can do is bring the record to its fullest potential. But how does one measure "fullest potential"? By how the track makes you feel.

In my book *Zen and the Art of Mixing*, I define a great mix as follows: a great mix is one that brings a production of a great song to its fullest potential by effectively manipulating the listener's emotions and focus, thereby forcing an appropriate and desired physical reaction while simultaneously causing the listener to sing.

I realize that's a mouthful, but essentially, if a track makes you sing and causes some other physical reaction—whether it makes you dance, stomp, or raise your fist (even goosebumps count as a physical reaction)—then it's a great mix. If you can't stop singing to your production, if it does everything you wanted it to when you set out to make the record, you can't ask for much more. Your production has most certainly been brought to its fullest potential.

The whole goal is to get a reaction from the listener, preferably tens of millions of listeners all over the world. This is how an unknown song becomes a hit—many people react to it. If a track doesn't make *you* react, then how the hell is it going to make anyone else react? You're producing it! I mean, you already adore the song, right? So if a song that you adore doesn't cause you to sing and move, then how is it going to do that for anyone else?

Unless you're highly skilled at mixing, you will be doing a great disservice to your band and clients if you mix their record. Let me put it this way: I have mixed a great many albums, and I can tell you that there is nothing more difficult to mix than my own productions. It's so much easier to mix as a third party that in some ways it's an entirely different job. The tracks are fresh and exciting. I'm not married to any parts. I'm oblivious to the political baggage and the arguments that were involved. I've unaware of any parts that didn't make the session. And I can be super-aggressive, knowing that I have a producer with a vision who will act as my backstop.

The mixer as a specialist has been around since the early '80s, when large-frame consoles stocked with automation began to appear in studios. The ability to program a mix with mutes and fader rides made it an art in its own right, and the perceived importance of the job increased significantly.

Before mixing became a specialty, an engineer was responsible for both recording and mixing a project. The problem? Maybe 1 in every 10 engineers is actually a good mixer. In fact, a producer is far more likely to be a better raw mixer than an engineer. The problem with producers as mixers is that they rarely possess the attention to detail necessary to bring a mix home. This probably has a lot to do with the mind-set of the job. Producers are right-brained thinkers who evaluate the whole, and recordists are left-brained thinkers who focus on the minutiae. Mixing requires equal parts of both, and if you've spent your entire time working on a record in one or the other hemispheres, it becomes difficult to view it from the other side.

Your recordist is likely to ask you if he can mix the project, and if he's a good recordist it's worth finding out if he's a good mixer too. If not, then you need to find a mixer, preferably someone who refers to himself as one. Mixers are considerably more expensive than recordists—such is the nature of a job whose importance has been elevated beyond all reason. That doesn't mean you can't find a killer mixer to fit within a reasonable budget. You just have to ask.

The bar for accepting a mix project is considerably lower than producing. I don't need to adore a song to mix it, although I do have to find something redeeming in the music. A mixer operates much like a producer in that he must work within the confines of a budget. When a producer approaches me about mixing a project, I can either quote a firm number and pass on anything less (in which case I don't get the gig), or I can accept the gig for short money on the strength of the music itself. If I love the music, and it seems like an easy record to mix, there's no reason for me to turn down a reasonable offer, particularly if I want to fill a void in my schedule. That said, if that producer then hires someone else to mix his next full-budget album, I'm unlikely to say yes the next time he approaches me for another favor.

These days many mixers often have their own mix suites, and can mix an album for a flat rate, without additional studio costs. Some mixers still prefer to mix on a console, and this will bring the price up considerably. Whether you attend a mixing session or not is up to you and, to some degree, your mixer. I won't perform analog console mixes for anything less than my full price and unless the band and producer are physically there to sign off on them. Recalling an automated mix takes several hours, and that's just to get it fairly close. The better maintained the studio and the better the assistant, the closer the recall will be, and it can be pretty damn accurate under ideal circumstances. Unfortunately, the quality of studio assistants and maintenance is generally lower now than it was in years past, which makes mixing on a console a significant drag for unattended sessions.

If your mixer has a mix suite, and is using a computer to mix, there's no need to attend the mix session. A really good mixer will usually get the mix pretty close to what you're looking for, and you can go through the notes process with him remotely. Of course, there will be times when you get a mix back that seems to miss the mark. This will happen no matter who is mixing for you, and no matter how often he absolutely kills it.

When attending a mix session, don't get involved too early. A mixer needs time to discover the production, figure out which parts work with which, and work out an arrangement. If you're in there fucking with him, he'll be reticent to try out his more radical ideas. There is a certain randomness that is necessary in mixing. You've had days with the track, and your mixer is hearing it for the first time. He needs to discover how everything works in the track in a compacted period of time, and doesn't need you in there preventing him from doing his job. Besides, it's only going to drive you crazy.

There's nothing worse than sitting in the back of the room, listening to an outrageously loud hi-hat and wondering why the fuck your mixer isn't hearing it. He's probably listening to some other part that's bothering the shit out of him at that moment. Such is the way mixing goes. Let him mix for a few hours before you start checking up on him. Even if he misses the boat completely, it doesn't take long to make adjustments to a mix, even seemingly radical ones.

Mixes take anywhere from a few hours to a few days, depending on the mixer and the size of the job. In general, a mix shouldn't take more than a day, and particularly fast mixers can finish a mix in about six hours. I prescribe mixing fast, as it prevents confusion, and forces the mixer to keep his eye on the big picture. Really, the only thing you should be concerned with is the quality of your mixer's work. Once you find a great mixer, stick with him.

If you really want to understand the thinking that goes into high-level mixing, I'd like to take a moment to once again recommend you pick up *Zen and the Art of Mixing*. Not only is it a good companion book to this one, but it's also full of detailed information that will make *you* a better mixer. The better you are at mixing, the better you'll be at recording and producing, because you will start to listen to your productions from the perspective of the end game.

Mastering

If we're going to discuss the process of mastering in general, then we first need to go over loudness. I went into loudness in great detail in *Zen and the Art of Mixing*. Frankly, I can't explain loudness more effectively or succinctly than I already have, so I will reprint this particular explanation here.

Theoretically (and traditionally), the mastering engineer's sole job is to prepare the client's master for manufacturing while staying within the given parameters of the delivery medium—whatever that medium happens to be. All delivery mediums have parameters that must be adhered to for proper reproduction. A 12-inch vinyl record has a maximum run time in the neighborhood of 30 minutes and an optimal run time of about 15 minutes, depending on the bass level and overall volume of the program; a proper playback speed of 33 or 45 revolutions per minute; and a limitation on the amount of low- and high-end frequency information that can be reproduced based on the run time of the side. A CD has a maximum run time of about 72 minutes, with a bit rate of 16 bits, a sampling rate of 44.1 kHz, and a maximum level of 0 dBFS (decibels relative to full scale) before clipping. The mastering engineer's job is to take your master in whatever form you deliver it (tape, CD, WAV file, SDII file, etc.), make sure it conforms to the specifications and limitations of the destination delivery medium, and prepare the master for the manufacturing company. These days the master is typically delivered as a PMCD (pre-master CD), which is a sealed CD master that the manufacturing plant uses to press the final product.

The mastering engineer's role has expanded greatly over the years. These days, the mastering engineer also tends to make mix judgments, and attempts to maximize the impact of your mixes through the use of a processing chain. The processing chain can include any number of digital and analog EQs, compressors, limiters and faux tape-saturation devices. This may sound all well and good, but at some point, maximizing impact was confused with maximizing level. There was a time when the credo of the well-regarded mastering engineer was "do no harm." This noble sentiment has been replaced over the years with the "take no prisoners" mantra of a war—more specifically, a loudness war.

Loudness is the apparent level at which a CD plays through a consumer playback system. The louder the mastering engineer can make your CD, the louder your CD will sound in comparison to other CDs, and the louder your song will sound in iTunes (although the Soundcheck option will match the playback level of all your tracks in iTunes). Loudness began as a way to get a perceived advantage. If your CD played back louder than other CDs, then people would more readily take notice. It's the same principle behind the loud commercials we've lived with for so many decades. If the commercials are louder than the television show, they're harder to ignore.

Loudness is achieved mostly by reducing the dynamic range of a mix. On any CD in which the loudest parts hit digital zero, the overall dynamic range is determined by the extent of the low volume information. If the loud parts on a CD are played at a comfortable volume and the soft parts are so quiet that you actually need to be in a sound-isolated listening room to hear them, then that CD has an enormous dynamic range. As exciting as a large dynamic range can be, it's useless in any real-world environment. This is mostly due to the masking effects of the constant background noise in our lives.

Mixers and producers figured out the pitfalls of a broad dynamic range long before the mastering engineers put their thumbs on that particular scale. It was the classical music producers who were crazy happy over the increased dynamic range of digital reproduction, not the popular music genre producers, who were already engaged in a vinyl loudness war of their own.

The original loudness war from the late '70s and early '80s cooled down once CDs came out. The producers decided to take advantage of the improved dynamic range that CDs offered, and the mastering engineers on the whole kept the program level under −3 dBFS (other than perhaps some transients), mostly because early converters typically degraded the sound above that level.

It was the introduction of brickwall limiters like the Waves L2 that set off the current 15-year loudness war. A brickwall limiter will prevent any transients from ever passing beyond a set maximum level. Mastering engineers quickly realized that by smashing down the transient peaks into square waves, one could easily reduce the dynamic range without ever risking outright clipping. By pushing the loudest parts of the mix down with a brickwall limiter, the mastering engineer could reduce the dynamic range of the mix, which resulted in a CD that played at a higher average level than other CDs. CD players with jukebox turnstiles made these differences in level obvious, since the new loud CDs actually played louder than other discs. Record companies liked the idea of having their newest artist's CD play louder than other CDs, and it didn't take long before radio airplay became part of the justification.

Radio stations have used severely effective brickwall limiters for many decades. The FCC requires this because it helps prevent transmission bleed into other bandwidths. Once label executives caught wind that mastering engineers now had these "magical radio limiters" at their disposal (which they've always had!), it didn't take long before the mythological concept of "radio ready" mixes spread throughout the industry. In reality, there is no advantage gained by putting a severely brick-limited mix on a radio station that is already brick-limiting the signal. In fact, loud records actually sound much worse on radio, but that obvious disadvantage doesn't seem to alter the perception within our industry.

While I have a pretty good idea who actually started the loudness war, it's almost pointless to lay blame on one particular person, as it was a relatively gradual occurrence. At some point, someone—a producer, record company exec, or mastering engineer—started pushing the envelope to gain an advantage. One man's advantage is another's disadvantage, and so the war was on.

The record companies began rewarding mastering engineers for their ability to maximize loudness. The louder the mastering engineer could make a CD, the more money she could charge the record companies. The major labels literally incentivized mastering houses to make CDs as loud as they possibly could, even if that meant obvious clipping at the reproduction stage. All bets were off once that happened, and by the time some mastering engineers were capable of charging $10,000 for a half day's work, sound quality was no longer important.

It wasn't long before mixers, who were also part of the profit-sharing infrastructure, and who could also reap the monetary benefits of loud records (albeit more indirectly), realized that their favorite mastering engineer could make the CD louder if they delivered mixes that used less stereo field and more upper midrange. And as if that wasn't enough, the loudest of the loud mastering engineers magnified apparent loudness by boosting the high frequencies of a mix. The end result was what we have now: overly bright, depthless, distorted records. And thus, the total annihilation of dynamic range and listenable music was complete.

Here we are at the crossroads. There is no more level to be gained. There is no way to make your CD louder than your competitors', since there's no way to make music louder. As an industry, we're already pushing the level past the capacity of the converters. We're well beyond reasonable

EQ curves where brightness is concerned. With tempo fluctuations long eradicated, we've destroyed the last true dynamic we had available to us from a production standpoint. We've destroyed the impact and depth of an entire generation of productions, and we've rewarded the consumer for seeking convenience over quality by reducing sound quality to such an extent that it's become irrelevant. Nice, huh?

The great irony of the loudness war is the undeniable role it has played in changing how consumers listen to music. Whereas music was once a visceral and interactive listening experience—one that captured the full attention of the fan—loudness, brightness, and the consequential distortion has reduced music to nothing more potent than background noise. Ironically, the widespread production of music capable of cutting through all but the most overbearing background noise has had the effect of causing the average listener to turn their music down, not up. The rampant turning down of music has had the consequence of making music nothing more important than background noise, thereby reducing its overall relevance and value. While there are certainly other factors contributing to the metamorphosis of how people listen to records, I'm not sure music would have become the stepchild of the entertainment industry had the music industry not treated it like one first. (Although the overall swallowing up of record companies by the mega-entertainment conglomerates certainly didn't help matters.)

While it might be interesting to actually research (and divulge) who started what in the evolution of the loudness war, I fear that doing so would only serve to elevate certain producers and mastering engineers to an even more iconic status than they already enjoy. It doesn't really matter who pushed what envelope when and for what reason. It's human nature for us to compete. In modern times this causes us to push the envelope beyond all reason, and this is exactly what we've done as an industry.

Just so there's no misunderstanding, this loudness summation is basic at best, and doesn't provide the full breadth of the digital loudness war. To lay blame purely on the mastering engineers as a community would be unjustified. There are very few in this business with clean hands where loudness is concerned, and it's been a natural spiraling frenzy propagated mostly by greed. I provide this information so you have some understanding of the history, so you can hear for yourself the ramifications of apparent loudness on the effectiveness of a mix, and so you can understand what the hell your soon-to-be-fired mastering engineer has done when he delivers you a master that sounds as flat as a pancake.

Again, the mastering engineer is in charge of preparing the mixes for the final delivery medium—nothing more, nothing less. I realize this flies in the face of what one might read on the Internet, but I can promise you, the idea that the person with the least flexibility to affect the product is somehow the most important person in the process is complete nonsense. The last thing you want as a producer is to involve yourself with a mastering engineer so aggressive that he demonstrates no respect or sensibility toward your hard work as a producer. You want your mixer to be aggressive, not your mastering engineer.

The biggest consideration in choosing a mastering engineer today is the loudness issue. As such, it's important for you to educate yourself in this regard. If you listen to a CD pressed in the early '90s and compare it to the same CD pressed in the 2000s, the later pressing will likely be considerably louder, and sound considerably worse. It's not just the sound that takes a hit; the impact of the record is negatively affected, too. A record with a reasonable dynamic range tends to sound punchier, and is generally more inviting, than a record in which loudness was the goal. Exceptionally loud records are assaultive and uninviting. Even at low monitoring levels, it becomes difficult to ignore a loud recording. But then, that's the point.

The loudness battle has gotten significant attention over the years. Some producers and artists are bucking the trend, but they're seemingly few and far between. There are really only two ways I can see for the loudness war to finally come to an end, and frankly, only one of them is actually possible. The first way is for a rather dynamic record to become an enormous international hit of epic proportions, breaking every sales record in existence. That would be the impossible way, since so few people actually buy records anymore. The second way is for reproduction devices to automatically adjust the playback level. This technology is available now. It's merely a matter of it becoming a standard feature. In the meantime, we must compete, and sometimes that means pushing for some loudness.

An aggressive mastering engineer will manhandle the track to maximize loudness. Brickwall limiters are just one weapon he uses to meet that goal. Compressors will also reduce dynamic range. The problem is that a stereo compressor on a mix will alter the balances considerably. As a mixer, I take great umbrage when a mastering engineer puts a compressor on my mix. I spent hours getting the balances right, I've already used a compressor on the mix (and if I haven't it's for a pretty good reason), and I certainly don't need some guy going in and changing my balances. That said, sometimes a compressor is a reasonable tool for a mastering engineer to use, just not on a great mix.

EQ is also handy for loudness. There is a bump in our hearing in the 2–3 kHz range. This happens to be the fundamental frequency range of a crying baby—go figure. Mixes in which the upper midrange and above are boosted will therefore sound louder to us. We call this "apparent loudness." So, if you crank the top end of your mix and smash it with a brickwall limiter, you will produce a record that can't be ignored, regardless of what volume the consumer is listening to it at. Of course, the track will have no depth, and will most certainly irritate the hell out of everyone in the room. But it won't be ignored!

Practically speaking, as a producer, you need to consider loudness. You need to compete to some degree; otherwise, those loud, bright tracks will make yours sound dark in comparison, which will require the listener to turn up the volume on yours (heaven forbid!). If the consumer turns your track up to a comparable level, it will technically sound better, but even with that, we have trouble resetting our brains from excessive brightness. It's kind of like entering a dark house on a bright day. It takes a few minutes for your eyes and brain to reset. This means that your track could be at a distinct disadvantage when played next to other tracks.

I can't advise you on how loud is too loud. It kind of depends on the record itself. I can tell you that the most expensive and the least expensive mastering engineers have the same thing in common. They can both provide you with atrociously loud and unlistenable records. If that's what you want, so be it, but don't bother spending time in the studio worrying about recording quality. Just throw the mics up and hit Record, because it won't matter by the time you're done.

I'll warn you now, there are some mastering engineers who are incapable of following direction where loudness is concerned. Oh, some of these guys will give you lip service, but at the end of the day, they figure you don't know the difference anyway, and will often ignore your wishes.

The best way to evaluate a mastering job is to listen to the record in your favorite venue. I listen in my car, and I'm not listening for sonic quality so much as what the track does to me. Much like evaluating a good mix, if you find yourself singing and moving in the intended manner, then it's a good job. If you find yourself confused, then and only then should you compare the mastered mixes to the flat mixes.

It's difficult to directly compare a raw mix to a mastered one due to level differences. I don't bother going back and forth between a mastered and an unmastered mix. Even if you can successfully match the playback volume, alternating between short bursts of music is a useless test—one that will only serve to over-saturate your ears. You really have but one main concern when it comes to your completed record, and that's emotional impact. You need more than just a few bars of music to evaluate impact, so you should listen to a full verse and chorus of the unmastered track and then listen to the same full section on the mastered one. Whichever track makes you feel better is better. I realize that may seem like a rather unscientific test, but then judging emotional impact is an art, not a science.

A good mastering job on an album will cost on average between $1,000 and $3,000. Some mastering engineers cost less, and some cost considerably more, but it's best to look for people who fall close to within that range. If you're unsure of a mastering engineer, you can always ask for a test master, which many mastering engineers are more than happy to provide. Whatever you do, don't send your track out to 10 different guys. For starters, that's not cool, and you won't be able to judge between that many mastering jobs, particularly if most of them are competent.

If you're making a record for a label, it's possible they will have a preferred mastering engineer. Labels will often take the record out of the producer's hands come mastering time. You must stand up to them if they attempt this. There's a reason why they don't want you involved in the mastering process. They want to make the record as loud as possible, and they don't want you standing in the way of that. As much as you have to play politics when dealing with a label, you can't allow them to just go in and butcher your hard work like that.

Of course, once you draw a line in the sand regarding mastering, the typical solution is for your label to agree to a shootout. But the label is almost always going to prefer the louder record. Label execs don't know how to evaluate a mastered record. They're going to choose the louder and brighter job every time. Given this, you would do well to avoid a shootout, and to deliver a record that has enough loudness to compete but not so much that it's unlistenable.

Wrapping Up the Project

Regardless of whether your tracks were mixed on an analog console or in the box, recalling your mixes even a year later will be nearly impossible. In fact, you actually have a better chance of a recall in the analog setting than the digital one, given the constant upgrades in operating systems, DAW software, and plug-ins. Given this, you should make sure to save your alternative mixes and files for the future.

Once the record is mastered, ask your mixer to provide you with the following mixes: instrumental mix (no vocals), TV mix (no lead vocal), and stems. You want these mixes printed at the sampling and bit rate used for the session. All of these mixes are useful down the line for edits, should the track be used for a commercial or a movie. The TV mix allows the singer to perform live to the track on TV. Bands don't usually use TV tracks, but they're also handy for karaoke, should the song become well known. The instrumental is released in some genres, and it too can be used for track performances on TV.

Stems are typically eight tracks of submix that combine perfectly at unity gain to make your two-track mix. They are usually used for movies to give the re-recording engineer some control over the mix. At first that might seem a bit radical, but songs in movies have to work with the rest of the audio, including Foley and dialogue. The re-recording engineer must be able to change the balances based on the rest of the audio, the most common being a momentary reduction in the vocal to accommodate the dialogue.

Increasingly, mastering engineers are requesting stems. Given this trend, some mixers, myself included, will refuse to deliver stems until the album is released. Unless the track is slated for a movie, I won't deliver stems until well after the album has been mastered. If a mastering engineer ever requests stems from you, fire him on the spot. I don't care if the mixes are atrocious. He's not a mixer, and has no business whatsoever attempting to mix the record, no matter how bad he thinks it sounds. Seriously, here's how the conversation should go:

Mastering engineer: "Do you have stems?"

You: "You want to mix the record?"

Mastering engineer: "Well, no, I… "

You: "You're fired."

See how simple that is?

If the mixes are bad, you need to fix that at the mixing stage. Mastering engineers don't have the sensibilities to mix. They think in terms of sound, not in terms of the big picture and the emotional impact. So, for a mastering engineer to even suggest that he'd like to mix your record—and that is *exactly* what he's suggesting—is outrageous and should be taken as nothing less than a personal assault.

Perhaps if enough producers begin to tell enough mastering engineers with mixer envy to fuck off, this practice will be all but eradicated. It's not good for young mixers who are learning their craft to have someone else redo their work, and it's not good for our business to accept further deferment of production decisions to overpriced sonic janitors. It hasn't happened to me yet, mostly because I know how to mix. As far as I'm concerned, it shouldn't happen, period. Not to anyone.

I've said my piece. Here's your typical eight-track stem configuration:

Bass (mono)

Lead vocal (mono)

Drums and percussion (stereo)

Harmony instruments (stereo)

Background vocals (stereo)

Your mixer will know how to lay out stems on those tracks that diverge from this simple example.

Once you've collected all your alternate mixes and properly backed them up in multiple locations, you're done. Sessions end with a flutter, not a bang. The band and its support team are going to go out and sell your hard work. Meanwhile, you're going to go find your next project and get yourself another lottery ticket. After all, every album that you make as a producer has the potential to make you money well after you've completed the album.

You gotta love that.

Chapter Three

The
Politics

Your approach to politics when working with a band is what separates the men from the boys in producing. We've discussed some of the basics throughout the course of this book, the most important and obvious being to cozy up to the brainchild.

How much power the brainchild or leader wields is almost directly proportional to how many songs she writes for the band. The more songs the leader writes, the more power she has within the structure of the band. There's a good reason for this. The songwriter is the one person in the band who can't really be replaced, not without significantly changing the identity of the band. Cover bands notwithstanding, the band exists because of the songs, and whoever writes the songs is king (er... or queen).

Occasionally you'll come across a band in which there are multiple songwriters, and this changes the dynamic considerably, although with some predictability. The power structure of the band will almost always mirror the songwriter relationships within the band. For instance, two songwriters who usually write as a partnership will typically carry equal leadership weight within the band. A band carrying four separate songwriters will typically function as a democracy for band business, but will rotate power creatively based on who wrote a given track.

Some bands work out songs together and share credit equally between the members. This is by far the healthiest business structure for a band. Everyone gets paid equally, which prevents the drummer from insisting that his two shitty songs make the album. Given this scenario, it's not a bad idea to have a business discussion with the band. Otherwise, you could be hog-tied into recording and prioritizing less important songs in order to accommodate a somewhat business-savvy band member.

I realize I'm repeating myself here, but for purposes of review, there are only three major music revenue streams when it comes to bands: record sales, live performance (which includes merchandise), and publishing. For all intents and purposes, record sales no longer exist. Too many acts are willing to treat the product as a loss leader for the other two revenue streams, and that's not an unreasonable business model, given the nearly complete erosion of intellectual property protection. Obviously, some acts still sell records, but today's 1 million in album sales is the equivalent of yesterday's 10 million in album sales. The chances of anyone making money on sales these days are so low that this can no longer be relied upon as an effective method of profit sharing. Hopefully, this will change in the future, but as of this writing, that's the reality.

Since the record itself won't bring in significant revenue, it's often used as a loss leader for ticket sales. Live performance monies can be a lucrative revenue stream, and the band typically shares equally in these revenues. Touring is the crux of the band's business, but it carries a rather large overhead. As a result, many bands require tour support, which is a nice way of saying they need a subsidy from a label or large management company. As the band becomes more popular, its need for support begins to drop.

Publishing is the Mother of All Revenue Streams. It's where the big money is at in this business, and without sales, the only stream that can generate "mailbox money." A hit song, one that is spun relentlessly on radio, streamed on the Internet, licensed for commercials and movies, played in clubs, and successfully covered by others, will generate revenue for decades. Whereas live touring requires the band to tour in order to generate revenues, the songwriter will make money for the rest of her life, well after the band entity itself has disbanded.

Given these realities, any band member who is not a songwriter in the band will only make money on the band's efforts when they're on tour. Once the drummer comes to this realization, he will often attempt to write songs, and will likely insist upon some of his songs making the album. If the drummer gets two songs on a 10-song disc, he will receive one-fifth of the writer's royalties for the album. The problem with this logic? The record sales that do exist today are trending toward online song purchases. This would tend to preclude the drummer from making any money on his shitty bullshit song. I realize there are drummers in this world who are talented songwriters in their own right, and I don't mean to be picking on drummers, but it seems to be the most economical way to make my point. At least it was until I wrote this disclaimer.

If you find yourself in a situation where you have the worst songwriter in the band demanding song representation on the album, you must either capitulate and record those songs, or finesse the issue. If you merely ignore the problem and steamroll over the band by refusing those songs (whether done early or upon completion), you could blow up the entire project. It's in the interest of the band to put out as many great songs as possible. The best way to accomplish that is for the songwriter(s) to give the band a stake in the songwriter's royalties. Enough of a stake so it makes sense to everyone in the band to choose the songs based purely on quality.

It's impossible to come up with a fair percentage for the band to receive without understanding the band's contributions. Even then I would be reticent to offer any hard numbers. If the songwriter typically comes into rehearsal with a completed song in which he spoon-feeds parts to the band members, then the band is not particularly integral to the process beyond performing the songs. Given that scenario, a nominal percentage of the publishing would be downright generous. If the songwriter typically comes in with half-baked ideas, and the band works on the song as an entity, then the others should be entitled to a share of the songwriter's royalties. Technically, only those involved in the lyric and melody are the songwriters. But if the band entity is an integral part of the process, it makes sense for the songwriter to reward the band for their contributions in the form of profit-sharing revenues.

Politically, it would be foolish for you to suggest this sort of business arrangement in an open forum. This discussion must be had directly with the songwriter of the band, and should be presented wholly in business terms, not moral ones. This explanation must be based on the contributions of the band, the realities of the business, and the importance of a happy band. If the band is the venue in which the songwriter can best release his songs, then the band is not without significant importance. All you want to do is present the dilemma and the solution, and let the songwriter figure it out from there.

This is not a discussion you should have with a band unless it's proving to be a problem. You don't want to fuck with a band that is happy with its business arrangements, even if you think they're unfair. You risk blowing them up by doing that, and they will renegotiate their terms if and when it comes up. The problem is if your mere involvement is perceived as raising the stakes significantly. Then the songwriting royalties can become an issue.

Sharing Credit

Bands and artists alike frequently ask to share production credit. I've done this in the past, and I don't recommend it. In this book I've laid out for you exactly what producing is. In concise terms, it's both a leadership role based on morale management and creative vision, and an organizational role based on resource management. Regardless of what you bring to the party in terms of song enhancements, creative contributions, arrangement, song form, parts, and overall presentation of the band, *they* will get all the credit. They're the band. They get credit for being the band, which is everything. They need to take credit as producer, too? I think not.

From the band's perspective, they are a major part of "producing" their album. This is true. After all, they wrote the songs and demoed them up in a way that attracted you. But the credit is "Produced by," and in all but rare cases that task is performed by one person—you. Sharing your credit as producer is as ludicrous as you sharing credit for being in the band. Believe me, if you do your job right, by the time you're done successfully creating the album, they will consider you part of the band. Of course, that feeling will fade quickly as they spend months on the road and you move on to produce other bands.

The one time you might consider sharing your producer's credit is if you're asked to perform duties as an engineer/producer for a long-established band with many albums under their belt. Even then you should resist this demand unless it's the difference between winning and losing the gig. Just keep in mind that any time you draw a line in the sand, you risk losing the gig.

This entire book is one big argument against sharing credit. Don't be afraid to shoot such a request down outright when it comes up early. A young band will rarely push this issue beyond an initial inquiry, particularly if you lay out your reasons in a clear, concise, and firm manner. Consider a request to share credit as the most important test of your leadership and communication skills. Pass this test, and the band will have accepted you as the leader of the project.

How to Rule

I think I've made this pretty clear throughout the book, but let there be no doubt: producing is not a dictatorship. It's the band's album. They're the ones who need to be proud of the finished product. They're the ones with their pictures on the cover, not you. The band is who is most branded by the results, not you. You will work on many albums over the course of your career, and one album out of many will only brand you if it's hugely successful.

That said, you're not there to cater to their every whim; you're there as an expert—a leader who understands how to make an album. You're beholden to a budget and you share in profits if the album does well. Your expertise on how to accomplish the best album possible for the band is what puts you in this position. Therefore, you're not there to serve purely at the pleasure of the band. You're there to lead them through the creative process within a structure. If you consistently yield creatively to the will of the band against your stated vision, you are no longer making the album you promised. A yes man has no value to a band, or any other creative entity, for that matter.

So, how the hell do you reconcile the idea that you are hired by the band with the idea that you must maintain some control over the creative process? Very carefully.

Really, it all comes down to the setup. There's a reason why I'm adamant that you be wholly honest at all times—it sets the tone for open and honest communication. There's a reason why I suggest that you not only have a vision, but that you sell the band on your vision, because it puts you in the leadership position. There's a reason why I suggest you wait until after preproduction before you even begin to talk contracts, because it gives you the opportunity to get the band wholly on board with your vision without feeling stuck. You're the one with the vision and the plan, and once the band buys into that completely, the only way they get to hear your completed vision is to buy into your leadership.

That doesn't mean there won't be disagreements. It doesn't mean your client won't make attempts to pull you and the project off vision. It doesn't mean you won't have a problem band member hell-bent on putting a wrench in the works. All of those things can and will happen on occasion, no matter how clear you are in your communication. But if you were honest, forthright, and clear in your vision, if you laid out the plan—both the musical plan and the recording plan—you have multiple witnesses to this, and there can't be much argument against sticking with a plan that everyone has agreed upon. The entire presentation system as I've laid it out for you is meant to force the band to stick with you until the very end, and when one band member revolts temporarily, the others will keep him in check.

Given the nature of producing, and despite the fact that you work for the band, there will be times when you must stand your ground. The temporary mutiny of a single irritant is nothing more than a test of your resolve. Stand firm. An attempt by the brainchild to involve you in a three-hour Science Experiment during the tracking session is a test of your focus. Stand firm and keep the session on track. If the singer is a terrible guitar player, yet insists on laying down guitar doubles, it's an internal power play. Stand firm. Of course, since you're working with a band, it's rare that you will have to stand firm without the support of others. You can and must use this support to your advantage.

Whenever you work with a group on a creative project, alliances will constantly shift. It is unusual for cliques to remain unified and unchanging throughout the process. When the band is split evenly, it puts you in the position of tie breaker. When the band is split unevenly in your favor, you can leverage the support necessary to push through your agenda. When the band is split unevenly out of your favor, you need only sway one or two band members to your side. From the shrewd position of pure political calculation, you can use divide-and-conquer techniques to get your way all day long. The problem is that that sort of leadership is divisive in nature—hence the term "*divide* and conquer." This would seem to make you the anti-producer. When you're short on time, you may have to use these kinds of political calculations just to keep the session moving forward. But overall, you want to engage in consensus building; otherwise the alliances could become firmly entrenched.

Compromise is a part of all record-making. When you deal with a large team of people who have varying opinions, there must be some give and take from everyone involved. Again, as the leader, you set the tone. If you are seen as a compromiser, then everyone in the band will be willing to compromise. Any time a situation comes up where you can find some middle ground that doesn't negatively affect the product, you should.

Every person on the team will compromise throughout the course of an album. The art of compromise from a leadership position is to agree when a decision makes no difference, to offer other viable alternatives when it does make a difference, and to stand firm when all reasonable alternatives have been exhausted. If your brainchild has an idea he wants to attempt, why would you want to shoot it down? You don't want the band shooting down your crazy ideas. So don't shoot down theirs. You must lead by example, and you will be seen as nothing short of a hypocrite if you don't hear out ideas. At the same time, if your brainchild's ideas come fast and furious and completely lack focus, you can't possibly entertain them all. You have a responsibility at that point to keep the session on track, and you have the authority to keep the session focused.

You must also take into consideration the level of passion exhibited in any given protest. A drummer who is adamantly against a drum fill will likely trump the rest of the band that loves the fill. The drummer who describes herself as "not particularly fond" of a fill has essentially admitted that she will yield to the consensus of the group. That said, if fixing the fill is as easy as grabbing one from another take, why wouldn't you go out of your way to solve the issue for the drummer no matter how strongly she feels about it? Unless the drum fill is somehow critical to the production as-is (and that's possible), then why not help make the drummer more comfortable? The act of acquiescing in a situation that doesn't require it will give you significant political capital later on. It sends the message that you're not going to stand firm unless it really matters to the production. It also sends the message that you want everyone in the band to be happy with their record. These are good messages to send.

As much as the songwriter has more weight in the band, and as much as you want to give the brainchild more weight, she can't be given carte blanche. A four-to-two majority against the brainchild and you is a tough spot to be in politically. To go against the entire band can cause feelings of resentment. Often the band will acquiesce to the brainchild, but if they're standing firm, you would be foolish to act as anything other than arbitrator here. Placing your thumb on the scale in favor of a single person in the band is ill-advised unless the issue has to do directly with her own personal performance. A guitar player who is unhappy with his part trumps the rest of the band in regard to those parts. A brainchild who is unhappy with the guitar player's part does not.

While it's true that the songwriter or brainchild is the person with the power, you mustn't ignore or discount the rest of the band. One of the more compelling reasons to cozy up to the brainchild in the first place is to help you navigate the politics of the band. It's not so you can give yourself permission to treat everyone else like second-class citizens. The band members are just as aware of the natural pecking order as you are. Given this, you should go out of your way to give them a sense of importance. If the entire band isn't performing to the best of their abilities, your production will suffer.

Given this, you should avoid voting positions that are not in your favor. Producing can't be done well by committee, so don't put yourself in a position where you only get one vote out of many. Issues will come up, and if most of the band is unhappy, you really have no choice but to find an alternative. If that doesn't work, then you should probably defer the problem.

Deferring Decisions

As we've already established, it's generally best to avoid deferring decisions when it comes to producing a record. Politically, however, there are times when it's necessary to table a discussion. Whether you're dealing with a split band that is far too entrenched in their positions to negotiate, or an emotionally charged brainchild, politically speaking, deferment is a useful tool. There is no point in allowing a debate between two sides that are incapable of hearing anything other than their own positions (that includes you). Use time to your advantage.

The passage of time will allow people's emotions to settle down, which will result in a band more likely to compromise. You can also use success as emotional leverage to open up a dialogue for solving difficult problems. Success tends to emulsify hardened positions, and serves as an example of the good things that can happen when everyone works together. Of course, whatever you do, don't return to your problem track on the heels of another disaster.

Deferment will also allow the band to live with the track in its controversial state. If you give the band a rough mix of the track as it stands, they will likely listen to it a number of times before you return to working on it. Many times, a controversial part will grow on people, and if it doesn't, then you will likely be given all sorts of solutions to the problem when you return to the track. This goes for you as a producer as well. If you are uncomfortable with a part, live with it before you shoot it down. Of course, if deferment doesn't seem to resolve the issue, you always have the power of veto.

The Power of Veto

Technically, you don't really have veto power unless the band is willing to give it to you. But even if you have this option, it's in limited supply. How much veto power you have can only be measured by how much political capital you've accrued, and you must sometimes spend that capital elsewhere. Therefore, you should reserve your limited power of veto as if you have but one veto at your disposal. Frankly, that's probably an accurate estimate.

You can use all sorts of tools to sway a band, starting with logic and demonstration. Furthermore, exercising veto power without any political backup whatsoever likely won't work. You must have some kind of support for your position from within the band.

If you make light of your veto power, you might be able to buy yourself some soft vetoes. Just the mere threat of a veto, expressed in a joking manner, can soften positions, if only so they might avoid that scenario. When you joke about your veto power, it makes the band think you have more power than you actually have. Use this technique solely to keep people in an attitude of compromise.

Setting the Mood

Humor is one of your best weapons when it comes to running a session. As much as making a record is serious business, the goal is to make it a fun experience. And why not? If you can keep your band in a good mood and make the process fun, they'll be far less likely to focus on inconsequential bullshit. Arguments are infrequent when people are having a good time, and as the leader, if you can keep the focus away from the stakes involved, you'll make your life considerably easier.

Your bedside manner is important to the vibe of a session. Even though you might be in a shit mood, it's critical to put on a game face for your band. They rely on you to keep the mood up, and are watching you for any indications of problems.

Prioritization

Whenever you record more songs than will make the album, you must be prepared to cut your losses based on the song prioritization list. If you allow your band to divert your attention to a low-priority track early on, you could be mismanaging your time resources. There is no way to predict with perfect accuracy which tracks are going to cause you problems and which will seem effortless. You do not want to put yourself in a position where a lack of focus on your part either causes you to dump an important song, or diminishes the quality of the project overall. A priority list is useless if you're not going to actually use it to prioritize.

There are times when it's a good call to choose a low-priority track if it's going to offer some kind of relief for your session. A goofy track can be useful for lightening up a dismal mood, in which case you could argue that the track is momentarily of the highest priority. Time and morale management are the fulcrum for keeping your session on a relatively even keel. While it's important to complete your highest-priority songs, it's rare for your list of must-have songs to rise above five or six. This gives you plenty of leeway to use lower-priority songs as a respite from the grind.

The goal is to track 12 to 15 songs in order to finish a minimum of 10. Unless things go drastically wrong, you want to track all of the songs before abandoning them in the overdub process. If an easy song is likely to give you much needed success, you should use that to affect the overall mood of the session.

The Art of Presentation

Your best weapon against a political crisis is presentation. Sometimes you want to shock the team with a radical idea. Sometimes you want to soften them up first: "I've got an idea, and I'll warn you now, it could be genius or it could be pure shit." I demonstrated this tactic earlier in the book as a way to prepare the team for a bold idea, but there are other benefits. Warning the band that an idea is radical can buy you a little time to explore it, especially if you're worried that the concept could dramatically change the overall vision. A sudden and radical suggestion can be useful if you want to assert some control over your session, or if the band is completely open and malleable.

The beauty of ideas is that they lead to other ideas. If I know what I'm looking to accomplish with a suggestion, I'm far more likely to present it confidently, and without explanation. I need only spark my own alternate ideas when my path is clear. If I'm not sure about an idea, and I'm looking for the band to help me improve upon it, I'm likely to present it in a more diffident manner.

A large part of your job as producer is sales. Before you ever set foot in a studio, you have to sell yourself, sell your enthusiasm, sell your vision, and sell your worth. The sales job doesn't end there. Any time you find yourself dealing with resistance, you must sell your idea. This is best achieved through demonstration.

You never want to engage in an argument that can be easily proved or disproved by a demonstration. The whole process of making a record should be one demonstration after the next, all of which lead up to your vision. Arguing concepts in the abstract that can be implemented in reality is a waste of everyone's time. If there is a point of contention as far as the direction of a production is concerned, investigate the options on the production itself. Don't spend time debating that your way is the right way, only to disallow a reasonable request to try something else.

You never want to dismiss your band members' concerns as problems that can be fixed later. If you're telling the band that they will know at all times where they are in the record, then you can't then suggest that everything will be fine later. You can agree that there's a problem and defer it until you can come up with a solution. But don't ever tell a band that you can "fix it in the mix" (even if it's true). If you can fix it in the mix, you can fix it right then and there, too.

You want to avoid festering concerns within the band. It's critical to communicate what is going on. If you're struggling with a track, share that with the band. They can help you with it.

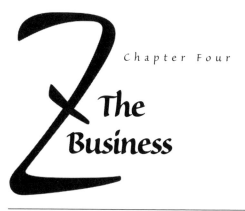

Chapter Four

The Business

Had I written this book just five years ago, this chapter would be on how producers get paid, including nearly step-by-step instructions on what you should fight for and against in your contract. As it stands, the old model is fast becoming irrelevant. The business is in total flux; it has been for a few years now, and it will be for at least another few.

As we've discussed, the only viable revenue stream in which to profit-share is publishing, and while it's becoming more commonplace for a producer to be paid in this manner, it's still a relatively new demand. As such, you could very well meet considerable resistance if you attempt to negotiate a back end consisting of publishing. Your juice as a producer will greatly affect how much resistance you encounter, as will how long the band has been around. Any band that's been in this business long enough to have paid out a producer based on the record sales model is likely to have a serious problem with paying you in publishing. That's because until quite recently it was taboo to even suggest it.

Publishing royalties are paid out in a number of ways. There are mechanical royalties, which pay out based on the sales of the album (which are just as useless as artist royalties). There are performance

royalties, which pay out based on radio spins and Internet streaming, and which will account for most of the band's revenues. And
then there's licensing, which pays out when the song is placed in a
movie or commercial. Licensing is completely negotiable, and can
pay out anything from a few thousand to many millions of dollars,
depending on the song and its purpose.

Mechanical royalties are set by Congress as a statutory rate, but
when the artist and the songwriter are one and the same (and this
includes bands), this is typically reduced to 75 percent of the
statutory rate in the contract. That may seem odd. How is it that
Congress sets a statutory rate, which the labels can then negotiate
down? Well, the statutory rate is what must be paid to the songwriter. When the songwriter and the artist (or band) are one and
the same, this becomes a legal point of negotiation. Since bands
write their own material, it's likely that they won't get the full
mechanical rate on their album sales.

According to David Touve, an assistant professor of business at
Washington and Lee University, the average spin on terrestrial radio
in the United States pays out between $0.000186 to $0.000372 *per
listener.* A single spin on a major radio station can reach millions,
so a record that's being spun many times a day on thousands of radio
stations can generate an enormous amount of revenue. In reality,
however, performance royalties aren't calculated on a per-listener
basis. That's an average figure that was calculated scientifically
through Mr. Touve's research.

Publishing is the gift that keeps on giving. Once you have a hit,
other artists will cover the song, over and over again. Even if the
song isn't a hit, there's always a chance that someone will cover it
later and make it one. If someone successfully covers the song
decades later, you will be a beneficiary of that sudden boost in
publishing revenues. Even better, if a big corporation decides that

they're willing to pay millions of dollars to license a song for a national advertising campaign, you make money too. A lot of money, even if your percentage is relatively small.

Now, it's important to understand that publishing is made up of two distinct halves—the songwriter's half, and the publisher's half. The publisher administers the monies for the songwriter, although this can be done by the songwriter herself; it is not a requirement to have your catalog administered. When we talk about being paid out of the songwriter's publishing, we are talking about her half of the monies only. Since it's unlikely that you want to administer the publishing for less than 50 percent, you're only going to take your royalty out of the songwriter's half.

Some of you might be thinking, "Well, why not take it out of the publisher's half if there's no publisher involved?" Well, if there's no publisher, then it doesn't really matter which half you take it out of. If the songwriter sells her publishing down the line, or if a label takes the publishing as part of the deal, then you will have to take it from the songwriter's half regardless.

The best way to convince the songwriters in the band to pay you points on the publishing is to simply explain the realities of the business today. Points on album sales are a useless revenue stream when the band is simply going to put their music online for free in the hopes of attracting people to their shows.

The current business model in its most simplistic form is as follows: 1) Get famous. 2) Capitalize on your fame. That's it. A famous band with a popular song will attract fans, to whom they will sell tickets, which gets them media exposure, which translates into all sorts of publishing revenue streams. Even if a band pushes back against the suggestion that they'll be giving away their songs, it's really the only way a band can get noticed right now. Protectionism doesn't work when your competition is giving away their product.

At this point in the game, you should *encourage* a band to release their material online for free. Obviously, if you're paid through sales, then it's not in your interest to encourage them to give the product away.

A number of books have been written on the business of music, including Donald Passman's *All You Need to Know About the Music Business*, which I highly recommend. Make sure to get the newest edition, because it's all changing at a remarkable clip. When it comes right down to it, the money payouts in music are so convoluted and complicated that you must often rely on industry-standard practices. Of course, I'm not sure there *are* standards any longer, which is kind of my main point here. Label deals have changed significantly over the past five years as well. This is where your attorney comes in, and you will need one when it comes to negotiating contracts with a band, now more than ever.

Frankly, the ins and outs of how a producer gets paid, while important, are a function of what you can negotiate between your lawyer and theirs. This is especially true when dealing with labels. I prefer to negotiate my terms as simply as possible with bands, particularly independently funded ones. An unknown band is a long shot, and there's no point in spending several thousand dollars to negotiate a complicated contract, particularly since the band can rarely afford an attorney of their own until there's a label involved.

Even when there are attorneys involved, I prefer to negotiate the terms directly with the band and manager. Keep it simple. If the band is a success, you'll make money. If they're not, you won't. No breakage. No deductions. No reserves. Just pay me a percentage of the songwriting royalty stream. Which raises the question, "What percentage?" There are no standards, but everyone that I know who is currently doing this is getting between 5 and 10 percent of the publishing. Where in that range you fall depends on a great many factors, and where the standard ends up is anyone's guess.

How We Got Here

There are a great many reasons why record sales decline each year. It all started with the atrocious business habits of the music industry itself. The transfer of record labels from small businesses run by music lovers to mega-corporations run by bean counters was the beginning of the decline. The music corporations put short-term gains over long-term business plans, and as a result, bands that did not sell records on their first effort were dropped before their second. Even a band with an enormous radio hit was unlikely to release a sophomore effort. Not only did this help to promote a rather fickle consumer culture, it also completely destroyed the development of catalog for the industry as a whole.

A band that breaks on its third album sells all three albums. This invests fans in the band, which all but guarantees more successful albums. Had Pink Floyd existed under the business model of the '90s, there would have never been a *Dark Side of the Moon*, *Wish You Were Here*, or *The Wall*. Catalog sales accounted for an enormous volume of sales in the '80s and '90s, so for the industry to ignore future catalog was nothing short of catastrophic to the business.

Then there was that decade from the early to mid-'90s when albums were not only overpriced, but often had no more than one good song. The teenage consumer was burned time and time again paying $17 for albums by bands with no chance in hell of ever making another album. Bring in Napster, and the conditions were ripe for consumers to give the industry a big "fuck you" as they downloaded their music for free. You rip me off, I'll rip you off. No problem.

I can promise you that the loudness wars didn't help matters. At the height of the insanity, labels were routinely spending $500,000 to produce albums that sounded so atrocious that a kid in his bedroom with Pro Tools and a Waves L2 could compete sonically. Loudness and distortion on records caused the end user to turn the music down, which had the result of making music nothing more than background noise. Loud records on radio were as assaultive as the commercials themselves. No longer was music an interactive experience where the listener sat down and listened to an album. Loudness made music uninviting, which in turn devalued it further. If you can cause someone to turn a record up, that's a positive reaction to the music. When you cause someone to turn the music down, that's a negative reaction to the music. In an effort to give their tracks an advantage over others, record labels and producers managed to foster a negative reaction to their music. A negative reaction means no sale.

Of course, most people want to blame downloading as the main problem, and at this point I'd agree. But let's not pretend that the music industry (and the movie industry) hasn't done everything in its power to promote a download culture. Downloading, to some degree, is a symptom of the poor stewardship of the record labels. Years of putting out overpriced, undervalued, uninviting, burn-and-turn products has all but begged consumers to stop paying for product. What little product does sell is no longer bundled into a collection of songs (once called an album), but is instead sold as a single solitary song.

While we can certainly put plenty of the blame on a short-sighted industry, the lack of protection for intellectual property in this country has all but put the nail in the coffin where sales are concerned. It's killing the book industry too, and the movie industry is next if things don't change drastically. Torrent sites located in China and Russia provide users with just about any movie, book, or song in existence for free. The only purpose of these sites is to make money by allowing people to steal the hard work of others. This book that you're reading now has a 90 percent chance of being illegally downloaded. If that's how you got this book, then consider that I have not made a single dime from your enjoyment of it. Yet you're going to take all of the great advice that I spent a lifetime acquiring and months writing, and do what? Make records that others are going to steal?

If you downloaded this book, you are one of tens of thousands of others who did. As a result, I have to question why I'm writing books only to give them away. Unlike a band, I can't tour and make income by selling tickets to shows. I make money from sales and sales alone, and if I can't sell books, there's really not much point in writing them. Not at the expense of my family, who not only must deal with the temporary reduction in my earning power as I take the time off to write a book for an advance commensurate with dismal projected sales figures, but also my total unavailability as I immerse myself in the project. Why should I make a sacrifice like that for two checks a year that barely buy me a nice dinner? I mean, if my books are unpopular, then I should give it up. But when my books are exceptionally popular, shouldn't I be able to reap the rewards of that?

I have watched my friends leave the record industry, or plod along as best they can, hoping and praying for things to change. If labels can't make money, and artists can't make money, then we can't make money. If you stole this book, you're part of the problem, and while it's easy to justify that because "everyone" does it, you will change your tune when it happens to you. When you create a popular work that reaps you little to no reward, you will start to wonder why you're doing it in the first place. A fucking banker makes money every time there's a transaction. There is no value in monetary transactions for society as a whole. Yet here we make products that significantly affect people's lives, and we make next to nothing? Sorry, but that's fucked up.

You have a limited time in your life in which to make records. The likelihood that you will be able to make records in your 60s is low, which means you're going to either need to retire, or develop some other skill. If you never profit-share, you will never be able to retire. There is no way to accrue enough money to give you a sufficient nest egg purely as a work-for-hire in this business.

Hey, I'm not trying to bum you out here, and I'm not whining about the 50,000 or so people who have stolen each of my other two books thus far. I'm merely explaining the facts to you. I understand what it's like to feel violated by planned obsolescence when it comes to software. I understand what it's like to feel ripped off after purchasing a CD with only one good song. I understand how and why this has all happened. But if you downloaded this book for free by paying some Russian $10 for the ability to do so, I suggest you go online right now and purchase the book legitimately. Otherwise, it could very well be my last.

There is legislation in the US Congress now called the Stop Online Piracy Act (SOPA). As with most legislation, it's controversial, with some claiming that the legislation not only won't work, but that it will be the end of the Internet as we know it. The usual partisan lines have been blurred on this issue. Conservatives and liberals have landed on both sides, which should give you some sense as to just how complicated this issue is.

As currently written (and it will change), the SOPA legislation would give the government the ability to shut down those sites whose sole purpose is to illegally distribute copyrighted material. The naysayers complain that SOPA makes the government's powers too broad, which will surely result in government abuse— a reasonable concern. One assertion is that SOPA will bypass the Digital Millennium Act's "safe harbor" provisions (which protect sites like YouTube from copyright infringement suits if they exhibit consistent due diligence), putting YouTube and other sites in jeopardy of being shut down by the government. Some argue that the legislation will end the Internet as we know it, others call that hyperbolic, and still others suggest that there is no way to stay ahead of sites providing illegal downloads.

Whatever comes out of Washington, DC, in this regard will certainly be less than perfect. We already know this. By the time you read this, SOPA could be dead. That's irrelevant. What we must acknowledge is the larger point. The status quo is unsustainable. As an industry we must put pressure on the US government to come up with sensible legislation that works to protect intellectual property without dramatically limiting the power of the Internet. Perhaps that's impossible. I don't know. All I know is that tech companies make their money through the distribution of content, and media companies make their money through the protection of content, and we must meet somewhere in the middle to offer easy and affordable access to content without denying the creator the ability to profit from his or her popular work.

Ending on a Positive Note Is Good to Do

Now that I've successfully guilted you into purchasing this book (and my other two books!), and left you feeling defeated about intellectual property protection, we should probably end this on a positive note.

Effective producing comes down to effective communication. The better you are at expressing your thoughts, the more skilled you are at deciphering the thoughts of others, the better you'll be at producing. This is a job in which the ability to listen is a baseline skill, one that should not be relegated simply to the music itself.

What I have given you here is nothing more than a start and a way of thinking about things, both politically and creatively. As you make records, you will use this information in the way that works best for your personality and skill set, just as all of us who produce records have. Much of what I've offered here I've learned from a great many mistakes—both that I have made and that I have witnessed. You will also make mistakes, and those will define how you operate in the studio over time. You'll even pick up tricks as you work with others. Learning to produce is a lifetime process. At least now you have some idea of the thinking that goes into producing a record, from the first listen to the demo to the final approval of the master. I would encourage you to reread this book every now and then, as there will be some concepts that you will connect more readily to as you gain experience.

While it's true that the music business is in flux, this is an exciting time. Artists and bands are no longer reliant on major labels for distribution. A band can operate as a business without any label support whatsoever, and that was a rarity just a decade ago. As much as the Internet has fucked things up in this business, I'm grateful for it each and every day. It has empowered the *people* to become the arbiters of what's good. A band or artist who can tap into the zeitgeist can blow up without having to get by the gatekeepers first. If you can make a name for yourself, you can and will make money in this business, and best of all, you'll be making music for a living. It doesn't get any better than that!

Now, go forth and produce.

Finding Mixerman

Get general information about Mixerman, including excerpts from his first book *The Daily Adventures of Mixerman*:

mixerman.net

Hang with Mixerman and friends at The Womb Forums. Discuss anything and everything that has to do with making music; join in on the collaborative events; enjoy *The Mixerman Radio Show with Slipperman and Aardvark (names listed in order of importance)*; and make friends and contacts from all over the world.

thewombforums.com
youtube.com/thewombforums
The Mixerman Radio Show (at the Womb)

Find out what's happening on the Internet by joining Mixerman's social network pages. As Mixerman puts it, "Never miss out on a good *merde*-fling again."

Like! Mixerman on Facebook
Follow @mixerman on Twitter

To contact Mixerman directly: mixerman@mixerman.net

ALSO BY
MIXERMAN

The Daily Adventures of Mixerman

Backbeat Books

Mixerman is a recording engineer working with a famous producer on the debut album of an unknown band with a giant recording budget. He writes a gripping diary loaded with anti-heroes: the pretentious singer, the depressive guitarist, the drummer who's as "dumb as cotton," and the bassist who is mean and petty. Mixerman takes you through the recording process of a bidding-war band in over their heads with a famous record producer (also in over his head). Many find his diary entries side-splittingly funny. Some find them maddening. And a select few feel they are the most despicable accountings of record-making ever documented.

9780879309459   6" x 9" • 440 pages • Hardcover..$24.99

Zen and the Art of Mixing

Hal Leonard Books

In his first book, the author detailed the frustrating and often hilarious goings-on during the process of recording a major-label band. Now Mixerman turns his razor-sharp gaze to the art of mixing, giving readers reason to hope – if not for logic and civility in the recording studio, then at least for a good-sounding record. With a firm commitment to art over technology and to maintaining a grasp of each, Mixerman outlines his own approach to recording success, based on his years mixing records in all genres of music for all kinds of artists, often under trying circumstances.

9781423491507   5.5" x 7.75" • 296 pages • Paperback $24.99